# LONG LIVE THE MATADORS

# LONG LIVE THE MATADORS

## THE FEARLESS HISTORY OF TEXAS TECH'S MASKED RIDER

STACY STOCKARD CALIVA

TEXAS TECH UNIVERSITY PRESS

Copyright © 2024 by Texas Tech University Press

Publication of this book was made possible by the generous support of the Helen Jones Foundation, Inc.

All rights reserved. No portion of this book may be reproduced in any form or by any means, including electronic storage and retrieval systems, except by explicit prior written permission of the publisher. Brief passages excerpted for review and critical purposes are excepted.

This book is typeset in EB Garamond. The paper used in this book meets the minimum requirements of ANSI/NISO Z39.48-1992 (R1997). ♾
Designed by Hannah Gaskamp
Cover designed by Hannah Gaskamp
Cover photograph courtesy of Texas Tech University Office of Communications and Marketing

Library of Congress Cataloging-in-Publication Data

Names: Caliva, Stacy Stockard, 1983– author. Title: Long Live the Matadors: The Fearless History of Texas Tech's Masked Rider / Stacy Stockard Caliva. Description: Lubbock, Texas: Texas Tech University Press, [2024] | Includes index. | Summary: "A program history of the Masked Rider, the primary mascot of Texas Tech University, including a rundown of the riders' horses, as written by a former Masked Rider"—Provided by publisher.
Identifiers: LCCN 2023019550 | ISBN 978-1-68283-194-6 (cloth: acid-free paper)
Subjects: LCSH: Texas Tech University—History. | Masked Rider (Mascot) | Horses—Texas—Lubbock—History. | Horsemen and horsewomen—Texas—Lubbock—History.
Classification: LCC LD5314 .C35 2023 | DDC 378.764/847—dc23/eng/20230627
LC record available at https://lccn.loc.gov/2023019550

Printed in China
24 25 26 27 28 29 30 31 32 / 9 8 7 6 5 4 3 2 1

Texas Tech University Press
Box 41037
Lubbock, Texas 79409-1037 USA
800.832.4042
ttup@ttu.edu
www.ttupress.org

DEDICATED TO MIDNIGHT MATADOR,
LONG MAY HIS MEMORY LIVE.

"The Masked Rider is as much a part of Tech as the Double T."

**LINDA THORSEN BOND, "RAIDER SYMBOLIZES TRADITION,"**
***UNIVERSITY DAILY*, SEPTEMBER 19, 1968**

# CONTENTS

# FOREWORD

When I started my job as the Texas Tech Spirit Program Director in 2003, I was already aware that the Masked Rider was a big deal. I laugh now at how little I truly knew about the enormity of the enterprise. When I began working within the program, I realized how much each rider sacrifices: the hundreds of appearances they make, the daily care of the horse, the enormous effort put into ensuring the truck, trailer, and tack are always ready for the public eye, and this in conjunction with all the expectations that come with being a Texas Tech student.

I was honored to speak when Texas Tech's 43rd Masked Rider, Stacy Stockard Caliva, ended her term at the 2005 Transfer of Reins ceremony. As her supervisor, I had been able to observe her during the 2004–2005 school year. I remarked on her dedication, commitment, and love of the Masked Rider Program. Although she was just the second Masked Rider I had worked with, I sensed something extraordinary in the way she performed her role. As we ended the annual ceremony that year, I found myself hoping I would somehow have the opportunity to work with Stacy again.

In the nineteen years since that ceremony, I have watched Stacy's dedication to the Masked Rider Program grow stronger every year. In fact, thinking of ways to grow and improve the venture never seems to be very far from her mind. She has volunteered to help each Masked Rider since the time she stepped down. She is always available to assist with any task related to the operation.

When she told me she was writing a comprehensive book about the Masked Rider Program, I was delighted. This book is long overdue, and I am so grateful that Stacy has poured her indefatigable love of Texas Tech and the Masked Rider into this project.

The students who serve as Masked Rider are the cream of the crop of Texas Tech University. I believe that with all my heart. They are the most elite group of students this university has to offer. When they accept the position of Masked Rider, they become a part of something bigger than themselves. They are the face of the university and serve as one of its most visible representatives. This tradition would not be where it is today without the work of the sixty-two riders who took on this monumental role.

Seeing the Masked Rider lead the football team out onto the field has always been my favorite Texas Tech tradition. It still gives me goosebumps even after twenty years in my job, and I have seen grown men tear up when they talk about it. It is a tradition that touches people deeply.

I am excited that everyone will now be able to read and understand what those of us know who have worked with the Masked Rider Program. There is simply no greater symbol of Texas Tech University than the Masked Rider.

**STEPHANIE RHODE**
**DIRECTOR OF TEXAS TECH SPIRIT PROGRAM**

# ACKNOWLEDGMENTS

First and foremost, I will forever appreciate the support of my husband, Trey Caliva, and my parents, Joe and Mary Stockard, in this longtime project. You have shared in its joys and frustrations and have truly loved the Masked Rider Program and its people and horses. You three have contributed to the positive community that embraces new and former Masked Riders and celebrates this tradition.

To my daughter, Vivian: you spent many hours with me researching at home and in the reading room of the library before you were born, and I edited this book with you in my lap. Former Masked Riders came to your baby shower, and you met your first Masked Rider at ten weeks old—while wearing a onesie gifted to you by those former riders. I look forward to reading this book with you and the day when you will be able to read it to me.

Thank you as well to my family and friends who have been so encouraging in this endeavor and invested in its progress. I also greatly appreciate the support and accommodation of my colleagues in the Office of Advancement to complete this project.

Several years ago, I met Travis Snyder with Texas Tech University Press at a luncheon and pitched the concept of this book. Thank you, Travis, for your receptiveness to the idea and for allowing us to memorialize the history of the Masked Rider Program in this book. You and your team at Texas Tech University Press have been a joy to work with.

I couldn't be more thankful for the expert librarians at Texas Tech's Southwest Collection/Special Collections Library in finding literature and photographs: Weston Marshall, Shelby Newman, and Lynn Whitfield. Your helpfulness, resourcefulness, and enthusiasm uncovered rare pieces of our history that might have otherwise been lost to time. You are incredible at what you do.

Thank you to Ashley Rodgers with the Office of Communications and Marketing, who has photographed the program from the inside out since 2013, and Robert Rhode, our Spirit Program photographer who began taking photos of the Masked Rider, Raider Red, Cheer, and Pom in 2006. The help from you both in finding the last twenty years of photographic history was instrumental in documenting the modern era of riders. Having photographers who chronicle our milestones and the behind-the-scenes moments that lead up to them has made and will continue to make a significant impact on the recording of program and university history.

A number of former Masked Riders provided assistance with piecing together missing parts of history: JoLynn Self Frankfather, Ralynn Key Kirkpatrick, Corey Waggoner, Christi Chadwell Short, Lee Puckitt, Larry Cade, Daniel Jenkins, and Lea Whitehead Baze. Thank you, too, to former riders Laurie Tolboom Martin and Ashley Adams for so graciously contributing your professional photographs to this project. I greatly appreciate the research of three others who were able to identify a few of our horses: Kim Lindsey and Alli Edwards with the 6666 Ranch for their help with two of our horses that seemed impossible to find, and my colleague, Haleigh Erramouspe, for finding the origins of our first unofficial horse during a different project and sharing her research.

I am also grateful for our program leaders and mentors, Stephanie Rhode and Dr. Sam Jackson, not just for your help with the program's history but also for supporting our horses and riders for a combined fifty years. Steady and dedicated guidance, oversight, and advocacy have been key components to the success of this industry-leading program. The Masked Rider would not be the same without either of you.

Last, thank you to the Helen Jones Foundation, Inc., for selecting this book to receive one of your grants. Your generosity and trust allowed us to create a beautiful history of a Texas Tech tradition deeply treasured by alumni and friends.

# LONG LIVE THE MATADORS

# INTRODUCTION

In September 2014, the Masked Rider Program held its sixtieth anniversary reunion dinner at the 50 Yard Line Steakhouse. Former riders shared stories with the group about their time in the saddle—some serious and some not so serious—that had been kept secret for decades. While the subjects ranged from family pictures with dad in costume and children in the saddle to a pet monkey that did not take to barn life, one commonality tied us all together: how much our time as a Masked Rider meant to us.

As the night drew to a close and everyone filed out, I said goodbye to one of our Honorary Masked Riders, Alvin Davis. He was wearing his signature red sport coat, black felt cowboy hat, and Double T tie. He turned back, looked at me out of the corner of his eye, and said, "Someone should write a book about this." I agreed and began this project shortly thereafter.

I served as the forty-third Masked Rider from April 2004 to April 2005 during my senior year at Texas Tech University, which was also the fiftieth anniversary of the Masked Rider Program. During that time, Chancellor David Smith and President David Schmidly led Texas Tech. Marsha Sharp and Bob Knight coached their basketball teams to the NCAA tournament. In football, Mike Leach and quarterback Sonny Cumbie took the Red Raiders to a 7–4 record in the regular season and a Holiday Bowl win over No. 5 University of California.

Midnight Matador and I traveled more than 12,000 miles that year and made about 110 appearances, all in Texas. Amos, as he was known to his friends, was the greatest partner a Masked Rider could ask for. He was stunning, strong-willed, and the smartest horse I have ever been around.

He had his share of cantankerous days—thankfully most not visible to the public—but his brilliance under his riders is well documented. Football games were his specialty. I trusted him to carry me through situations that cause most horses to come completely unglued. Nothing fazed him, which was probably his best trait as a Masked Rider horse, and he was full of personality. He loved visits from Raider Red at football games, usually took naps on the sidelines, and if he couldn't figure out what something was, his first instinct was to try to eat it, whether it was a pom-pom or actual food. Those who spent time around him knew the tactile abilities he had with his teeth.

When Amos's retirement became imminent in 2012, I could not even conceive of not taking care of him. Being Masked Rider opened so many doors for me, and I owed so much of the success of that year and in my life to Amos. I watched him carry riders throughout the years, and I knew they were all safe under his watch. He earned everything good in the world for his service to Texas Tech.

During the month-long selection process for determining who would care for him in his retirement, I was a wreck. I woke up thinking about Amos and went to sleep thinking about Amos. When Stephanie Rhode, our Spirit Program coordinator, called to tell me that Amos would get to live with me, my world felt whole.

It took about a year for him to settle into retirement after nearly eleven years on the job. Every time I saw him, I couldn't believe how lucky I was to care for him. Amos loved carrots, apples, baths, attention, and The Beatles, but he loathed mud, being woken up at night, and Corona ointment, which is like Neosporin for horses but with a potent lanoline smell—problematic for a mischievous horse who got into everything. He made exploratory bites on things he wasn't sure about, and one time I fished a hoof pick out of his mouth that he had picked up when I turned my back.

When he passed away from recovery complications following emergency surgery for a freak, unanticipated bout of colic in February 2015, I was heartbroken for months. No horse I have ridden or tested since has compared to Amos.

It is a surreal feeling to come home from the vet's office after that final goodbye, sit on the living room floor in dirty barn clothes, and watch your horse's death become the lead story on the 6 p.m. and 10 p.m. news, make national news, and become a trending topic on social media. After seeing news stories about his death that week containing several inaccuracies (including that he passed away on the operating table), I believed more than ever that the Masked Rider tradition needed a single place to hold the most thorough and accurate history of our program, its riders, and its horses.

Just as Amos deserves to have his legacy remembered, those who contributed to the Masked Rider Program deserve to have the history they made documented. No matter how long ago we served, we are introduced as former Masked Riders and asked about our time in the saddle. It is a point of pride to know you contributed to a tradition that so many people hold close to their hearts.

This book shares why finding a mascot became a relentless search for Texas Tech and how secret closed-door conversations turned into a Gator Bowl surprise. It details how the program has grown and evolved over the decades into one of the most recognized and well-organized college mascot programs in the country. In it, you will learn how each of the fifteen black horses came to be selected as mascots—whether they came from pivotal Texas ranches, the racetrack, working ranches, the show ring, or even the Texas Tech breeding program. Told primarily through interviews the riders gave during their respective tenures, it offers a glimpse into their thoughts and feelings in their own moment of time in the program. What started with a cape made by the Home Economics Department has become the most depicted subject in Texas Tech's campus art collection.

Intertwined with the history and evolution of Texas Tech, the story of the Masked Rider encompasses more than sixty-five years of victories, heartbreak, and an occasional horse ride inside a building.

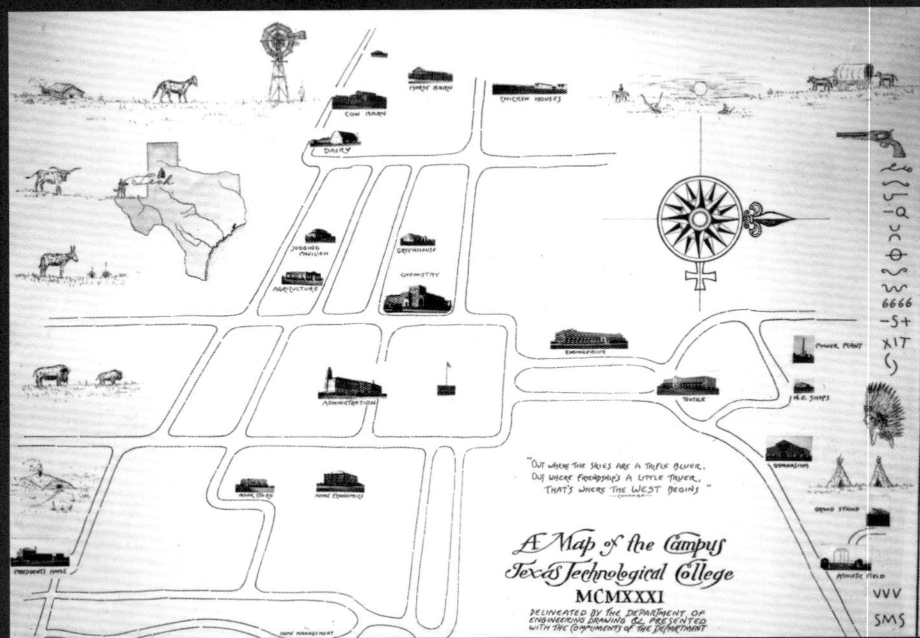


This 1931 campus map by the Department of Engineering shows the early locations of buildings of Texas Technological College. The horse barn is located near the top center of the map. Other animal husbandry buildings are found in the same section. (Courtesy Texas Tech University Southwest Collection/Special Collections Library, hereafter the Southwest Collection)

This aerial view of the agriculture structures on campus in the 1938 *La Ventana* features the Agriculture Building (no longer in existence) and the Judging Pavilion (still standing and in use) in the foreground, along what is now 15th Street, facing west. The Dairy Barn is to the left, and the horse barns are to its northwest. (Courtesy the Southwest Collection)

# 1

# THE SHORT TENURE OF BLACK INVADER

Lubbock, Texas, sat in a flat, barren expanse in West Texas in the 1920s. Its population totaled just over 4,000—an amount doubled from the previous decade. In comparison, Dallas had nearly 159,000 residents at the time, and more than 138,000 people lived in Houston.[1]

West Texans wanted a college in their region for their growing populations. Then-governor James Ferguson falsely said West Texas A&M College (a branch of Texas A&M) would be established in Abilene, but instead it was in Canyon. Thanks to outrage from West Texans at the deception, a state exploratory committee was created, settling on Lubbock after visiting thirty-seven towns. Ferguson had already made enemies in the state university system in preceding years. He had feuded with the University of Texas (UT) at Austin during a failed attempt to defund the institution for its refusal to fire a list of professors who opposed him. State Senator William H. Bledsoe of Lubbock, chairman of the investigating committee, called for Ferguson's impeachment. Ferguson, who was now also indicted for embezzlement and misuse of state funds, resigned before the impeachment process could begin.[2]

Six years later, Governor Pat Neff signed the bill filed by Senator Bledsoe and State Representative Lewis Carpenter, making Texas Technological College official on February 10, 1923.[3] When Texas Tech opened its doors September 30, 1925, it welcomed 914 students into six buildings on the campus set west of Lubbock.[4] The buildings sat at a distance that looked as though they were miles from town and miles apart from each other. From a viewpoint looking in three directions, only the six Texas Tech buildings could be seen among the sea of dirt and sand. The walk from the administration building—the first structure built on campus—to the engineering building was a block-long dirt path.

In the 1930s, Lubbock's population exploded to 20,000 residents, and Texas Tech grew to nearly 4,000 undergraduate and graduate students. The town and college grew in prominence. The college even poured proper sidewalks for its pedestrians.[5]

Around the same time, mascots had become a marketing staple in creating a brand identity for a product. In the early 1900s, RCA's Nipper listened to his master's voice; Buster Brown and his dog Tige peddled shoes; Sailor Jack and his dog Bingo graced Cracker Jack boxes; and Leo the Lion opened every MGM movie. By 1933, the Budweiser Clydesdales had been introduced to the public, Elsie the Cow had helped Borden win the milk wars of the late 1930s, and in 1944 Smokey Bear became the illustrated mascot for the United States Forest Service with his live eponymous counterpart born and rescued in 1950.

Similar to product marketing, mascots brought identity to colleges and were also thought to bring good luck. In the 1930s and 1940s, Texas Tech students went crazy for animal mascots. Fraternities had dogs as mascots. Reptiles became laboratory mascots. Even the Pre-Law Club had an animal mascot.

Members of the Tech Band fraternity Kappa Kappa Psi rescued a small, grubby black-and-white terrier on a rainy day one spring. They named her Babe, and she lived in the band house.The fraternity placed a pledge pin on her collar, and she became the first female member of Kappa Kappa Psi. Babe attended marching band practice, accompanied the Tech Band to football games, and was usually free to run around the band building. She gave birth to two puppies, Pepper and Dammit, which were adopted by Assistant Band Director Joe Haddon and trombone player Chuck Wilson, respectively.[6]

But many established universities had live-animal mascots, so why did Texas Tech have nothing of its own? Students and community members frequently wrote editorials in the campus newspaper, the *Toreador*, questioning the lack of a mascot and chiding the college for failing to select one.[7] The owner of Varsity Bookstore—a longtime Lubbock staple—offered a cash prize for the best suggestion.[8] The school had just recently changed its nickname from the Matadors to the Red Raiders, and people were still trying to figure out exactly what a Red Raider should look like.

Southern Methodist University already had five black Shetland ponies serve as Peruna the Pony mascots by the time 1950 rolled around. Louisiana State had Mike the Tiger. Baylor University brought Joe College the black bear to away games by train. The University of Texas established Bevo, the Texas Longhorn, as its mascot in 1916, and Texas A&M University's first Reveille dog mascot appeared in 1931.

During halftime of an October 1925 football game, Marvin T. Ward, a county commissioner and the superintendent of Tech's grounds and buildings, presented a yearling bull to the college. Branding irons were heated by fire on the field, and the bull was branded in front of the crowd with 30–0, the score of Tech's first football victory. Spectators would attempt to ride the bull calf as halftime entertainment.[9]

The young bull with the Matadors' winning score of 30–0 against Montezuma College branded on its side appears at a football game in fall 1925. (Courtesy the Southwest Collection)

Borden Dairy Company volunteered their bull calf, Beauregard, the son of Elsie and Elmer, to stand in as the mascot for the 1951 homecoming weekend.[10] Some groups rallied around children dressed as matadors, embodying Tech's first nickname.[11] One community member suggested that a male student dress as a matador, and female students dressed as picadors (the men on horseback at bullfights who spear the bull) could flank him. Fortunately, that one never got off the ground.

The football team found various mascots. The 1934 team adopted a stray dog named Mattie.[12] In January 1936, Tech football players Jesse and Broadway Browning roped a wildcat while on horseback on a Fluvanna ranch over the Christmas break. They tied it up behind the gym and fed it raw meat. They suggested the wildcat be the mascot for the game that weekend, if not longer. When the *Toreador* asked how the two overcame the danger of roping the angry cat, Jesse replied he wasn't worried because he "had on [his] chaps and a leather jacket and gloves, but it was still pretty risky business."[13] However, Tech was not ready for a live predator as a mascot. Indeed, one of Baylor's bears attacked Tech football coach G. B. Morris on the sideline in 1948.[14]

In 1936, Texas Technological College student Arch Lamb sensed discontent among the Red Raider football fan base.[15] To foster school spirit, he founded the

Jesse and Broadway Browning show off the wildcat they caught on their father's ranch in 1936 for the university yearbook, *La Ventana*. (Courtesy the Southwest Collection)

Saddle Tramps, an all-male pep squad group. After gathering ten charter members, Lamb expanded the group by adding forty more members. In that group of forty was a student named George Tate.

Tate and Lamb held a common bond of being three to four years older than their peers. Tate started school at the college in 1930, renting a house owned by a retired preacher. A year into the Great Depression, his two roommates ran out of funds by Christmas and returned home. Tate moved into the preacher's home and worked off his rent. By the end of the 1932 school year, though, Tate had to return home to help his family on their farm.

In 1935, Tate had a disagreement with a contrary neighbor that escalated to a fistfight.[16] Tate landed a punch that knocked the neighbor to the ground. The neighbor stood back up with a .38-caliber revolver and aimed for Tate's stomach. A wrestling match ensued for control of the gun, and the neighbor shot Tate in the upper leg.

Tate drove himself ten miles to the hospital in Plainview, Texas, but after several days he didn't think the hospital would let him leave. He crawled out of a window and hopped in an escape vehicle driven by his brother-in-law. The fiasco was enough to make Tate want to stay out of trouble at his home and return to college.

As part of the New Deal, the National Youth Administration paid $15 a month to college students, but recipients must have a job. Ray C. Mowery in the Animal Husbandry department provided Tate with a job at the Texas Tech horse farm (then located where the College of Media & Communication currently sits) repairing harnesses for the teams of Percherons. Mowery later promoted Tate to grading papers and doing lab work.

Once Tate joined the Saddle Tramps, Lamb came to him with a clandestine project:

> Arch thought we ought to have what they called a Red Raider Rider. I was a member of the Saddle Tramps, and Arch came to me one day and said, "George, can you get a horse?" "Well, there's a saddle horse out there at the horse barn where I work." Well, he said, "Now we have to keep this quiet if we want to surprise everybody." He asked if I'd do what he wanted me to, and I said yeah, I sure will.[17]

Lamb set about having a costume made. He enlisted a clothing class taught by Lila Allred Kinchen and his future wife, Mina Wolf, to sew a mask and cape, similar to the ones worn today but not as elaborate, according to Tate.[18]

Lamb selected the Texas Christian University football game on September 29, 1936, for the premiere of the Red Raider Rider. The event-packed weekend included the groundbreaking for the Museum of Texas Tech, an announcement of a record 2,670 enrolled students, and a convocation, during which Lamb formally introduced the Saddle Tramps.[19]

On the "wet, rainy night" of September 29, 1936, Tate took Tony, a palomino-colored riding horse, and met Lamb and the Saddle Tramps at the football stadium.[20] "I should've gone and asked if I could borrow the horse," Tate said in a 1990 interview. "But I said, well, if we want to make a mystery thing out of it, I'll just slip him out."[21]

Over the years, there has been some confusion about whether the horse Tate rode was named Tony or Silver. In a 1990 oral interview, Tate called the horse "Tony," saying it was the only riding horse Texas Tech had and acknowledging it was a palomino, a color of horse with a yellow body and white mane and tail. The minutes for the September 26, 1936, Board of Regents meeting recognized the gift of a palomino stallion to Texas Tech. A September 1936 press release by the university said Texas Tech received the "prized stallion" Silver from Hal H. Vaughan, an oil man from Shamrock, Texas. Silver competed at the Texas Centennial Central Exposition in Dallas that year and was believed to be the first palomino owned by an educational institution. The press release also claimed Vaughan had the country's largest herd of palomino broodmares.[22]

In his new costume of a red shirt, black trousers, black mask, and red and black cape—and borrowing his roommate's boots (that were three sizes too small) because he did not own a pair of his own—Tate surprised fans by leading the Saddle Tramps onto the track of the football field. The group paraded around the track together before the start of the game.[23]

"We didn't make this wild ride around the field," Tate said.[24] Later interviews with Tate and Lamb suggest that a run around the field did take place sometime that fall. "By the time I got back by Berle Huffman, who was assistant coach and also a track coach, he said, 'I'd like you to get that horse off this track. You're messing it up.' . . . So I didn't stay around too long."[25]

Texas Tech went on to shut out national powerhouse Texas Christian University and its quarterback "Slingin'" Sammy Baugh, a two-time All-American and future Pro Football Hall of Fame inaugural class member, 7–0 that day.

Tate made one or two more appearances during the 1936 football season, then hung up his cape for good.[26] In his interviews, he comes across as a modest agriculture student. But during the year he rode the horse, he served as the senior class vice president and president of Block and Bridle and, like Lamb, was listed in *Who's Who in American Colleges and Universities*. Tate graduated the following spring in 1937 and became a teacher in Eola, located in Concho County in Central Texas.[27]

"I wasn't the first Red Raider Rider because I was popular," Tate told the *Texas Techsan* in a November/December 1984 article, "but because I could get a horse and saddle."

"We called him the Red Raider Rider," Lamb told the *Texas Techsan*. "Few people have spoken much about it because they didn't want to take anything away from Joe Kirk Fulton as the first Masked Rider, but there was an earlier rider." Others allegedly followed Tate as a ghost rider sporadically through the early 1940s, but names have never been revealed nor the rides documented. "At many alumni functions," former Saddle Tramp Rob Lake shared in an interview with the Southwest Collection Library, "a few exes have divulged to the Saddle Tramps that they, at one time or another, had made appearances as the rider. And, they have always prided themselves in having kept the secret."

Lamb philosophically explained the importance of quickness and anonymity in the *Texas Techsan* article. "We thought the Red Raider Rider should represent the school spirit of Texas Tech. . . . Now what is school spirit? It's kind of like a phantom. Like the soul of a man, you can't put your finger on it, can't draw a picture of it. School spirit just appears when you need it, then disappears until it is needed again. Same thing with the rider."[28]

Tate made history as the first unofficial Masked Rider. Sadly, his uniform—the only physical evidence of his service—was destroyed. "I lost it in a house fire in 1952," he said with a twinge of remorse in a 1984 interview. He hesitated. "I sure wish I had it."[29]

Lamb's and Tate's vision didn't catch on permanently, and Tech still searched for its first mascot, which came in an unlikely form.

The Animal Husbandry Department, now the Department of Animal and Food Sciences, debuted a young black Aberdeen Angus bull as a prospective mascot during a football game on October 18, 1952. The Saddle Tramps and cheerleaders made his game-time appearance possible. Formally named Black Invader of Tech, the sixteen-month-old, 900-pound bull was born and raised on the Texas Tech campus. The college showed him at the Panhandle-South Plains Fair in Lubbock, the State Fair of Texas in Dallas, the Hockley County Fair in Levelland, and the Tri-State Fair in Amarillo. In typical 1950s show-cattle fashion, the bull stood about four feet tall on short, squatty legs and was as wide as he was tall. Paul Wiley, an animal husbandry major from Whiteface, handled the animal, which sported a red blanket with a black border and black Double T with "Black Invader" written just below in black block letters for public appearances. The bull became the face of the first concerted effort among the campus community to name a mascot.[30]

Tech planned Black Invader's first away-game trip for the next weekend: a match against North Texas State University (now the University of North Texas) in Denton on November 8, 1952. Texas Tech held a pep rally around the courthouse in downtown Denton the day before the game, and spirits were high.[31] Unfortunately, Black Invader, who was staying in the basement of a NTSU fraternity house, received some unplanned grooming. During the night, a group of about thirty-five "pranksters" overpowered his guard, Jack Harris, and clipped "NT" onto each of his sides. Handlers attempted to paint over the damage, but the bull became agitated. Luckily, his custom blanket covered the clipping.[32]

An animal husbandry professor decided that an "expert" clipped the bull due to the quality of the clipping. But the department's biggest concern? Black Invader's hair might not grow out in time for him to compete at the Fort Worth Stock Show in January.[33]

A rare photo of Black Invader at a football game is featured on the front page of an October 21, 1952, copy of the *Toreador*. (Courtesy the Southwest Collection)

In April 1953, Black Invader finally made it to the ballots. After a petition for a vote spurred on by the cheerleaders, Student Council elections included a vote to have a black bull be named the official mascot.[34] Although some students voiced concerns that naming a bull as mascot could earn Texas Tech the reputation of a "cow college," others believed it properly signified the Spanish traditions of the institution.[35] (While Black Invader's Angus breed originated in Scotland, it probably was the most manageable bull that resembled the exceptionally aggressive black Spanish fighting bull.) With 1,249 votes, Black Invader became the first official mascot of Texas Tech.[36]

But Black Invader's unplanned haircut proved to be a bad omen for the mascot. Affection for the bull waned on campus. The football team began to believe that instead of bringing good luck to the team on game days, the bull was a jinx. The Red Raiders fell to 3–7–1 in the 1952 season during his debut, and for the fourth time, Southwest Conference members rejected Tech's bid to join the conference.

Shortly after students named Black Invader the official mascot, the bull was sold for just $250 in a purebred consignment sale. His low selling price was blamed on a lack of Angus bidders at the auction. Attempts to replace the bull for the 1953 football season failed due to a lack of interest and motivation. By the end of the year, Black Invader and black bulls in general quietly slipped off the radar and the football field. Texas Tech was again without a mascot.[37]

Joe Kirk Fulton sits atop what is likely Blackie underneath the bleachers for the September 30, 1954, football game against West Texas State College, now known as West Texas A&M University. (Courtesy the Southwest Collection)

2

# A SENSATIONAL ENTRANCE

During the mascot-less 1953 season, the Red Raiders went 5–0 in conference play and earned a trip to the Gator Bowl. The football program had never looked better, and the college was gaining respect and validity across the state. DeWitt Weaver entered his third year as the head coach of Red Raider Football, and joining the Southwest Conference became a priority. While Texas Tech was succeeding in the Border Conference, the Southwest Conference would show the country that Texas Tech deserved to be among the ranks of the top universities and add an air of legitimacy for the college's academic and athletics programs.

Southwest Conference member schools voted on which schools should and shouldn't be admitted. Tech fans believed Southern Methodist University was to blame for the failed 1952 bid. They waged economic war against Dallas, cutting up their Neiman Marcus credit cards and mailing the remnants to the store. Allegedly, the act pushed store chief Stanley Marcus to encourage SMU to change their vote in Tech's favor.[1]

Coach Weaver wanted to do everything possible to gain admittance to the conference, including developing a proper mascot to make Tech more desirable to voters.[2]

Moody Alexander worked as a student trainer under Coach Weaver during that time. In a 2008 interview with the *Texas Techsan*, he explained how the idea for a horse mascot allegedly began stewing during a Rotary Club luncheon for the players, coaches, and football staff in preparation of the Gator Bowl. "[O]ne of the players remarked that people in Florida think everybody in Texas rides a horse," Alexander told Bill Dean. "We all agreed, and someone suggested that, since I was on the Student Council, I should look into it."

Alexander said he brought up the idea to Coach Weaver. "In fact, he said that he had always thought we ought to have a horse," Alexander recounted.[3] Weaver likely already had a plan in mind.

Coach Weaver asked a favor from a couple of friends, Evelyn and R. H. Fulton. He brought his idea to their son, Joe Kirk, a junior animal husbandry major: lead the team onto the field at the Gator Bowl on horseback.[4]

Equine mascots were a rarity for major universities in the 1950s. In 1936 at the United States Military Academy (more commonly known as West Point), a mule became the first ridden official equine mascot for a major university. Mr. Jackson

Fulton rides at another football game in 1954. (Courtesy the Southwest Collection)

(named after Stonewall Jackson) retired from work as an Army pack mule and went into service as the school's designated mascot. He presided over two Black Knights football national champion wins during his twelve-year reign.[5]

The Masked Rider predates all other Division I horse mascots. Its 1954 inception came before the University of Southern California's Trojan and Traveler (1961), the University of Virginia's Cavman (1963), Murray State University's Racer One (1976), and Florida State University's Chief Osceola and Renegade (1978). The Masked Rider also served as the model for Oklahoma State University's Spirit Rider, who first appeared in 1984 and was created by a Texas Tech alumnus.

The University of Oklahoma's Sooner Schooner, pulled by two white ponies, made its debut in 1964 and wasn't officially named the mascot until 1980. Southern Methodist University's Peruna the Pony first appeared in 1932, but it has always been a miniature horse or pony too small for riding and is always led

Fulton takes off for the pregame run with the football team behind him in a fall 1954 game. (Courtesy the Southwest Collection)

by hand. The University of Wyoming's Cowboy Joe has also been an unridden pony since its start in 1950.

The Denver Broncos welcomed their first live mascot horse, an Arabian stallion called Thunder, in 1993. The Kansas City Chiefs debuted their live horse mascot in 1963 as well—a horse named Warpaint, ridden bareback by a man dressed as an American Indian chief. Warpaint's rides ended in 1989 when the horse entered his twenties, and the duo was replaced with an actor who rode victory laps on a motorcycle. The team revamped the tradition in 2009 with a Chiefs cheerleader, who happened to be a two-time Pinto Horse Association World Champion in the saddle. The Chiefs ended the program in 2020 after discussions with the American Indian Community Working Group.[6]

On January 1, 1954, Joe Kirk Fulton pulled on his Levi's jeans, his boots, a red shirt, and a black felt cowboy hat. His black cape lined with red satin boasted a black Double T crafted by Lila Allred Kinchen (later an associate professor of clothing and textiles), using material purchased by the Athletics Department. Fulton, though, has been the only Masked Rider who did not wear a mask. During his time, the mascot was referred to as the Red Raider or Red Raider Rider.

Fulton rode Blackie, a black gelding—loaned to him by Jim St. Clair[7] of the Levelland Sheriff's Posse—that had gone to Jacksonville for the Gator Bowl parade. He borrowed a trailer and saddle from his father, R. H. Fulton. Joe Kirk led the team out on the field, galloped one loop around, and vanished. *Atlanta Constitution* sports editor Ed Danforth penned the now-famous quote: "No team in any bowl game ever made a more sensational entrance." Danforth also called the entrance "typically Texas."

Coach Weaver had a hunch Joe Kirk was up for the job of galloping a horse through a football stadium. Word got out that Joe Kirk had allegedly ridden his horse into the Student Union Building one day, and soon after, Coach Weaver asked Joe Kirk to his office and proposed the idea.

While many claimed to have originated the idea of the modern Masked Rider with Coach Weaver, Fulton said time and time again the idea came from Weaver—but with a caveat.[8] "He wanted a masked rider," Fulton recounted in 1980, twenty-six years after his Gator Bowl ride. "He called me, visited with me about the idea, and asked me if I thought it would work."[9]

Four years later, Fulton said, "I've heard about fifty different people take credit for that idea since I have been out of school, and whether it was original with DeWitt, I can't tell you, but I can tell you that my conversations were with DeWitt. He came to me."[10]

Perhaps the idea originated with George Tate's costume and rides in 1936, which was what Arch Lamb believed: "[T]here was an earlier rider."[11]

Coach Weaver and Fulton knew that the fans loved the first run; however, neither anticipated that seventy years later the Masked Rider Program would have developed into the tradition it has become.

Fulton continued his regular mascot duties during the 1954 through 1955 football seasons. Blackie remained his preferred mount, but occasionally he rode Pretty Day. His costume generally stayed the same, with the addition of a few flashy pieces over time. Fulton wore custom black chaps with red fringe and the words "Red Raiders" in red letters down each leg. He used a red-and-black-striped corona-style saddle pad, breast collar, browband, and noseband. The wool corona-style looked puffed and fluffy: when seen from a distance, it almost looked as though it were

During his first full football season in 1954–1955, Fulton's costume and tack grew more elaborate. (Courtesy the Southwest Collection)

Fulton continues his run around the end zone. (Courtesy the Southwest Collection)

A photo of Jim Cloyd and Tech Beauty appeared on the cover of the October 1956 *Texas Techsan*. (Courtesy the Southwest Collection)

Cloyd sits atop Tech Beauty in this 1957 photo from *La Ventana*. Tech Beauty is wearing her hackamore, a bridle for young horses, and Cloyd wears the first iteration of the Masked Rider uniform. (Courtesy the Southwest Collection)

made from yarn. It was a colorful addition very popular in the 1940s and 1950s, and the pads are still used today with traditional western parade saddles.

Fulton's years did come with a couple of missteps. He accidentally ran into a Louisiana State University cheerleader and dodged flying whiskey and beer bottles hurled from the student section. He also unintentionally ran the Texas A&M University yell leaders off the track at Kyle Field during their school song.

At the end of his service, Fulton received a commemorative silver belt buckle. The buckle continued for decades as the sole token of thanks students received

A group of students flank the Texas Tech mosaic in the Southwest Conference Circle, also called the Saddle Tramps circle. The Central Power Plant can be seen in the background. Undated. (Courtesy the Southwest Collection)

for their time as the Masked Rider. The small silver oval buckle featured a gold Double T flanked by a gold 1950s stylized version of the Masked Rider and horse on the right and a gold football on the left. A gold-colored rope bordered the buckle. This style of buckle was last made by James Maddison of JM Buckles and awarded in 2006 by Dink Wilson. The outgoing rider now receives a larger, modern-style buckle of their design.

Once Fulton hung up his spurs, Jim Cloyd served as the second Masked Rider for the 1956 football season. The Block and Bridle Club, the head of animal husbandry, and the dean of agriculture selected riders jointly. Athletics then approved the selected candidate. According to former Athletics Director Polk Robinson in a 1961 edition of the *Toreador*, "The riders are always good horsemen with a high scholastic rating and good leadership abilities." Starting with Cloyd and continuing for fifteen more years, the Masked Riders previously served as horse herdsmen at the Texas Tech Farm before taking on the mascot role. Funnily enough, Cloyd had himself never owned a horse and when asked if he would ever purchase one replied, "I'm not sure because wherever I work, I am always provided with plenty."[12]

Cloyd came to Texas Tech ten years after graduating high school and brought an exciting past. The Navy veteran had been trained on radar but grew up ranching and worked on the 6666 and Matador Ranches before arriving on campus. Recalling the change from working as a cowboy to serving in the Mediterranean Theatre during World War II, Cloyd said, "The only real trouble was that the sun nearly blinded me when I had to take off my wide brim hat for that little white one."[13]

Cloyd's first year also ushered in a more formal costume with a matador feel. The cape was now made of satin, and a black bolero hat entered the picture, as did a black oval-shaped mask and a Spanish-style red satin shirt with golden yellow accents, red satin pants, and black boots.

The program also acquired official tack thanks to Joe Kirk's father, R. H. Fulton: a $500, sixty-five-pound black saddle designed for ranch work crafted by notable saddle maker S. D. Myres of El Paso.[14] Oversized graduated silver conchos adorned the stirrups, pommel, cantle, and double skirts. Over the years, a black leather breast collar has replaced the horse's corona-style breast collar featuring the words "Texas Tech" tooled in red on the horse's right and "Red Raiders" on the horse's left. R. H. Fulton also provided an official bumper-pull horse trailer painted red with black-and-white trim. For away games, riders pulled the trailer using a car borrowed from a local dealership and returned it to its dealership Monday morning. Hub Motor Company of Lubbock donated the car during Cloyd's year.[15]

The spring of Cloyd's first year came with long-awaited news for Texas Tech. After a twenty-nine-year campaign, the university finally received an invitation to join the Southwest Conference during the spring meeting in Fayetteville, Arkansas, on May 12, 1956. Texas Tech had overcome the final obstacle: Southern Methodist University's voters. Student Association president Glen Cary told the *Toreador*, "This is the greatest day in the history of Tech."

In celebration of their admittance to the Southwest Conference, Texas Tech built the Southwest Conference Circle between the Engineering Key and Jones AT&T Stadium. The circle featured eight terrazzo mosaics arranged in a circle on the ground, identifying the name and mascot of each member school. A 1950s-style Masked Rider represented the Texas Tech panel. The Southwest Conference Circle would become home to pep rallies and homecoming bonfires for years to come until the university population outgrew the space.[16]

The year 1956 brought a new horse to the program: a Quarter Horse mare with feminine features named Tech Beauty. The three-year-old black mare is distinguished in photos by her two hind socks. Tech Beauty was bred by and foaled on the Tech Farm, which was located on the southeast corner of 15th Street and Flint Avenue on campus. The college owned both her sire, Amigo, and her dam, Tech Bonnie. She had lived on the Tech Farm from the day she was foaled on June 22, 1954.[17]

Cloyd and Tech Beauty had a special relationship—one he would treasure for decades after his time at Texas Tech. Cloyd and his staff supervisor, Dr. Fred Harbaugh, developed her name and registered her with the American Quarter Horse Association. Cloyd broke Tech Beauty before she became the Masked Rider's horse, and she became the official mascot with only six months of under-saddle training.[18] At two years old, Tech Beauty became—and remains—the youngest horse to serve in the program. Tech Beauty was also the first Masked Rider horse owned by the university.

Cloyd's time spent with Tech Beauty was so meaningful to him that he handwrote a message on a 1987 Masked Rider ceremony RSVP, requesting that references to Blackie be changed to Tech Beauty: "I would appreciate your

Tech Beauty in her paddock at the horse farm. Undated. (Courtesy the Southwest Collection)

Tech Beauty lopes in her paddock with the Texas Tech horse barn behind her. Undated. (Courtesy the Southwest Collection)

correcting program info. to reflect that I was the first rider of Tech Beauty since I broke her to ride during the summer of 1956."[19]

He also typed a letter to the Special Feature Department in El Paso's *Sundial* newspaper—and copied then-Texas Tech Athletics Director Polk Robinson—in regard to a 1965 Sunday magazine section feature about the Masked Rider. He pointed out he only rode her in a hackamore (a bridle that relies on pressure on the bridge of the nose instead of a bit, typical equipment for horses new under saddle) and shared that even in her young age, Tech Beauty "never proved fractious or unmanageable even when [confronted] with Baylor's live bears or University of Houston's live [cougar]."[20]

After serving as Masked Rider from 1955 to 1957 and graduating from Texas Tech, Cloyd tried to get a job at Disneyland driving a stagecoach, but the required union card cost $128. He shared with *Livestock Weekly* that he turned down the opportunity: "I told them if I had $128, I wouldn't need a job." After stints breaking horses, selling sewing machines, and teaching at Texas Tech, he successfully ran for sheriff in Canadian, Texas.[21]

As sheriff, Cloyd was in a shootout with a pair of bank robbers and apprehended them when he shot one of the robbers in the side. Years later, he ran into the robber who was now working at a feedlot. The reformed robber apprised Cloyd of a group planning on stealing cattle from the feedlot. When the would-be thieves arrived, the robber told them they better watch out for Cloyd. "Look what he did to me," he said and lifted his shirt to expose the scar from the bullet's entry wound. No cattle were stolen that night.[22]

Donald "Polly" Hollar and Tech Beauty in 1957. (Courtesy the Southwest Collection)

Donald "Polly" Hollar took the reins from Cloyd in 1957 and served two terms aboard Tech Beauty as well. Hollar was born in Guthrie, Texas, the home of the 6666 Ranch. One report states he borrowed a 6666 horse during his first year as Masked Rider.[23] His father, E. W., worked as a cowboy for the Pitchfork Ranch and later served as the sheriff of King County. The nickname Polly came from 6666 cowboys. Hollar helped out the ranch cook and had to pass a hateful parrot every time he took out the trash. The parrot always tried to bite Hollar, so the cowboys called him Polly.

Hollar was one of nine children. During his Masked Rider year, his mother Vera won the Paducah, Texas, Lions Club Woman of the Year Award. Hollar's father was the King County sheriff at the time, and the family lived in the sheriff's quarters at the jail in Guthrie, Texas.[24]

While at Texas Tech, Hollar competed on the Texas Tech Rodeo Team in bull riding and saddle bronc riding. After graduating with a bachelor's in animal husbandry in 1959, Hollar became a rancher and cutting horse trainer, winning the 1974 and 1994 American Quarter Horse Association (AQHA) world championship show senior cutting horse classes and $550,000 in lifetime earnings.[25]

In January 1958, the *Toreador* printed a very special upcoming birthday announcement: Tech Beauty was in foal by Handfull, a winning Quarter Horse stallion owned by Gene Smith of Cone, Texas. On July 14, 1958, she delivered a healthy chestnut colt with a blaze and four stockings named Skips Beaut. As James Hamm wrote in the *Toreador*, "After her recent recovery, Tech Beauty appears to be in shape for several more years for her pregame activities. Hats off to a Gallant Lady."[26]

Tech Beauty is pictured with her first foal, Skips Beaut, in summer 1958. (Courtesy the Southwest Collection)

Hollar and Tech Beauty make their pregame run through the Saddle Tramps in 1957. (Courtesy the Southwest Collection)

Hollar handed over the title in 1959 to twenty-year-old J. H. "Hud" Rhea. The lanky animal husbandry major and Monterey High School graduate lived with his family west of Lubbock on the Levelland Highway. Rhea appears in one of

Hollar watches a football game sitting atop Tech Beauty in 1958. The first trailer can be seen behind them to the left. (Courtesy the Southwest Collection)

J. H. "Hud" Rhea atop his horse, Beau Black, during his tenure as the Masked Rider. (Courtesy the Southwest Collection)

Rhea poses atop the Texas Technological College sign. The words on the sign are covered with a sticker on top of the photo. (Courtesy the Southwest Collection)

the more historic Masked Rider photos featured on the cover of a *Texas Techsan* alumni magazine. He stands atop a Texas Technological College sign in his red costume with gold decorations smiling with right hand waving and left hand on his hip. The sign he stands on now sits on the grounds of the Museum of Texas Tech.

Tech Beauty was still on maternity leave during Rhea's tenure. According to a September 1959 Texas Tech press release, Rhea rode his own horse that he had raised from a foal: a black two-year-old registered Quarter Horse stallion named Beau Black. Rhea described Beau Black as "one of the family . . . and he acts like it." Beau Black lived with the Rheas and their three mares while undergoing roping and cutting training.

Rhea told the university his "one great concern when leading the Red Raiders onto the field before each game is riding around the field at a full gallop. But he is confident of Beau Black's even temperament."

The concern came from the fact that the horse was a stallion, and stallions can be unpredictable and aggressive. Stock-horse breed associations prohibit youth riders from exhibiting them, a rare number of amateurs own and handle them, and they are typically left to professionals. In the horse industry, most male horses are castrated, or gelded. These geldings are more docile and even-tempered.

Rhea drew his confidence in Beau Black from the 1959 football season opener, a September 19 game at the Cotton Bowl where Texas Tech beat Texas A&M University. "All in all, he didn't get very excited in Dallas last week," Rhea told the Tech Department of Public Information. "He behaved pretty well for a two-year-old stallion."[27]

Rhea rode Beau Black for his two terms. The horse remains the only stallion to ever serve as a Masked Rider mount. Rhea later became a horse show judge, moved to Roswell, New Mexico, and became the president of First National Bank in Roswell.

Dean Killion arrived at Texas Tech in 1959 as the new director of the Goin' Band from Raiderland. Under Killion's leadership, the Goin' Band experienced a renaissance. The enthusiastic innovator shaped the band into the nationally known powerhouse it is today.

As soon as Killion came aboard, he began adding more pageantry to the pregame and halftime shows. He developed the "Tech Step" and the run-on from the tunnels at pregame and onto the field at halftime. The run-on helped move the growing band quickly onto the field. Killion also developed the "surround-sound" style of marching and playing, including the Band 1 and Band 2 concept—an even split between the band so spectators in every seat could hear the Goin' Band. Band members frequently refer to their "foot and a half of real estate" on the marching field—a term coined by Killion. He also added the traditional spats to the marching uniform. Aside from making improvements to the band during football games, Killion created the Court Jesters, which is the basketball band.

Killion also made the pregame more elaborate and ceremonial. These pregame improvements led to the Masked Rider's theme song.

Fresh from completing his master's degree in music education from the University of Illinois, Richard Earl "Dick" Tolley accepted a position as brass instructor with Texas Tech's School of Music for fall 1959. The trumpet player from Scranton, Pennsylvania, had previously served as an Army musician and choral director. Tolley composed the music for what is known as the Red Raider Fanfare—"Go! Fight! Win!" and "Two-Bits"—as well as "Ride, Raider, Ride" (often called the "Horse Music") in 1961. The Goin' Band plays the Red Raider Fanfare and immediately follows it with "Ride, Raider, Ride."[28]

"Ride, Raider, Ride" signals the Masked Rider's run. Its fast tempo and flurry of piccolo and trumpet lines reflect the feel of seeing the horse and rider sprint down the field.

Tolley remained at Texas Tech as a professor of trumpet and associate director of bands until his retirement in 1991. Killion retired as director of bands in 1980 due to declining health after undergoing brain surgery to remove a tumor. He passed away in Lubbock in October 1997. By the time Killion retired, the Goin' Band had doubled in size to 400 marching members, and the Masked Rider's pregame run and "Ride, Raider, Ride" became forever intertwined. The Masked Rider remains the only collegiate mascot to have a theme song that was written specifically for it.[29]

Kelley Waggoner of Henderson, Texas, became Masked Rider in 1961. The veterinary science major and father of eighteen-month-old twins Danny and David and one-and-a-half-month-old Lance Allen served as the horse herdsman at the Texas Tech stables. He made his debut that May, leading the Texas Tech Rodeo's grand entry aboard Tech Beauty, who returned from her time as a broodmare.

Rhea appeared with Beau Black on the cover of the Lubbock phone directory during his 1960–1961 season as the Masked Rider. The pair is pictured in this promotional photo that accompanied a press release with Texas Tech twins Grace and Kathryn Flechtner. (Courtesy the Southwest Collection)

Kelley Waggoner's twin boys sit in his saddle on Tech Beauty during a home football game in this photo that appeared in the *Lubbock Avalanche-Journal* in November 1961. (Courtesy the Southwest Collection)

Waggoner told the *Daily Toreador*, "When I was first asked to be the Red Raider, it was impressed upon me that it was my duty to promote goodwill and school spirit, and I have sincerely tried to do my best to do this. . . . It has certainly been an enjoyable experience."

Waggoner's football season, though, ushered in the first major changes to the Masked Rider's game-day duties. Since Joe Kirk's first full season, the horse and rider had traveled everywhere the football team played and galloped a lap to lead the team onto the field. But in fall 1961, coaches at other schools expressed their concern that the horse's runs tore up their football field turf. Horses' hooves exert a great deal of pressure at the gallop, and their metal shoes, which help them grip the ground, can cause divots and holes.

Sideline foot traffic also became a concern. At the University of Arkansas, four people stood in the end zone during Waggoner's lap, but his "superior riding . . . saved an accident" as he was able to maneuver around them.

Waggoner finished his undergraduate career by winning the 1961 Dub Parks Memorial Award for being the outstanding member of the Tech Rodeo Association and garnered a nomination for Mr. Texas Tech in 1962.

News broke on December 2, 1961, that Student Association President Carlyle Smith had formed a special committee to reconsider away-game runs. On December 12, 1961, the Student Council voted to recommend that the Athletic Council limit the pregame runs to home games only, and while the horse should not run at away games, it should still accompany the team, which was on par with other Southwest Conference teams. The special committee explained its decision by stating, "Dangers in the past have become reason to believe this tradition could prove dangerous to people who are not acquainted with it."

The Student Council also slipped in one additional recommendation to the Athletic Council: that the Red Raider be named the official school mascot since the horse and rider had not yet been designated as such.

Texas Tech's mascot was finally officially named.

In 1962, red-haired Bill Durfey took the Masked Rider's reins. The animal husbandry major grew up on a ranch in Wellington and came to Tech—"the best school in Texas," according to Durfey—on scholarship. Dr. Ralph Durham, Dean of Animal Husbandry, selected him: "I thought Durfey was as good a horseman as I ever saw."

Durfey stayed busy as a member of Tech's Rodeo Team, meat judging team, and Block and Bridle Club. He was also a big fan of Tech Beauty.

"She was great," Durfey told the *Lubbock Avalanche-Journal* in an October 2, 2011, article. "She was a very good Quarter Horse. When we would line up at the beginning of a game, it was like she was at the starting gates at a racetrack."

When Durfey took the mare to College Station for the Texas A&M game, the Aggies scored a last-minute touchdown at the end of the game to take a 7–3 lead. A large group of Corps of Cadets members rushed toward the pair, but when the horde was twenty yards out, a single Corps leader stepped between Durfey and the crowd. He called off the rush, and Tech Beauty was safe from what Durfey suspected was a kidnapping.

Durfey's year brought two new additions to the Masked Rider Program. The first was a sponsor for the vehicle that pulled the trailer provided by R. H. Fulton.

Waggoner remained active with the Rodeo Team. He is shown here at the May 1961 Texas Tech Rodeo where he served as general manager. (Courtesy the Southwest Collection)

Scoggin-Dickey Buick Company in Lubbock donated the use of a vehicle for out-of-town games for five years. The second was a bit more pivotal.

In 1962, Dr. Dale Zinn, an animal husbandry professor in his early thirties, arrived at Texas Tech. The Oxford, West Virginia, native earned his bachelor's and master's degrees at West Virginia University and his PhD at the University of Missouri–Columbia. Zinn had also served a stint in the US Air Force. In addition to teaching, his various roles during his thirteen years at Texas Tech included coaching the livestock, wool, and meat judging teams, managing the meats lab, and serving as chair of the animal husbandry department. He was also the faculty advisor to the Masked Rider and tasked with selecting the Masked Riders, a duty previously taken on by Dr. Ralph Durham, the chair of the animal husbandry department.

Bill Durfey in costume in a photo taken during his 1962–1963 season as the Masked Rider. (Courtesy the Southwest Collection)

Douglas "Nubbin" Hollar became the Masked Rider in 1963, and he and his brother Donald "Polly" Hollar became the first set of siblings represented in the program. Douglas knew how the Masked Rider gig worked. When Donald served, Douglas traveled from their hometown of Guthrie, Texas, to watch Donald and Tech Beauty make their runs. Originally born on the historic Pitchfork Ranch, Douglas later lived with his family on a farm and then in the town of Guthrie. Douglas never thought he would be the Masked Rider. "Not a chance!" he told the *University Daily*. During his youth, the chubby Douglas stood a hair over five feet tall, earning him the nickname Nubbin. But as he aged, he outgrew his nickname; he took the reins at five feet, nine inches tall.

Durfey and Tech Beauty gallop past the Double T by the north end zone at a football game in 1962. (Courtesy the Southwest Collection)

Durfey with Tech Beauty on the Texas Tech campus in October 1962. (Courtesy the Southwest Collection)

In this 1963 photo from the *La Ventana*, Durfey and Tech Beauty meet Texas Governor John Connally on the sidelines at a football game. (Courtesy the Southwest Collection)

Just like his brother Polly, Nubbin began his tenure as a Masked Rider on Tech Beauty. He rode the horse every other day in the same saddle his brother used. However, Hollar's year held quite a few more obstacles than his brother's.

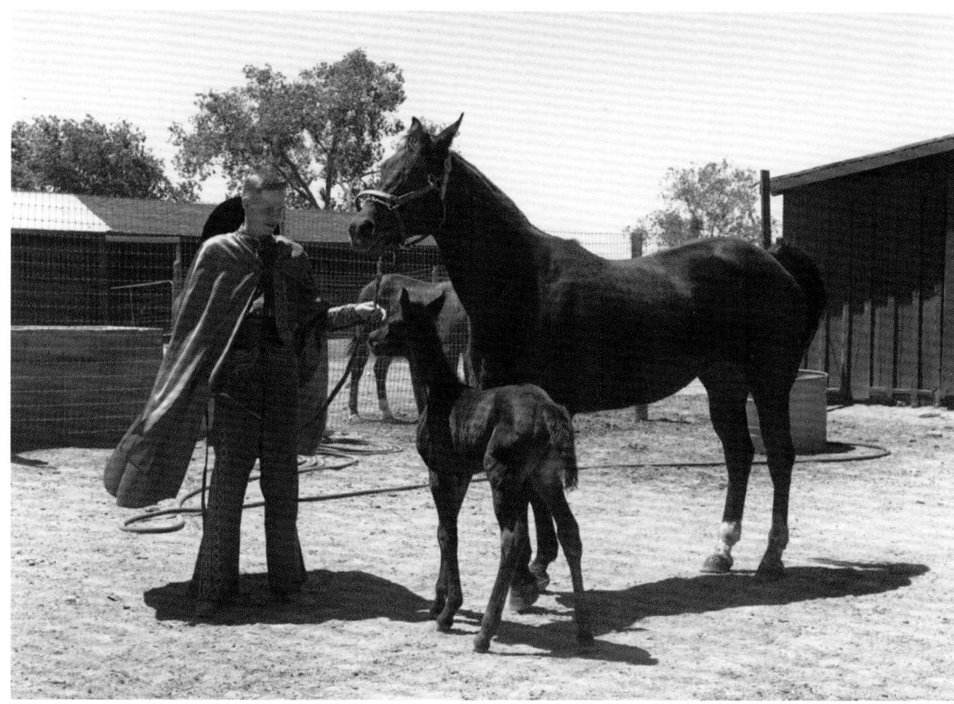

Durfey visits Tech Beauty and her second foal, Tech Beauty II, at the Texas Tech Farm. Undated. (Courtesy the Southwest Collection)

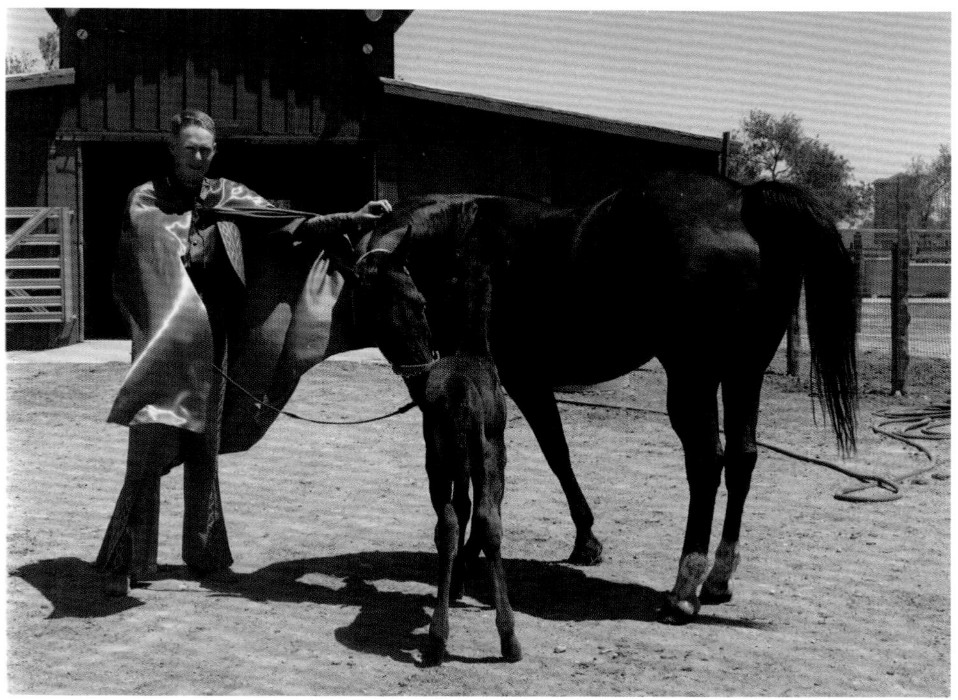

Durfey and Tech Beauty and her second foal, Tech Beauty II, at the Texas Tech Farm. (Courtesy the Southwest Collection)

Durfey and Tech Beauty and her second foal, Tech Beauty II, at the Texas Tech Farm. (Courtesy the Southwest Collection)

Hollar and Tech Beauty traveled to Austin for the September 28, 1963, football game against the University of Texas, but the Longhorns did not allow the pair to make their customary pregame and touchdown runs. Texas Tech fans noted "that big Texas U cow got to stroll around as much as he pleased," according to a *University Daily* recap of the game.

On the eve of the Texas A&M game, unknown thieves stole Tech Beauty from her stall at the Tech Farm late at night on October 4, 1963. Hollar discovered her missing the morning of the game. Charcoal Cody, a black roping horse owned by a Lubbock businessman, filled in for her at the game. Charcoal Cody's owner dyed the gelding's white facial markings black so the crowd wouldn't notice Tech Beauty was missing. But the frantic search continued for the mare.[30]

At about 2:30 a.m. Sunday, a *Lubbock Avalanche-Journal* reporter called Hollar with a hot tip: Tech Beauty could be found in a barn outside Idalou, a small town east of Lubbock. Hollar, future Masked Rider Dink Wilson, animal husbandry chair Dr. Ralph Durham, Boyce Hart, and Harold Heely scoured the area with no luck. Finally, when they were returning from the search at 1 p.m., the group found her tied to a feed trough in a shed three miles south of Idalou.

Her halter was upside down, which caused rope burns on her head. She was

Douglas "Nubbin" Hollar with Tech Beauty during his 1963–1964 season as the Masked Rider. (Courtesy the Southwest Collection)

Hollar and Tech Beauty pose with the 1963 Texas Tech football team. Notable players on the team are No. 44 Donny Anderson, No. 81 Dave Parks, and No. 22 Roger Gill. (Courtesy the Southwest Collection)

tied between the shed wall and the feed trough, so she had not been able to lie down since her theft, nor had she been fed or watered since Friday night. Most notably, the thieves spray painted "AMC" for A&M College in aluminum paint on her sides. Other than superficial injuries and being stiff, tired, hungry, and thirsty, however, Tech Beauty was fine and happily loaded up into her trailer to come home.

Tech Beauty was one of many alleged victims of Texas A&M students over the years. The next month, Aggies stole Bevo from the University of Texas and took the longhorn for a joyride to College Station.[31] Two years earlier, University of Texas students stole one of Baylor's bears named Ginger, panicked, and hit the bear in the head with a wrench, killing her. Years earlier, in 1955, another bear, Pancho, was kidnapped twice in one season—returning on one occasion with "A&M" painted on his sides.[32] University of Texas students claimed to have taken Southern Methodist University's Peruna V in advance of their game in Austin in 1959, but they kidnapped the wrong pony. The perpetrators shaved off its mane and tail and took the animal to the game. Their mistake was revealed when the real Peruna showed up to the game in perfect condition with his true handlers.[33]

The actions against mascots led to a resolution presented by either Baylor or

A rider who appears to be Douglas Hollar rides past the Goin' Band from Raiderland aboard Charcoal Cody. Undated. (Courtesy the Southwest Collection)

Douglas Hollar with Tech Beauty II on the left and Charcoal Cody tacked up on the right during Hollar's 1963–1964 season as the Masked Rider. (Courtesy the Southwest Collection)

An unidentified Masked Rider on Tech Beauty rides in a parade down Broadway in this photo from the late 1950s or early 1960s. (Courtesy the Southwest Collection)

An unidentified Masked Rider on Tech Beauty rides down Broadway past Gaylord's Fashions in the Texas Tech homecoming parade in the early 1960s. (Courtesy the Southwest Collection)

SMU representatives—depending on which paper you read—to the student-run Southwest Conference Sportsmanship Committee meeting on December 30, 1964, in Dallas. The resolution asked for serious disciplinary measures for students in SWC schools involved in the destruction, damage, or theft of another school's property, including mascots.

The student representatives from Texas A&M and the University of Texas opposed the resolution, claiming the measures were "impractical." Despite additional opposition from other schools who believed their universities already had sufficient punishments in place, the resolution passed. A University of Texas representative next proposed the dissolution of the committee, deeming it "essentially useless," and threatened to withdraw their membership at the next meeting if the committee's role was not expanded. Their proposal failed, and

Hollar poses with the torch after setting the 1963 homecoming pep rally bonfire at the Southwest Conference Circle. (Courtesy the Southwest Collection)

The Saddle Tramps donated a mural of Tech Beauty in her remembrance. The sign remained at the north end of the stadium for years. This image appeared in the September 22, 1964, issue of the *Daily Toreador*. (Courtesy the Southwest Collection)

Texas Tech Student Association President Ronnie Botkin said while he agreed the committee should have an expanded role, the University of Texas "has not put as much into the Committee as it should have."[34]

Hollar made one off-season appearance with two horses: Tech Beauty and her yearling, Tech Beauty II. Both wore Double T blankets at a February 18, 1964, appearance at a cage game against Texas Christian University.

Hollar also is the first Masked Rider documented to have the honor of starting the homecoming bonfire. For a number of years, Masked Riders were given the torch to light the traditional homecoming bonfire at the Southwest Conference Circle on campus. Some lit the fire on foot, and others performed the lighting ceremony on horseback. A photo of Hollar lighting the bonfire in the 1964 *La Ventana* is the first reference.[35]

On March 18, 1964, Hollar made what would be Tech Beauty's final appearance: riding in the ABC Rodeo parade in Lubbock. On April 13, Tech Beauty grazed in her wheat pasture at her home at the Tech farm. The now ten-year-old mare was one month away from foaling. Nubbin checked in on the horse at noon, and she appeared fine. But at 5 p.m., he could tell something was wrong.

He took her into the Tech horse barn for an evaluation with Texas Tech veterinarian Dr. Fred Harbaugh. The pair stayed with Tech Beauty throughout the night. She passed away at 4 a.m. Monday, April 14, 1964. Dr. Harbaugh conducted a postmortem and discovered she died due to colic caused by an unknown virus of which there was no cure. Her death occurred just two weeks before her fifth foal was due.

Lubbock residents James Finley and Dr. R. C. Roney donated a young black Quarter Horse named Sugar Loaf to Texas Tech for Hollar to ride at the games the following football season, but no records other than an archived photo and press release make any further mentions of the horse.[36] It seems Sugar Loaf never made an appearance as the Masked Rider's mount.

At a September 19, 1964, football game, the Saddle Tramps unveiled a memorial above the north end zone at Jones AT&T Stadium to Tech Beauty: a roughly twelve-foot-tall painting of Nubbin Hollar in full game-day costume atop Tech Beauty.[37] The Saddle Tramps, Texas Tech's male school spirit organization, had formed a working relationship with the Masked Rider Program. The Tramps stationed themselves on the sidelines at every five-yard marker during home football games. They ensured the horse and rider had a clear path for their runs. The Saddle Tramps funded the project completed by Lubbock advertising artist James Carty at a cost of more than $300. The painting remained a fixture at Jones AT&T Stadium for more than a decade.

The sudden loss of Tech Beauty left a hole in the hearts of many riders and Texas Tech fans. She had become the community's mascot. Red Raiders stuck beside her through foaling, a kidnapping, and dozens of home and away games. Her replacement turned out to be a familiar face.

Tommy Martin and Charcoal Cody at Jones AT&T Stadium. (Courtesy the Southwest Collection)

# 3

# CHARCOAL CODY

Bill Price was a card-carrying member of the Professional Rodeo Cowboys Association. The US Navy veteran worked as a roughneck on West Texas oil fields, played the drums for a band he started, cowboyed on a ranch near Lovington, New Mexico, and became a steer and calf roper and world-champion roping horse trainer. Bill later settled in Lubbock, opening the Bill Price Western Shop and even winning the Wendy Ryon Memorial Award for Western Retailer of the Year.

Bill also owned Charcoal Cody, a twelve-year-old roping horse registered with the American Quarter Horse Association. Pro Rodeo Hall of Famers Troy Fort and Toots Mansfield had even roped off the horse at one time. Sired by the King Ranch's famous Bill Cody and out of a Jack McClure mare, the black 14.2-hand, 1,200-pound gelding quietly subbed in for Tech Beauty during her kidnapping and for parades when she was in foal.

Charcoal Cody became the fourth horse of the Masked Rider Program and served for nine years. In an interview with the *Lubbock Avalanche-Journal*, one of Price's employees said, "Mr. Price could have made a valuable rodeo horse out of Charcoal Cody, but Tech means a great deal to him. Sure he's gotten some advertising out of it, but the reason he donated Cody goes a lot deeper than that."

Douglas "Dink" Wilson of Matador rode the horse for its first full football season in 1964. Wilson remarked that Charcoal Cody was "a real good horse" that was "easy to control and really likes to run."

Wilson, a junior range management major from Matador, Texas, broke horses during the summers on a ranch in Midland but regularly made the Dean's List at Tech. The *Daily Toreador* reported, "You'd never get the impression he is an 'egg-head.'" When asked how he would sign autographs if asked given his nickname, he said, "I guess I'd just sign 'em 'Dink' if anybody ever wants one."[1]

The *Daily Toreador* reported that Dr. Durham handpicked Wilson during fall 1964 registration, but later in 2011, Wilson shared with Texas Tech a more accurate version of events. He and the previous rider, Douglas Hollar, were roommates, and Wilson had served as Hollar's Masked Rider assistant. Hollar called Wilson a week before the 1964 football season and asked if he would take over Masked Rider duties so he could concentrate on his academics.

In the *Daily Toreador* profile, Wilson shared many sentiments that still resonate with riders today: "I was a little nervous at the barn before the game, but at the stadium I was too busy to worry about anything. . . . I like being able to sit that close to the game. The only trouble is that I can't tell how much yardage was made on any particular play. . . . Cody did a good job and wasn't bothered

Douglas Hollar rides in a parade with Charcoal Cody during his 1966–1967 season as the Masked Rider. (Courtesy the Southwest Collection)

by the cannon, the band music or the crowd."

In a Texas Tech video interview years later, Dink was asked about his most memorable experiences, and he recalled a Baylor game:

> They had this bear chained to the goal post, and one of the cheerleaders came out and said, "Mr. Red Raider, please don't run over our bear." And I said, "What are you talking about?" "Well, we heard you come down and ran over our bear." And I said, "There ain't no way you can drive this horse over that bear." And this boy was really concerned that I was going to. I rode up 30 to 40 yards from that bear, and of course the horse went to snorting and blowing. It was kind of unique, and that boy was really relieved I wasn't going to try to get his bear.[2]

Wilson planned on graduating in December 1964 and becoming a full-time rancher, but he ended up staying and serving an additional year as Masked Rider, completing his service in 1966. Hollar returned to the saddle for two more terms from 1966 to 1968.

The 1960s brought a shift in priorities for Texas Tech. Tractors replaced workhorses, and the real estate on the corner of 15th Street and Flint Avenue was deemed too valuable a space for livestock barns. In the summer of 1966, the university razed the horse barn and corrals that housed numerous Masked Rider horses over the years and made way for the new $4.5 million Business Administration Building. The horse facilities were moved to a location on Tech Freeway (now Marsha Sharp Freeway) where the Texas Tech University Health Sciences Center currently sits.

The move began in October 1961. Soon after Texas Tech finished building its meat lab, the School of Agriculture started moving into its new farm on the Tech Freeway. The new farm structures alone cost $500,000, and the total value of the 1,400 acres plus the facilities reached $7 million.

The facilities had space for 800 beef calves, 100 milking cows, 50 dairy calves, 1,000 laying hens, and 4,000 broilers. Centers for horses, sheep, and pigs came online as funding became available.

Another change came to the Masked Rider Program in 1967. Modern Chevrolet in Lubbock began a long-standing relationship with the Masked Rider Program, providing the vehicle used to pull the trailer to Masked Rider appearances.[3] The most popular vehicles for their donation were Chevy El Caminos and station wagons.

Johnny Bob Carruth, an agricultural education major from De Leon, Texas, took the reins to Charcoal Cody for two terms between1968 and 1970. Carruth's only issue with the senior horse occurred at a game during his first term, when the horse "bucked all the way down the football field."

"Charcoal Cody was an exciting and dynamic type of a horse and was really suited to the Masked Rider Program, and everybody in the stands and in the stadium just loved it," Carruth told Texas Tech's Office of Communications and Marketing in 2014.

The Masked Riders staged their first reunion at the University of Arkansas game on Saturday, November 23, 1968. Clyde Prestwood, the athletic academics counselor, planned the event, which included honoring the eight former riders at a brunch that morning and recognizing them at halftime.[4]

At the same time, Texas Tech football was outgrowing its stadium. In the 1960s, the field at Jones AT&T Stadium sat below street level. Instead of its current bowled-in seating, though, the north end zone simply had a grassy slope adorned with a flat concrete Double T surrounded by Southwest Conference

**We're proud of the Red Raider**
**Our Charcoal Cody shows it.**

***Bill Price's***
**Western Shop**

**2854**
**34th**

Bill Price's Western Shop took out ads like this one in the 1968 SMU football game program to showcase their donation of Charcoal Cody's use. (Courtesy the Southwest Collection)

team names. The horse and rider rode around the sidelines, banking their turn on the hill just below the Double T.

Following the 1969 season, the university began a second expansion of Jones AT&T Stadium. Crews used railroad tracks to move the bleachers on the second level of the stadium to the back, creating more room for seating and a bowled appearance. More importantly for the Masked Rider, Texas Tech went from grass to AstroTurf, and the slope above the north end zone that connected the field to the grass surrounding the Double T was separated by a wall, creating a track-type border around the field. The Masked Rider would no longer run up the hill during runs but would remain on the track.[5]

Douglas "Dink" Wilson poses in costume at Jones AT&T Stadium in 1964. (Courtesy the Southwest Collection)

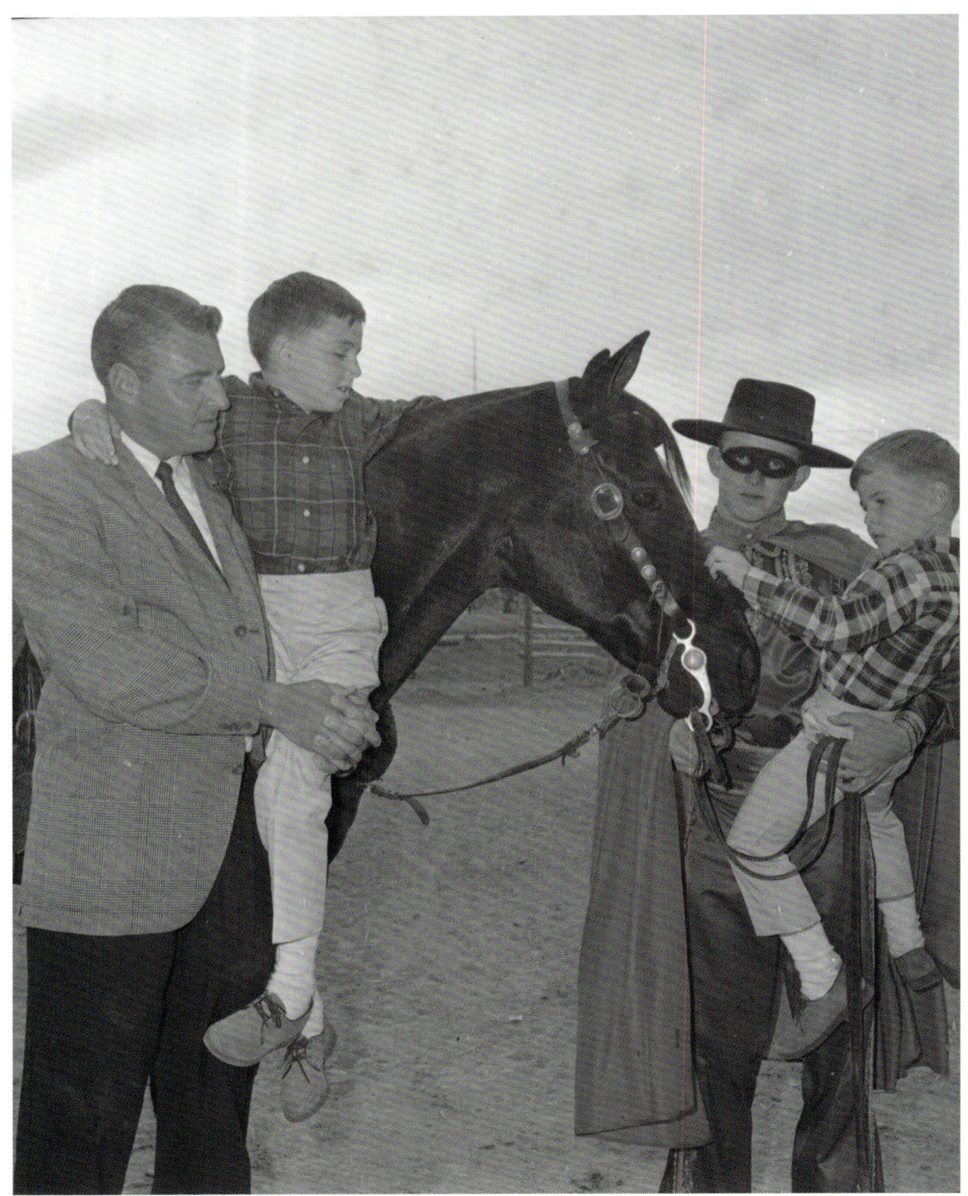

Joe Kirk Fulton and his sons, Kirk and Kyle (left to right), meet Charcoal Cody and Douglas Wilson in this photo that appeared in the *Lubbock Avalanche-Journal* on November 19, 1965. (Courtesy the Southwest Collection)

Douglas Wilson and Charcoal Cody at Jones AT&T Stadium in 1965. (Courtesy the Southwest Collection)

This unnamed horse and rider appear to be Douglas Wilson with three-year-old Tech Beauty II, in a photo likely taken in 1967. Behind the pair are the truck and trailer and the Chitwood/Weymouth/Coleman residence hall complex. (Courtesy the Southwest Collection)

Tommy Martin, a senior animal science major from Throckmorton, Texas, rode from 1970 to 1971. He made his first official appearance at the Red Raiders' football home opening game against Tulane on September 12, 1970.[6] Martin

Wilson and Charcoal Cody at Jones AT&T Stadium in 1965. (Courtesy the Southwest Collection)

An unidentified rider and Charcoal Cody make their pregame run with the El Camino and trailer in the background. Undated. (Courtesy the Southwest Collection)

Johnny Bob Carruth during his 1969–1970 season. (Courtesy the Southwest Collection)

took care of the horse for two years before his term because he worked at Tech's horse barn where Charcoal Cody lived. Martin said becoming Masked Rider "was a dream come true."

"Martin applied for the job as the Red Raider even before he had graduated from high school. . . . His application was kept on file with the rest," department chair Dr. Dale Zinn told the *Lubbock Avalanche-Journal*. Zinn advised Martin to shadow Carruth until he became eligible to serve in the position.

Martin and Charcoal Cody traveled with a couple of friends to the University of Kansas game in Lawrence, Kansas, but stadium officials refused to let Cody inside for fear his hooves would tear up the new turf—even though, according to Martin, Jones AT&T Stadium had the same turf. Instead, the pair remained on a hill by the scoreboard just outside the stadium's south fence and were subjected to being called Zorro by numerous University of Kansas fans. The Red Raiders won 23–0, and the pair made their touchdown runs on the hill. Martin's refused entry was the precursor to a rule that forever changed the Masked Rider's schedule.

As Martin's term wound down, the Southwest Conference's spring 1971 meeting handed down a decision that live animal mascots would no longer be

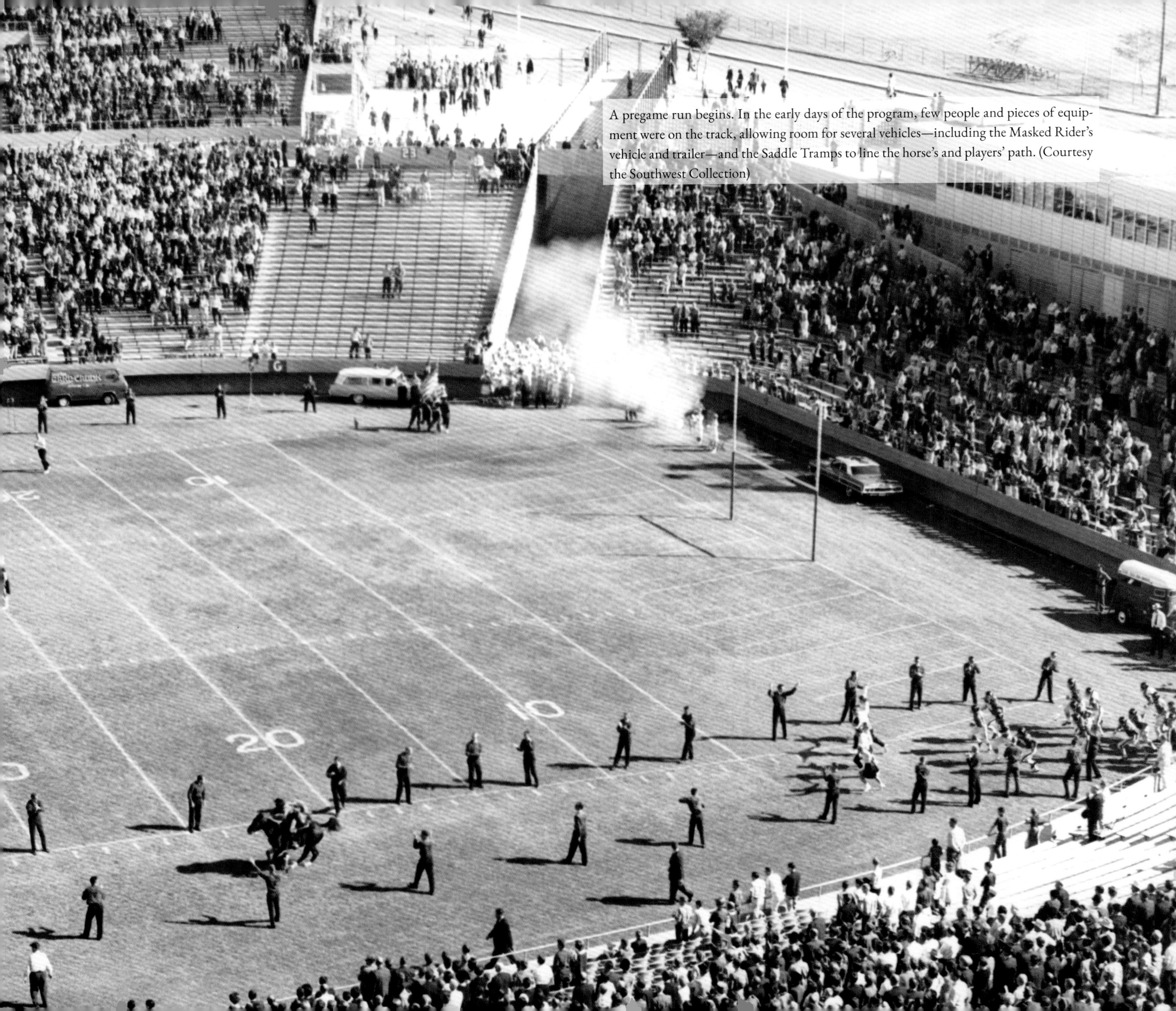

A pregame run begins. In the early days of the program, few people and pieces of equipment were on the track, allowing room for several vehicles—including the Masked Rider's vehicle and trailer—and the Saddle Tramps to line the horse's and players' path. (Courtesy the Southwest Collection)

Carruth rides Charcoal Cody through Saddle Tramps and balloon releases for a pregame run in 1968. (Courtesy the Southwest Collection)

MODERN CHEVROLET Supports THE RED RAIDERS!



Gordon H. Rose, President of Modern Chevrolet, stands with Texas Tech's Athletic Director, Polk Robison, in front of three Chevrolet vehicles Modern supplies without cost for use throughout the school year by Red Raider organizations. Next to the Tech Band Wagon are drummer Lloyd Lebow, drum major Jim Irvin and majorette Donna Snyder. The Red Raider, Johnny Bob Carruth, sits astride his horse, Charcoal Cody, behind the Raider's El Camino and trailer. Representing the Saddle Tramps is President Bill Pittman, seen with their Chevrolet Kingswood Estate Wagon. Their heavy brass bell, "Bangin' Bertha," sits on its trailer at right.

modern CHEVROLET See MODERN and SAVE 1902 TEXAS SH 7-3211

No. 1 In West Texas For 12 Straight Years!

ASK ABOUT OUR NEW LEASE PLAN!

Modern Chevrolet advertises their donation of vehicles for the Goin' Band, Masked Rider, and Saddle Tramps in the *Lubbock Avalanche-Journal* on November 23, 1968. (Courtesy the Southwest Collection)

allowed at away games without the consent of the home team. Discussions about the rule had begun in 1970, and the 1971 vote just clinched it. Many other schools either did not have a live mascot, or they had mascots that could not travel easily. For Texas Tech, the rule meant major changes to the Masked Rider's role and travel schedule. Texas Tech would most likely not be permitted to bring a mascot at most away games because the horse was a large animal that could damage the turf with its hooves.

The Saddle Tramps began discussing the issue in the spring semester of 1970 for fear that many teams would ban the Masked Rider from their stadiums. In the summer of 1971, Saddle Tramp senior Jim Gaspard took action to create a mascot that would be acceptable for away games. During the summer session, he served as an advisor at Wall residence hall and had a room to himself—the perfect laboratory for his creation.

Gaspard drew inspiration from having observed costumed characters greet park guests during a visit to Disneyland. He thought a cartoon-based costumed mascot could provide the support needed at away games, but he did not want to step on the Masked Rider's toes.

In a 1990 letter to the Saddle Tramps, Gaspard wrote, "I was concerned that any new mascot would be perceived as an attempt to replace the Red Raider as the school mascot. And we didn't need another controversy on campus."[7]

Gaspard continued in secret, contemplating further potential contentions. Dirk West, a Lubbock cartoonist and owner of West Advertising, created characters depicting each Southwest Conference school for the *Lubbock Avalanche-Journal*. His caricatures of Ol' Red, which West also referred to as Shotgun Sam, had a cartoon-like appearance. Gaspard decided to create a cowboy mascot that would be more light-hearted in contrast to the serious Masked Rider. He inverted the Masked Rider's name of Red Raider to Raider Red.

Gaspard began constructing Raider Red in his Wall Hall dorm room. His

**FORMER RED RAIDERS HONORED—Seven Red Raiders of past years were honored at Saturday's game. From left to right they are: Joe Kirk Fulton, Jim Cloyd, Donald Hollar, J. H. Rhea, Kelley Waggoner, Douglas Wilson and Douglas Hollar. An eighth, Bill Durfey, was unable to attend. (Staff photo by Richard Mays).**

Carruth atop Charcoal Cody in front of the first reunion of former Masked Riders in this photo that appeared in the *University Daily* on November 26, 1968. (Courtesy the Southwest Collection)

In an early pregame run, the horse and rider bank their turn along the grassy hill above the north end zone. Stadium seat additions later filled the area. (Courtesy the Southwest Collection)

Tommy Martin rides Charcoal Cody at the December 19, 1970, Sun Bowl in El Paso. (Courtesy the Southwest Collection)

Raider Red chats with Randy Jeffers and Charcoal Cody on the sidelines during the new mascot's first football season. (Courtesy the Southwest Collection)

letter describes the care he took in Raider Red's creation:

> I began the project from scratch and experimented as I went along, keeping in mind the need for ventilation and minimum weight as well as general comfort for the wearer. Residents of my wing occasionally dropped in with suggestions or to critique my work. Some just smirked, shrugging me off as strange as wing dicks sometimes are. Raider Red's head was constructed of chicken wire formed to slip over my head and rest on my shoulders, with care to align the eye openings with mine. The ears were modeled after those of my girlfriend, and now wife, Dinah DeWitt '72 . . . papier mâché strips torn from copies of the *University Daily* and soaked in wallpaper glue were used to cover the chicken wire. Two giant six-shooters were also built from papier mâché. As I recall the finishing touches to the head were applied during finals, along with the red moustache, eyebrows and hair, and leather mask and headband.
>
> While I worked on the head, I found a student in the theater arts department who agreed to make the body costume, complete with pillow stuffings. I don't recall her name but remember she was great to work with and took on the project with much enthusiasm to recreate the Shotgun Sam character clothes and cape, as well as adapt some comfort features for the wearer. Tandy Leather donated the leather with which I made a holster for the guns and a belt to hold the wooden bullets. The leather boots came from the Salvation Army store downtown and were painted red and white.

Gaspard debuted the costume at the first Saddle Tramps meeting of the semester on August 18, 1971. The group liked the idea and voted to bring Raider Red to the first pep rally a few weeks later. The crowd loved Raider Red and recognized the Dirk West character. West gave his permission to use the Ol' Red/Shotgun Sam character, and Saddle Tramp Stan Alcott of Lake Jackson, Texas, appeared as Raider Red for the 1971 season. A new mascot was born. (A few years later, the University of Nebraska would adopt West's Herbie Husker illustration as its mascot, making West the originator of two collegiate mascots.)

Over the years, the Masked Rider and Raider Red have worked together at football games and many public appearances. Gaspard's concerns about offending the Masked Rider tradition never came to fruition. Fans appreciate both mascots and the different roles they take on game days and as representatives of the university. Raider Red, known for his mischievousness and playfulness, can travel with the cheer and pom squads to all football games, including the away games when the home team or stadium does not permit the Masked Rider to attend. Gaspard's idea was a success, and his original intent was forever preserved.

In addition to Raider Red, 1971 brought another Texas Tech staple. Tech graduate Glenn Dippel and his wife Roxie moved to Austin in 1961. Surrounded at every turn by the Hook 'em, Horns sign, the Dippels had had enough. Inspired by Raider Red's oversized six-shooters, the Dippels submitted the idea of the Guns Up hand sign to the Saddle Tramps and cheerleaders.

Randy Jeffers with Charcoal Cody on the left and Showboy Huffman on the right in 1971. (Courtesy the Southwest Collection)

Randy Jeffers in his 1971–1972 season with Showboy Huffman. (Courtesy the Southwest Collection)

Dr. Bill Dean, executive vice president of the Texas Tech Alumni Association, recalled that at first, fans did not understand the meaning of the hand sign, but after the Saddle Tramps and cheerleaders used the guns up to students at a few football games, the hand sign caught on. Masked Riders incorporated it into their pregame and touchdown runs.[8]

During Tommy Martin's year, the Animal Science Department selected a stand-in for the aging Charcoal Cody: a three-year-old Quarter Horse gelding named Showboy Huffman, owned by Texas Tech student Randy Jeffers.

Randy Jeffers, a pre-law and business administration major from Amarillo, rode Charcoal Cody from 1971 to 1972, the horse's last year as mascot. Jeffers's selection came from his experience in breaking, training, and showing Quarter Horses. He was first introduced to the program at a horse sale as a high school sophomore. Jeffers was in a bidding war over a colt with representatives from Texas Tech looking for a future Masked Rider horse. He won the horse and kept up with the university representatives. In an undated video interview from the late 1990s, Jeffers recalled his first ride: "I was so nervous, I couldn't remember the words to the *Star-Spangled Banner*." Despite Charcoal Cody's age, "When he got ready to go, you were on for the ride."[9] The horse and Jeffers fell while rounding the first corner of the stadium during the pregame run at the 1971 Texas Tech–Baylor game, but neither sustained injuries. The game-day veteran Charcoal Cody popped back up to finish his run and met Jeffers back at the horse trailer in the south end zone.

"We pretty well flew by the seat of our pants in those days," Jeffers reflected. "There wasn't anybody really in the administration that kept up with us much once the season started. We were pretty much on our own and no funding to speak of."

Jeffers rode Showboy Huffman (now five years old) from 1971 to 1972 for out-of-town appearances when Charcoal Cody was being used at home. Charcoal Cody retired in 1972 at the age of twenty-one. Showboy Huffman took the horse's spot on the field and at the Texas Tech horse barn for Jeffers's second term but left Texas Tech with Jeffers at the end of his service in 1973.

The 1970s ushered in more than a decade of illustrious partnerships for the Masked Rider Program and an era many alumni fondly recall as the Happy horses.

The Masked Rider and Charcoal Cody appear on the cover of the October 1975 issue of the *Texas Techsan*. (Courtesy the Southwest Collection)

# 4

# HAPPY DAYS FOR TECH

Clarence Scharbauer Jr. is a legend in the horse world: American Quarter Horse Association Hall of Fame member and former president, Texas Horse Racing Hall of Fame member, and recipient of the national rancher of the year National Golden Spur Award and Texas Thoroughbred Association lifetime achievement award. He was one of the first to invest in Lone Star Park in Grand Prairie, Texas, and became the key spokesperson for the track's Class 1 license application to the Texas Racing Commission. Many credit Scharbauer as the main reason Lone Star Park won the bid against other applications.[1]

But perhaps more notably, Scharbauer and his wife Dorothy owned Alysheba, the 1987 Kentucky Derby and Preakness Stakes winner, 1988 Horse of the Year, and 1993 inductee into the Horse Racing Hall of Fame. The Scharbauers bought Alysheba, the son of Alydar, at Keeneland as a yearling for a steal at $500,000. After his racing career, Alysheba stood at stud in Kentucky and later in Saudi Arabia before he was retired as an attraction to the Kentucky Horse Park's Hall of Champions. He lived out the rest of his days in the stall previously used by famed racehorse John Henry.[2]

But before Scharbauer's days in thoroughbred racing, he was a true cowboy. The Scharbauer family began ranching in Texas in the 1880s. In an interview with the *Daily Racing Form*, Ken Carson, Scharbauer's Valor Farm general manager and employee of twenty-nine years, shared his boss's younger days: "He's a cattleman, but he's also a serious cowboy. . . . He can do anything on horseback. He was a world-class calf roper when he was young. He's a heck of a horseman. He can walk around a horse and tell you everything about him. He's a seriously good horseman."[3]

It was during these early days that Scharbauer's and Texas Tech's paths crossed. The horseman loaned Happy V (pronounced Happy Five), a twelve-year-old black gelding, to the Animal Science Department to serve as the program's next Masked Rider horse.

Happy V's loan was made possible by Gerald Nobles, who would become the twelfth Masked Rider. Nobles and eleventh rider, Jeffers, had known each other since high school through AQHA shows, and Nobles became Jeffers's assistant. The two were scouting new horses, and Scharbauer happened to be Nobles's cousin.

"He had a black horse on one of his ranches that his ranch foreman rode," Nobles told Texas Tech in an undated video interview about Scharbauer and Happy V. "We went out and looked at this horse and rode him, and he decided he might donate him to Tech. After a little more arm twisting, we ended up with a new horse donated to Tech from Clarence Scharbauer."[4]

Gerald Nobles with Happy V during his 1973–1974 season as the Masked Rider. (Courtesy the Southwest Collection)

An unidentified rider makes a game-day run on the track at Jones AT&T Stadium. Undated. (Courtesy the Southwest Collection)

Both Happy V and Nobles were from Midland. Nobles, a twenty-two-year-old animal business major, became the twelfth Masked Rider from 1973 to 1974 after first inquiring about the position as a high school senior on a college visit. Nobles, like many of his predecessors, worked at Texas Tech's horse farm. The first home game in 1973 would be the inaugural football appearance for both, but Nobles was confident in the new horse whom he referred to as his "buddy."[5]

"I don't expect any problems though, but that first corner around the field is tough," he shared before the game. "It's not all that dangerous if the rider pays attention. . . . The trick is to keep the horse on the [synthetic] Tartan track. If one foot gets onto the grass field there can be trouble. The grass is real slick."[6]

Nobles's care and confidence resulted in a clean year for both and a solid foundation for Happy V's career as the Masked Rider's horse, save for one game: when Nobles and his team forgot the saddle. Nobles and his wife were recently married, and his new wife's family was in town for the October 13, 1973, game against Texas A&M, which made for a packed weekend of visiting. "Back then, we kind of paraded him around with a blanket on," Nobles said of the horse upon arrival at a home football game. "Then we opened the trailer to saddle him up, and we'd forgotten the saddle and left it at the Tech Farm."

Students dress Will Rogers as the Masked Rider in fall 1973. (Courtesy the Southwest Collection)

The game was nationally televised, so there was no delaying pregame or kick-off. Nobles's assistant, Dan Kinsel, got in a Texas Tech police car and rode—sirens blazing—to the farm to retrieve the saddle.

"I'll never forget the sound of the siren as the car came down the ramp with the saddle in it," Nobles said. "I threw the saddle on and girded it and swung my leg over the saddle as they finished 'Two Bits.' I couldn't have cut it any closer."[7]

Years later, Nobles reflected on his time at Texas Tech and in the saddle: "Attending Texas Tech was an important time in our lives. . . . We met and married while attending Texas Tech. Yet, it was the Masked Rider experience that opened so many doors for our future. We have met and are still meeting

Anne Lynch during her 1974–1975 season. (Courtesy the Southwest Collection)

people through the Masked Rider Program that are so warm, friendly, and with whom it is a pleasure to be associated."[8]

Each Masked Rider had an assistant who helped with appearances and some day-to-day duties. Typically, after a year of shadowing the rider, the assistant moved up to serve as the Masked Rider the following year. As Nobles and Happy V loaded up for their games from the horse farm, one assistant—Anne Lynch, an animal science major from Dell City—developed a dream.

Once Lynch became a junior, she asked to put her name on the Masked Rider candidate list. The request was quickly shot down. Why? "Because girls couldn't try out." Women simply weren't allowed to compete for the position. In Lynch's famous words, "Well that wasn't working for me."[9]

Up to that time, only one person selected the next rider: the chair of the Animal Science Department, who at that time was Dr. Dale Zinn. Students turned in their applications to Zinn, who then selected the rider "mainly on scholarship and horsemanship," as he was quoted in an April 9, 1974, *University Daily* editorial. Applicants must be full-time Texas Tech students with at least a 2.00 GPA, and Zinn or other Animal Science Department faculty members

Anne Lynch and Happy V during her 1974–1975 season as the Masked Rider. (Courtesy the Southwest Collection)

had previously seen them ride. When she applied, Lynch had to ride in front of a group that included Zinn and head football coach Jim Carlin.[10]

Lynch's selection made national news and even graced the pages of *Sports Illustrated*. Her tenure was met with disbelief, disdain, and doubt from people—most of them men—who believed that a female rider was a break with tradition, or that women were not physically capable of riding the horse or carrying on the tradition like a man would. People alleged Lynch's appointment was a publicity stunt, her selection was bought in donations, and university administration or donors pressured the program to select a female rider.

"The real spotlight should shine on the horse because that's the thing that makes the tradition," Lynch shared with the media the day the Animal Science Department announced her selection. "The rider isn't really the one who is supposed to receive the attention."

But she did. Letters to the editor of the campus paper began pouring in about the perceived mistake of selecting a female rider. One even criticized Lynch's age when she began riding: "Don't you think six years old is a little late for a 'ranch' girl to start riding a horse?" One of the most referenced letters follows:

To the Editor:
I am writing to you in regard to the Female Red Raider!!! From things that I have picked up from the student body along with my own personal concern, Tech has made a huge mistake!!!

The feelings of pride and heart pounded excitement that each and every Tech fan has experienced while watching the traditional ride, has just been crushed!! A girl . . . what next, women for the football players? What has the great Texas Tech college come to?

This job of being the great Red Raider has belonged to males from the beginning in 1954. It was designed for a male and male only! I can't exactly picture a girl lifting the "Raider Trailer" and hitching it to the El Camino!

Much more goes into this job than I think this girl realizes! Can you imagine watching the famed ride before each game and seeing long hair flying out behind the supposed "male costume?!" I can't!

I know of many, many qualified male students who applied much earlier for this job than this girl did with a much higher grade point, plus much more experience in riding! There was even training that occurred last semester for one boy to get that job! What happened??

This is a great concern of mine plus many others and it sounds pretty fishy!

If the tremendous spirit that Tech is known for is to be continued next year, then something had better be done, cause at this point, it has been buried under long hair and the wrong sex!!!

If you feel as strongly about this as I do, please show it by letting it be known!!!

Name withheld

The above letter sparked fury among women. More letters arrived lambasting the writer and calling out the decision of the "chicken-hearted" writer to send it anonymously.

The more level-headed critics did not level their accusations at breaking an all-male tradition but at the potential bias in candidate selection. That the decision was left up to just one man received the greatest amount of scrutiny aside from the gender issue.

"The rumors flying about as a result of the new Red Raider Rider, whether true or not, impeached the integrity of the selection system for the rider and ultimately threw the tradition of a rider into an unfavorable public light," Mike Warden wrote a bit dramatically in an editorial in the *University Daily*.

Anne Lynch and Happy V in 1974. (Courtesy the Southwest Collection)

Anne Lynch and Happy V prepare to light the homecoming bonfire during her 1974–1975 season as the Masked Rider. The lace she added to the edge of her mask is visible. (Courtesy the Southwest Collection)

"Although most criticism stems from objection to the selection of a *female* Red Rider, the real criticism of a biased selection system itself cannot go unheeded."

Even former rider Gerald Nobles sent a letter to the editor printed in the *University Daily*. He raised the point that one individual shouldn't be burdened with a decision that carried so much weight, which lent itself to undue influence from outside sources.

"Nowhere else on campus is such a responsibility placed on one individual," he wrote. "For instance, the cheerleaders, UC student heads, twirlers, and Who's Who are not chosen by one person. Therefore, what is to be done? A change must be made to relieve the one person of this responsibility! This would eliminate pressure from an outside person, which in turn would keep this from happening again. . . . I truly feel sorry for the people who must take the rap for the selection so that others can get their names in headlines."

The Student Senate got in on the action, passing a resolution to revise the system and proposing a five-person panel.

On the eve of her first football game, Lynch was anxious for her inaugural run, as all Masked Riders are. But she was also worried about people throwing ice and other objects at her at the game. When asked about her comfort with Happy V, she said, "He is a level-headed horse. Happy Five has been around crowds and the band now and I think he will do a lot better than last year. Last season he came out bucking at the first of every game."

Even quarterback Tommy Duniven was on Lynch's side, saying in the September 13, 1974, *University Daily*: "It's fine with me. I think Anne is a real nice girl and a good horsewoman—what more could anybody ask?" His only negative feedback was that "they made such a big issue out of it."

Lynch and Happy V made their public debut Friday, September 13, 1974, at a 6:30 p.m. pep rally. She lined the edge of her mask with black lace to show her pride in being the first female rider and took to the field.

Robert Montemayor's editorial in the September 16, 1974, edition of the *University Daily* summarized the contempt some held for Lynch going into the football game and how he saw the ride through his eyes. Not many could say it better:

> I WAS REALLY anxious to get to the Tech game Saturday night. Not that it was so much the opening game, or that our then untested quarterback, Tommy Duniven, was making his debut, or even the traditional, colorful performance by the Goin' Band . . . not any of this. I wanted to see Anne Lynch's ride around the tartan track.

Anne Lynch and Happy V watch a game from the sideline during a 1974 football game at Jones AT&T Stadium. (Courtesy the Southwest Collection)

Last year Anne caught quite a bit of hell, both for alleged bartering for the position and for the fact that she is a woman. I heard Anne Lynch rumors flying left and right. I heard Anne Lynch would give Tech's twenty-one-year-old male chauvinistic custom a bad name.

Saturday night the announcer at the game made mention just before the kickoff that it was a "first ever." Needless to say, her history-making ride was getting a pretty stout billing.

As the crowd went into its usual two bits, four bits spiel, she took off on Happy Five. Something happened that made me feel pretty damn good . . . there was not one single difference between her ride and Gerald Nobles's ride of last year. The crowd came to its feet in the same old way, the cheers were still there, the band played the same, the players came on inspired as usual and as she rode past the east stands in front of the student section, the cheers came in thundering fashion. There was no difference, the spirit was still there.

I talked to Anne a few weeks back and she told me then that some people were thinking she might fall. And it's no secret, some resentful people were wanting her to fall. I told her then she'd do all right, and she responded saying, "I don't think I'll fall."

Anne Lynch and Happy V pose for press photos at Jones AT&T Stadium at the beginning of her term. (Courtesy the Southwest Collection)

Anyway, Anne Lynch is here to stay for the duration of the football season. She hasn't broken a tradition. She simply has become a part of it.

In a *University Daily* story dated February 14, 1975, Dale Zinn announced revisions to the way the next Masked Rider would be appointed, beginning with the newly formed Red Raider Selection Committee. The committee would be comprised of a committee chair, two additional faculty members, two student members, and a Texas Tech graduate. That year, committee members included Dr. Dale Zinn, who served as chair and represented the College of Agricultural Sciences; Feller Hughes and Larry Cunyus as the student members and

Anne Lynch shares a laugh with Bob Hope on the sidelines at Jones AT&T Stadium during a 1974 game. (Courtesy the Southwest Collection)

Joe Jim King in a publicity photo taken on campus. (Courtesy the Southwest Collection)

Joe Jim King makes his debut in 1975. (Courtesy the Southwest Collection)

representing the Agriculture Student Council and Saddle Tramps, respectively; Dr. John Allen as one of the faculty members and representing the Department of Animal Science, and Dr. Richard A. Lockwood, vice president of the Health Sciences Center, as the other faculty member and representing the other colleges in the university. Johnny Bob Carruth, a former Masked Rider, filled the position of alumni member, representing the Ex-Students Association.

Applications and resumes were to be submitted to Zinn by February 28. Applicants needed to have junior or senior standing in the fall with a GPA of 2.0 or greater, and they were required to possess the qualities of leadership and personality to uphold the tradition of the Red Raider. Committee members received all applications March 3 and met on March 6 at 3 p.m. to hold a preliminary screening of the applications. Those best fitting the criteria received a letter notifying them of their selection as a finalist. The committee interviewed

Joe Jim King with Happy V at Jones AT&T Stadium in 1975. (Courtesy the Southwest Collection)

the candidates March 12 through 14, after which the finalists went through a horsemanship evaluation on March 17. The committee then selected the winning candidate and sent the name and supporting documentation to the university president, then Grover Murray, for him to announce the rider.

The committee later developed its own regulations and responsibilities and for those of the Masked Rider for the "care and exercise of the horse during the football season."[11]

Joe Kim King, a mustachioed animal science major from Brady, Texas, was selected as the 1975–1976 Masked Rider, becoming the first rider chosen by a selection committee.[12] He had competed against a field of six men and six women.

King would be the last Masked Rider Zinn had a hand in selecting. After thirteen years at the university, Zinn left Texas Tech and the Masked Rider Program in 1975 to serve as the dean of agriculture and forestry at his alma mater, West Virginia University.

"The committee interviewed the applicants to see how they handle themselves in an interview," Zinn told the *University Daily*.[13] "There were five finalists selected who had tryouts at the ranch with the horse. This is different from the past when there was no riding test." He added that the final selection took into account personality, riding ability, and horsemanship.

"I take sincere pride in being the Red Raider," King shared with his hometown paper. "The honor is the greatest way I know of representing Texas Tech and the student body. I'll do my best to uphold the tradition."[14]

"I had never heard of the Red Raider until I first came up to Tech to go to school," the former Texas Tech Rodeo Team member told the *University Daily*.[15] "I got interested in it through Gerald Nobles, who was the Red Raider when I was a freshman. He explained the duties of the job to me and I guess I have been interested in it ever since."

"I have worked at the Tech feed lot in the past year," King said, "and we often ride Happy V to keep him from getting too fat."

During an otherwise successful year, King was scheduled to appear in Austin at the University of Texas game on Saturday, September 27, 1975. He and Happy V stayed with his family in Brady under the care of his father J. S. King, a veterinarian. The night before the game, someone snuck into the stable and dumped a gallon of orange enamel paint onto the hindquarters, tail, and hindlegs of

Joe Jim King and Happy V get ready to light the homecoming bonfire in 1975. (Courtesy the Southwest Collection)

the horse.[16]

Upon finding Happy V the next morning, King and his father removed the paint with paint thinner and shaved matted portions of hair. The paint left painful chemical burns on the horse that made him uncomfortable, and Dr. King gave the horse a 50 percent chance of surviving the incident on Saturday morning, unsure of how the fumes from the paint would affect the horse. After being under observation the rest of the weekend, Happy V was eating and "perky." The Kings believed the horse did not suffer from inhaling toxic fumes.

"I never thought this would happen in Brady," King told the *University Daily* in a telephone interview following the incident, saying he kept Happy V in Brady to avoid such a possible episode.

"I don't know who did it, but it has this entire town in an uproar," he said. "I suspect it's probably some high school kid and sooner or later someone will start bragging about it. Believe me, I'll find out who did it whether it's two months or three years from now."

King quietly used a stand-in horse at the game against the University of Texas, and Happy V fortunately made a full recovery. King anticipated the horse would be ready in time for the next game two weeks later against Texas A&M—a prediction that came true. Guards were posted with the horse twenty-four hours a

Joe Jim King and Happy V gallop on the sidelines at Jones AT&T Stadium in 1975. (Courtesy the Southwest Collection)

Jess Wall poses with Happy V in front of the horse trailer and car at Jones AT&T Stadium in 1976 during the Transfer of Reins. (Courtesy the Southwest Collection)

Jess Wall and Happy V run down the sideline past the University of Texas Band on October 30, 1976. (Courtesy the Southwest Collection)

day leading up to the game. Even though Happy V still had a few traces of orange paint on his hindquarters, he and King made their next run on October 9, 1975.[17]

The culprits have still not been identified.

King ended his term on April 8, 1976, at an on-field transfer ceremony. King thanked Jerry Ince—a Lubbock native who worked in finance, real estate, and his family's Ince Oil Company—for donating a new custom one-horse, bumper-pull trailer for the horse.[18] King also shared his appreciation for Happy V and how he "owed a great deal of his enjoyment to the help of other people."[19]

From a pool of thirteen applicants, four men and two women had advanced to the riding test just four days earlier on April 4. On Thursday, April 8, 1976, Texas Tech President Grover Murray announced the fifteenth rider at a 10 a.m. press conference at Jones AT&T Stadium.[20]

Jess Wall, a junior agricultural education major and former chute dogger, took the reins. He had transferred to Texas Tech from Clarendon College in Clarendon, Texas, near his hometown of Perryton. Wall had started breaking and training horses on his parents' ranch at the age of ten, and by the time he

Jess Wall as outgoing Masked Rider places a mask on Larry Cade during their transition in spring 1977. (Courtesy the Southwest Collection)

Larry Cade with Happy V at his debut in 1977. (Courtesy the Southwest Collection)

Larry Cade shows his "guns up" with Happy V in a photo that appeared in the 1978 *La Ventana*. (Courtesy the Southwest Collection)

was twelve, he was showing horses at 4-H and AQHA shows.[21]

"His predecessors have built a tradition of honor at Texas Tech," Murray shared with the crowd, "and . . . the selection committee advises me that Jess Wall has the qualifications to carry that tradition forward."[22]

Wall had one concern: "The only problem we've discussed is the northwest corner [the sharpest turn of the track]," Wall told the *University Daily*. "That's the only major problem I can see. As well as [Happy V]'s trained, and if you know what you're doing, there'll be no problems for a new rider."[23]

As his year came to a close, Wall shared his perfect ingredients that make for a successful term: "being responsible to the kids, as well as to the trained horse. A lot of time needs to be spent on working out the horse, feeding, and exercising him right."[24]

The spring 1977 Masked Rider tryouts resulted in another first for the program: its first rider outside the College of Agricultural Sciences and Natural Resources. As the *Daily Toreador* announced, "[b]eing a champion horseman, calf roper, bull rider, ranch hand, a high school honor student, basketball player, and now a senior majoring in geology at Tech is what it took to become the 1977–1978 Red Raider mascot."[25]

At Jones AT&T Stadium on April 1, 1977, the chair of the Red Raider Selection Committee, Dr. A. Max Lennon, revealed that Larry Cade of Sonora would serve as the Masked Rider from 1977 to 1978. The veteran rodeo rider and show horse competitor won the spot out of sixteen applicants and became the first to serve from the College of Arts and Sciences.[26]

"I just wanted to be a part of Tech," Cade told the *University Daily* at the ceremony. Cade had previously served as mascot for South Plains Junior College two years earlier. "Instead of coming to Tech, getting my degree and leaving, I wanted to leave something behind."[27]

"I have a service to offer this university—my horsemanship ability—and I want to give it freely for the spirit of this campus," he told the *Texas Techsan*.

Cade was a zealous advocate for the Masked Rider during his term. The week of the University of Texas game in Austin, he walked into the office of the *University Daily* and told the editor he had a story the paper would be interested in.[28]

In the summer, he and Happy V were scheduled to attend the University of

Larry Cade and Happy V gallop on the sideline in a 1977 football game. (Courtesy the Southwest Collection)

Texas game in Austin to cheer on the team from the sidelines, similar to their appearances at the Baylor University game in Waco earlier in the season, but because of miscommunication and a difference in the interpretation of a rule, his invitation was revoked. The ordeal ended in two front-page, top-fold stories plus an editorial in the campus paper about a tug-of-war between Cade and Texas Tech Athletics Director, J. T. King. It also involved Texas Tech President Cecil Mackey and University of Texas Assistant Athletics Director Bill Ellington.[29]

The rule, created by Texas Tech's Athletics Council, stated that the Texas Tech Athletics Department would not pay for the horse and rider to travel to away games if they were not permitted to perform. In previous years, King had interpreted "perform" as appearing in person on the sidelines, not making a run around the track at the home team's stadium; however, in the 1977 season, he seemed to change that interpretation to the horse and rider making a run. Cade also defined performing at away games as he and previous Masked Riders had done: the horse and rider standing quietly on the sidelines.

This definition—running on the track versus standing on the sideline in a designated spot—was at the root of the dispute, but King hedged and said the University of Texas had installed a new track around their field and wanted to protect it. King also insisted to the *University Daily* editor that Joe Kim King and Happy V had not appeared at the Texas game in Austin two years earlier, and that Cade and the horse had not appeared at this season's Baylor game; however, King did appear with a stand-in horse at the University of Texas game, and Cade had appeared at the Baylor game.

In a process similar to current procedures, the sports information director—then Ralph Carpenter—was tasked with calling each team hosting Texas Tech before each football season began to request permission for the university's mascot to "perform." Teams visiting Texas Tech followed the same process for their mascots. That year, Carpenter said Texas, Rice, North Carolina, Arizona, and SMU had told him the Masked Rider would not be permitted to perform, while Houston and Baylor said yes. Carpenter would report the responses to King.[30]

Because Cade's invitation was revoked contrary to previous Masked Riders' recent visits to Austin and what Cade was told only months earlier, he decided to contact the University of Texas's athletics department and find out why. Cade spoke with Ellington at the University of Texas, and Ellington said the horse and rider could attend if they remained off the track and did not run. It seemed that King had changed his previous interpretation of the rule, and Texas was fine with the horse standing on the sidelines.

"When King found out that I had called Ellington and gone over his head, he blew up. He then told me that even if the president [Mackey] called him and told him to let me go, there was no way that he [King] would let me. He said that even if he lost his job over it there wasn't any way I was going to the Texas game at the expense of the Athletics Department."[31]

The same week of the dispute, Cade found out he would not be allowed to

This unidentified rider (who appears to be Larry Cade) during a parade in Midland. (Courtesy the Southwest Collection)

attend the Southern Methodist University game. The student editor Cade spoke to at the *University Daily* called SMU's athletics director, Dick Davis.

"[T]hat's nonsense," Davis told the editor, contrary to what Carpenter had been told during preseason. "The Tech horse and rider are always welcome here. The only school that I know of that doesn't allow the horse at their stadium is Rice. We want the horse and his rider to be here if possible."[32]

Cade did not end up going to Austin, and King retired the next year. Less than a month after the SMU game, Cade would have a new equine partner.

Happy V began feeling tired toward the end of Jess Wall's term in 1976 to 1977. The horse was prone to colic, and a nutritionist adjusted his feed, which kept his issue at bay. Wall believed the horse's illness started with the spray-paint abuse, a belief that most refute. He told the *Lubbock Avalanche-Journal* that Happy V experienced a lengthy recovery from the ordeal.

"The probability that the paint had anything to do with the death is very unlikely," Dr. Clyde E. Kelsey, vice president for development and university relations, told the press on November 16, 1977.[33]

A new nutritionist arrived at Texas Tech and changed Happy V's feed in 1977, but the colic returned. Stace Hutson, the Texas Tech horse herdsman at the time, stayed up with Happy V on the nights he would experience colic.

Larry Cade and Happy V appear on the cover of the Indoors/Outdoors section of the 1978 *La Ventana*. (Courtesy the Southwest Collection)

During the horse's previous term, Joe Kim King remembered Hutson calling the veterinarian two times when Happy V fell ill.

Happy V had a bout with colic on October 24, 1977, but quickly recovered.[34]

Two and a half weeks later, at 7 a.m. on November 15, 1977, Hutson went to feed Happy V and discovered he had experienced colic overnight and passed away. A postmortem revealed the horse died of a ruptured intestine.

His replacement was announced and presented to the press—with Cade and the new horse in costume—less than thirty-six hours later, on November 16, 1977, at the Texas Tech New Deal Farm.

Unlike the horses that would follow him, Happy V's body was turned over to a rendering plant after his postmortem. According to Robert C. Albin, chair of the Animal Science Department, there are hazards in decomposition, but rendering produces byproducts like glue and tallow.[35] The disposition of Happy V's body caused a small outcry among students and employees who were appalled that an animal that had served the university for so long would be treated like a standard farm animal in death.[36]

"Why can't Texas Tech set up a memorial for Happy V and other past mascots?" one letter to the editor—signed by Concerned Raiders—concluded, referencing memorials found at Southern Methodist University and Texas A&M University.[37]

Cade's debut of the new horse at the New Deal, Texas, farm also marks the first reference to moving the Masked Rider's horses to this new location. After years located at the first Texas Tech farm on the southeast corner of Flint Avenue and 15th Street on campus, followed by a relocation of the farm to between 4th Street and Brownfield Highway west of Indiana Avenue, the horses would be moved to make way for Texas Tech's medical school—what is now the Texas Tech University Health Sciences Center and University Medical Center.

West Texas faced a lack of medical providers, and the university tried for about twenty years to gain legislative support for a medical school. The battle was finally won on May 27, 1969, when Governor Preston Smith signed the legislation to establish the Texas Tech School of Medicine. The bill, however, lacked a funding component. The medical school found temporary housing at two former residence halls—first at Drane Hall and later at Thompson Hall—before it established a home of its own.

The original plan was to place the medical school in the vacant triangle of university land between Brownfield Highway, Indiana Avenue, and 19th Street for two reasons. One, it was assumed that Methodist Hospital—now Covenant Medical Center—located directly south on 19th Street from the triangle, would become the teaching hospital for the medical school. Two, Texas Tech President Grover Murray and the university's Board of Regents heavily opposed making Indiana Avenue a thoroughfare, creating a city traffic artery through campus. The location was approved in late 1971 and included in the 1972 master plan.

In 1970, the university hired an architectural firm for the design. Around the same time the triangle was being approved, the firm had ruled it out as too small for the school and its impending growth. Instead, the firm targeted Texas Tech's farm and surrounding lands on the southeast corner of Indiana Avenue and 4th Street, north of Brownfield Highway.[38]

By 1973, the medical school held its official groundbreaking, and construction began the next year.[39] The Texas Tech farm would be forced to move once again.

In the early to mid-1970s, Texas Tech acquired a 983-acre farm just east of New Deal, among other new leases and purchases.[40] The new farm was more than twenty miles north of the Texas Tech campus but provided needed research and teaching areas.

In 1974, the Board of Regents approved the plan to move the farm's operations from the Texas Tech farm on Brownfield Highway to the New Deal farm to make way for the medical school. By 1975, contracts had been awarded for improvements and construction of facilities at the New Deal farm. Phase I of the operation moved the beef and dairy cattle operations, and Phase II, which was also approved in 1975, moved the remaining operations to finish clearing the area for the medical school.[41] The beef cattle center finished construction in 1976, and the move of animals began.[42]

The new farm contained a horse center with a stall barn, paddocks, and a small indoor working area. It became the new home for Masked Rider horses beginning with the horses that came after Happy V, but the distance made it difficult for riders to visit the horses every day and left reliance on the horse center manager for daily care.

Happy VI succeeded Happy V. He was donated by another group of Texas greats: Anne Burnett Tandy, Mrs. B. F. Phillips, and the 6666 Ranch.[43] Tandy, known as "Miss Anne," was a strong-willed, well-educated Texas woman. She is most famous for owning and running the 6666 and Triangle Ranches. A dinner party she and her husband hosted in March 1940 resulted in the creation of the

Lee Puckitt with Happy VI during his 1978–1979 season. (Courtesy the Southwest Collection)

Lee Puckitt and Happy VI during his 1978–1979 season. (Courtesy the Southwest Collection)

Lee Puckitt and Happy VI during a pregame run in 1978. (Courtesy the Southwest Collection)

American Quarter Horse Association.

Tandy went on to help found the AQHA Hall of Fame and the AQHA Museum. She loved racehorses and ranch horses, so that's what the 6666 bred. Her ranches owned seminal Quarter Horse stallions Joe Hancock, Grey Badger II, and later Dash For Cash.[44]

Phillips, later and more commonly known as Anne W. Marion, was referred to as "Little Anne." After her mother's passing in 1980, she inherited the 6666. As its owner, she purchased legendary Quarter Horse racehorse stallions Dash For Cash, Special Effort, and Streakin Six. Little Anne also served on the Texas Tech University System Board of Regents from 1981 to 1986. Like her mother, she was inducted into the AQHA Hall of Fame and the National Cowgirl Hall of Fame, the latter of which she moved from Hereford, Texas, to its current location in Fort Worth near the Will Rogers Memorial Center. She also established the Georgia O'Keeffe Museum in Santa Fe in 1997.[45]

Miss Anne and Little Anne donated Happy VI, a 16-hand, solid black, thirteen-year-old gelding. The horse was a minor celebrity in his own right already: he served as one of the first mounts of Carl "Bigun" Bradley in Marlboro television commercials on the 6666.[46]

Looking to associate the most masculine men in America with their cigarettes, Marlboro's advertising executives landed on cowboys. Models and actors dressed as cowboys lacked realism, but an art director scout stopped at the 6666 Supply House in Guthrie where Bradley was working as the wagon boss for the 6666 Ranch, giving orders to other cowboys. Bradley was cast as the first Marlboro Man who was a true working cowboy.[47]

The working horse—and now television star—made his Texas Tech debut with Larry Cade in the saddle on Thanksgiving Day for the Arkansas game. "This horse is bigger than Happy V and after I get him groomed and he gains a little weight, I think he is going to show up real well at the games," Cade

Lee Puckitt shows his "guns up" sign while sitting atop Happy VI at a home football game in 1978. The trailer is behind them. (Courtesy the Southwest Collection)

shared with the *Daily Toreador*. Cade added that Happy VI handled better than Happy V.[48]

The gift of Happy VI—the second horse publicly donated to Texas Tech—joined what was a growing list of generous donations to help the Masked Rider Program. Ince-Miley Trailer Sales continued to provide the pair's horse trailer. Willie Lusk Boot Shop and True Grit Western Wear provided the boots and clothing. Burney Chapman provided farrier services. Lubbock Implement Company, Inc. and Frances R. Knox of Green Acre Stable provided financial backing to the program. In one unnamed year, an anonymous donor provided a $200 scholarship to the rider.[49]

Coke Hopping shows his "guns up" in an undated photo at Jones AT&T Stadium. (Courtesy the Southwest Collection)

Lee Puckitt, a twenty-one-year-old business major from San Angelo, took the reins next for the 1978 to 1979 school year. Puckitt began riding at the age of six and still competed in team roping. That year's football program described him as "lanky," including his height—six feet, five inches— and weight—175 pounds.[50] Puckitt's stature and build became standout features, with his height and the term lanky—sometimes both—mentioned by nearly every writer when they wrote about him, even in photo captions.

Puckitt was announced as the Masked Rider on Wednesday, April 27, 1978, making his first public appearance at the annual football scrimmage just two nights later. Because he was so "lanky," he made his debut in Cade's costume after "a hasty job of altering."[51] Puckitt also pulled the trailer with his own vehicle.

Puckitt made his first true football game appearance five months later, which was Happy VI's second football game. Just before the pair's first pre-game run together, Happy VI fell, but the pair hopped back up and made the run. "The horse at the start of the run only wanted to go backwards. After some persuading and after he tripped and fell, we were able to make our run," Puckitt said later.

"I had been going to football games for several years, and I always loved seeing the Masked Rider," Puckitt told the *Daily Toreador*, remembering his motivation

Coke Hopping welcomes Happy VI-II upon his arrival at the New Deal Farm. Burney Chapman and Happy VI wait in the background. (Courtesy the Southwest Collection)

Happy VI-II greets Happy VI as Burney Chapman picks him up for the 1979–1980 football season. (Courtesy the Southwest Collection)

for becoming the rider. "It's always a thrill to see the excitement and pageantry of it all, and I wanted to be a part of it."

"It was a lot of work to be quite honest," he conceded, "because you had so many things to do with the horse and schedules and appearances. But it was nice because I was able to travel and speak with people I might never have gotten to talk with. . . . I got to meet a lot of people and carry on a wonderful tradition from a great university."

Coke Hopping makes a run at a home football game in 1979. (Courtesy the Southwest Collection)

This October 19, 1979, photo from the *Lubbock Avalanche-Journal* shares a glimpse of the game-day breakfasts the Hopping family held in their yard for visitors to see Coke get the horse ready before games. (Courtesy the Southwest Collection)

Kathleen Campbell with Happy VI-II during her 1980–1981 season. (Courtesy the Southwest Collection)

Kathleen Campbell and Happy VI-II during her 1980–1981 season. (Courtesy the Southwest Collection)

Vergil "Coke" Hopping of Memphis, Texas, took the reins from 1979 to 1980. The Panhandle cowboy rode on Texas Tech's rodeo team before being selected as the Masked Rider.

Happy VI served a short two years before his retirement due to pulled tendons in one of his front legs.[52] "He has as much spirit as any of the cheerleaders," Hopping told the media. "But his leg just won't stand up to the job."

Happy VI returned to the 6666 Ranch to recover. Anne Tandy, her daughter, Mrs. B. F. Phillips, and the 6666 Ranch replaced the horse with a black gelding with a white coronet band, Happy VI-II. Suited for life as a working ranch horse, the gelding, called "Stormy" by the 6666, "was bred for stamina and speed."

Legendary West Texas farrier and 1966 Texas Tech graduate Burney Chapman trailered Happy VI-II from the 6666 and said the horse "was one of the best

Kathleen Campbell poses with Happy VI-II in front of the Will Rogers and Soapsuds statue during her 1980–1981 season as the Masked Rider. (Courtesy the Southwest Collection)

horses the college has ever had."[53]

The horse took over at an official presentation ceremony held at the Tech Farm in New Deal the morning of October 11, 1979. In his first media photo, Happy VI-II appears with Hopping as Happy VI stands grumpily in the background next to the horse trailer with Chapman. The photo caption also contains the first publicly written instance of the mascot being called the "Masked Rider" and not the "Red Raider."[54]

Happy VI and Happy VI-II lived at Texas Tech's New Deal farm. Because of the twenty to thirty-minute drive from the farm to Jones AT&T Stadium, Hopping often brought the horse to his parents' home on University Avenue and 57th Street for pregame preparation. His mother shared with the *Lubbock Avalanche-Journal* that over the season, a crowd grew to see Hopping get the horse ready and sign autographs. The family began putting out coffee, juice, and donut holes for the fans.

Hopping was the first Masked Rider to ride with the reins in his teeth, a practice now forbidden due to safety issues on the field.[55]

Kathleen Campbell and Happy VI-II make a game-day run at a football game in 1980. (Courtesy the Southwest Collection)

Kathleen Campbell of Portland, Texas, followed Hopping on Happy VI-II from 1980 to 1981 and became the program's second female Masked Rider, besting a field of twenty-two candidates.[56] The well-read dual history and French major won the horsemanship and personality categories at the Miss Rodeo Texas contest, served a stint as the Texas Tech Rodeo Queen, and later went to law school. The world champion exhibitor grew up showing on the Pony of the Americas circuit and made the top-ten rider list for Texas five years in a row. She also competed in hunter/jumper and dressage shows as well as playday events.

Campbell received the call from Professor Leland Tribble, who chaired the selection committee at the time, while she was in her horse judging class. When selected, she shared with the *University Daily* that "[b]eing named Red Raider represents achieving one of the highest goals I think I could ever achieve at Tech."

"This will be something entirely different," Campbell told the *University Daily* about riding at football games. "I hope I will be able to handle it—and I think I will." She also gave high marks to Happy VI-II: "He's a very intelligent horse, and I think he will be quite willing to learn to work together."[57]

Perry Church appears in lighted costume at Jones AT&T Stadium in 1982. (Courtesy the Southwest Collection)

# 5

# A DECADE OF FIRSTS

When Kathleen Campbell's term ended, one of the biggest developments in program history occurred: the first publicly recorded modern iteration of the Transfer of Reins ceremony. Although the ceremony did not have a name at the time, it was advertised to the press and had a formal program. Held on March 11, 1981, at Jones AT&T Stadium, it marked the first time a special ceremony recognized the outgoing rider, and the incoming rider was formally introduced to the public.[1]

Judith Henry, assistant to the dean of students and chair of the Masked Rider selection committee, served as master of ceremonies.[2] Men's Athletics Director John F. Conley presented Campbell with a letter jacket in recognition of her service to Texas Tech Athletics—another first and a tradition that continues to this day. She also received a certificate of appreciation and a photo of herself with Happy VI-II.[3]

Robert H. Ewalt, vice president for student affairs, announced Kurt Harris of Stratford, Texas, as the new Masked Rider.[4]

Harris, who competed on Texas Tech's Livestock Judging Team with David and Dan Waggoner—the twin sons of fifth Masked Rider Kelley Waggoner[5]—was an honors student studying to become a veterinarian. He said for most of his life he had trained and shown halter, performance, and racing Quarter Horses. Harris had plenty of vet training and horse handling in his professional life already as a stallion and mare handler at Stratford Stallion Station and an assistant at his local veterinary clinic.

"I have always been a Red Raider fan," Harris told Texas Tech, "and I have personally known some former Red Raiders. When I was in junior high, I saw the Red Raider in real life for the first time. Since that time I have always dreamed of being one."[6] He later shared, "I think the Red Raider actually encouraged me to come to Tech. I have always been a Red Raider fan and now I am the Red Raider."[7]

The year 1981 also brought the first official endowment for the Masked Rider Program. Previous donors had publicly presented in-kind donations of horses, tack, vehicles, and trailers. Some contributions also came from area businessmen as well as financial support from the Department of Animal Science and the Athletics Department.[8]

The Masked Rider Committee (formerly known as the Red Raider Committee) set up the Red Raider Endowment, a perpetual fund to help the mascot program become self-supporting.[9] The Saddle Tramps made the first

Kurt Harris and Happy VI-II ride in the 1981 homecoming parade. (Courtesy the Southwest Collection)

contribution of $2,000. In March 1982, the Student Foundation donated $4,000 raised through their "Senior Challenge" annual fundraising drive.

Judith Henry estimated the annual cost of the mascot program was $5,000, which included a $1,000 scholarship for the Masked Rider. Beginning in 1981, the Student Foundation donated the funds for the scholarship.[10]

Sam Jackson stood on the sidelines at the 1981 Texas Tech–Baylor game. Jackson, then a senior at Stephenville High School, had planned on attending Texas A&M University. But that day changed his plans.

Kurt Harris is announced as the next Masked Rider for the 1981–1982 season. (Courtesy the Southwest Collection)

Jackson's father, Dr. Bill Jackson, bred, trained, and showed paint horses. Bill would go on to serve as president of the American Paint Horse Association in 1993 and lead the association during a time of exponential growth and the construction of its new headquarters.

Bill also knew the father of the current Masked Rider, Kurt Harris. For the Baylor game in Waco, the Jacksons invited Harris, his assistant Perry Church, and Happy VI-II to stay with the family in Stephenville. Jackson ended up on

Goin' Band members make friends with Happy VI-II on the sidelines during a fall 1981 football game. (Courtesy the Southwest Collection)

the sidelines at the game with the Masked Rider crew. Instead of visiting Texas A&M in the spring like he planned, he went to Lubbock for a visit and stayed with Harris.

Jackson chose to attend Texas Tech after his visit, majored in animal science, and won national championships on both the livestock judging team and the wool judging team. But the Baylor game served as the introduction of Jackson to a lasting relationship with the Masked Rider Program that would begin more than a decade later when he returned to Texas Tech as a faculty member.

Perry Church poses aboard Happy VI-II. Undated. (Courtesy the Southwest Collection)

The now famous lighted cape and hat made its debut with Harris in the 1981 fall semester for the football Light Show. All the lights at Jones AT&T Stadium were turned off for the Light Show, and the Masked Rider galloped a lap in pitch black. Lights similar to strings used on Christmas trees edged the brim and crown of the bolero hat and the Double T of the cape. The Goin' Band also performed their halftime show in the dark with light effects, and lights circled landmarks around the field, such as the Double T in the grass in the north end of the stadium.

The Masked Rider's lighted gear was designed by one of the engineering departments. The rider carried two motorcycle batteries stacked one on top of the other in a backpack contraption. The power cord to the hat connected to the cape, and the cape connected to the backpack. A later version placed the batteries in a cantle bag that was tied onto the back of the saddle. The cantle-bag version connected the hat to the cape to the saddle. The entire rig weighed as much as

Harris and Happy VI-II take a game-day run during a fall 1981 football game in Jones AT&T Stadium. (Courtesy the Southwest Collection)

The Masked Rider waves a rally towel as he makes a run past the crowd on Happy VI-II. (Courtesy the Southwest Collection)

the saddle, if not more.

Perry Church, who served as Masked Rider after Harris, shared his memories of the battery pack with Texas Tech. "When we got through with those rides, we were so black and blue. . . . We were the guinea pigs to get that started."

The lighted cape and hat also allowed the Masked Rider to take a role in the annual Carol of Lights tradition, which is the lighting of the campus Christmas lights and tree, and holiday lights parades in West Texas. The Masked Rider in a lighted hat and cape leads the procession at the start of the ceremony.

Perry Church, a Friona, Texas, native, first saw the Masked Rider in a Midland parade when he was in junior high.[11]

"I told everyone who was with me at the time that I wanted to be the Masked Rider," Church told Texas Tech in a 2011 interview. "It was one of the reasons why I chose to come to Texas Tech. When I finally got here and tried out, it was truly an honor to be named Masked Rider and represent the community and the school."[12] He initially tried out for the position in 1981, served as Harris's assistant to learn the ropes, then took the reins for the 1982–1983 season.

Vice President for Student Affairs Robert H. Ewalt, who would later become the namesake for Texas Tech's student recreation center, revealed Church as the twenty-first rider. Church, a senior agricultural economics–finance major, had started riding when he was three years old.[13]

Church developed his riding skills working horseback on his grandfather's ranch near Stanton, Texas, and apprenticed with AQHA judge and trainer Jack Kyle. He remembered Happy VI-II's calm demeanor, but once the first measures of the fight song began after a score, the horse knew it was time to run.

During one of his scoring runs at the November 13, 1982, game against Southern Methodist University, a spectator's hat flew onto the track. An SMU spirit squad member ran out to retrieve the hat in the path of Church and Happy VI-II, who were in a full gallop. The impact knocked out the spirit squad member, and she spent a week hospitalized recovering from face, head, jaw, teeth, chin, and leg injuries. She sued Texas Tech, its board of regents, and Church two years after the incident.[14]

The collision led to a review of safety procedures. Instead of making a full lap around the Jones AT&T Stadium track for touchdowns, the horse and rider would run from the southwest to northwest corners of the stadium along the track. The horse and rider would then walk from the northwest corner along the track clockwise to return to the southwest corner.

"They've made some changes for safety reasons," Church said looking back, "and I'm proud of that, too." He added, "When you have the cape on that's one thing, but people actually know who you are, so you have to carry yourself in a positive manner," referring to the public role the Masked Rider has continued to embody for Texas Tech. "You have to remember that you are representing the school at all times. It was tough, but it was well worth it."[15]

"We may not always have an outstanding team and people may not remember who the Red Raider really is, but they do remember a man on horseback galloping around the stadium."[16]

Buried on page 10 in the Monday, August 30, 1982, issue of the *Lubbock Avalanche-Journal*, a photo of Church and Happy VI-II adorned an announcement: Rainbo Baking Company would begin a campaign to benefit Texas Tech Athletics and drive excitement for the season.

The campaign had started with media messages from Rainbo about Texas Tech Athletics. Next, Rainbo inserted Red Raider decals into loaves of bread

A homecoming mum in 1982 with a Masked Rider at its center. (Courtesy the Southwest Collection)

Jennifer Aufill poses in front of the Texas Tech University seal with Happy VI-II during her 1983–1984 season as the Masked Rider. (Courtesy the Southwest Collection)

for two days, followed by donating five cents per specially marked loaf of bread to the Red Raider Club for four weeks. Rainbo also financed several projects and brought in three country-and-western acts to play for a barbecue on September 18, 1982—a date designated by the Lubbock City Council as Red Raider Day.

One of the other projects financed by Rainbo as part of their fundraising campaign was "[a] new song, a country and western ballad entitled 'Red Raider Comin' At You'" written by Dallas songwriter Ken Sutherland and performed and recorded by Red Steagall. The lyrics describe the Masked Rider and the lore the tradition inspires.

Rainbo distributed the song to local radio stations and also sold the record in Lubbock. From the sale of each record, amounts between $1.25 and $2.00

Zurick Labrier poses with Happy VI-II before the Texas Tech University seal during his 1984–1985 season. (Courtesy the Southwest Collection)

Labrier in front of the end zone at Jones AT&T Stadium during his 1984–1985 season. (Courtesy the Southwest Collection)

went to the Red Raider Club.[17] Records were also given to football season ticket holders and to anyone who requested one. The song was used heavily during the football season and in highlight videos. After the 1982 season ended, it faded away, and the remaining records were relegated to a closet in the Texas Tech Athletics Department.

About two decades later, the records were unearthed when the Red Raider Club was moving to a different building. They were donated to the Tech Hecklers, a group that supports Texas Tech Baseball, as a silent auction item at their First Pitch Luncheon fundraiser for the team. The Tech Hecklers soon requested that the song be played at baseball games. Soon, it was played regularly at baseball games and occasionally at football games as well.[18]

The song became a sentimental staple among Texas Tech fans.

Jennifer Aufill of Lubbock became the third female Masked Rider, taking the reins for the 1983–1984 year and proudly curling her hair and wearing red lipstick.

Aufill's father, Jack, was an animal production alumnus from Texas Tech.[19] He stayed in Lubbock and started the local horse auction Jack Aufill Sales, which became the longest-running weekly auction in Texas. He ended up with a total of three horse auctions and added rodeo producer to his dossier.

Jennifer grew up with horses, and by the time she was three years old, she was riding horses into the auction ring for her father. "I was daddy's 'little boy,'" she told a magazine years later, recalling her upbringing. Her father would send one of his hands to pick her up from school, and she would change into her jeans and boots during the drive, riding horses until dark.

Like the riders before her, Aufill remembered Happy VI-II's calm demeanor, especially at football games: "A lot was going on[;] it was loud." But she didn't get nervous "[b]ecause I was on a really gentle horse that didn't get scared easily." Aufill once had to lean down from the saddle to push a coach aside and out of the horse's path.

"You can be the best rider in the world, but if you don't have a good mount because there's so much more going on around you—if you're having to mess with the horse the whole time—you can't enjoy what's going on or look for things that are happening and really enjoy the moment," Aufill said in a later interview with Texas Tech. "And this horse was a really good horse to ride. He was super gentle. He was super easy to get along with. He'd put his head down and just walk along. They'd play the fight song, and he'd get all excited. He knew the song they played when we scored, and he knew he'd get to run. He was just automatic."[20]

The horse's one imperfection was a sparse tail, caused by what she guessed was another horse chewing on it. Aufill used tail extensions to give Happy VI-II a full tail befitting the "beautiful horse."[21]

Zurick Labrier of Masterson, Texas, became the 1984–1985 Masked Rider on March 7, 1984. The junior animal production major had ridden "ever since I was old enough to hold myself on a horse."[22]

While a senior at Dalhart High School, Labrier went to a Texas Tech football game and decided he wanted to be a Masked Rider. "One of my goals when I came to Tech was to try out for the Red Raider," Labrier said. "Tech has a lot of pride and tradition in the Red Raider and, because of my background with horses, that encouraged me to try out. I felt I had something to offer."[23]

The Transfer of Reins ceremony brought several new developments.

Continuing the tradition of scholarships, the Student Foundation presented Labrier with a $1,000 scholarship. The Saddle Tramps bestowed on him the Joe Kirk Fulton Award.[24] To commemorate Aufill's term, Texas Tech Athletics presented her with the traditional letter jacket. Texas Tech development office spokesperson John Anderson announced that $15,000 had been raised for the Red Raider Endowment.[25] The amount included the combined $6,000 from the Saddle Tramps and the Student Foundation. Anderson said most donations came from former Masked Riders. "We would like to raise the whole $50,000 before homecoming next year," Anderson announced.[26]

"The Masked Rider Committee has set the goal of raising the $50,000 between now and the 1984 Homecoming," Joe Kirk Fulton said in what was possibly the first public reference to the Masked Rider Committee instead of the Red Raider Committee. "The start has come, to a great extent, from former masked riders, and now the campaign will be a people's campaign."[27]

Although the fund reached just $20,000 by August 1987, the 1984 Transfer of Reins marked the first public ask for endowment assistance.

Soon after the Transfer of Reins, Labrier made an appearance at Haynes Elementary School in Lubbock. The former competitive roper who spent time working on his grandparents' New Mexico ranch and with his father at a feedlot near Dalhart was now answering questions from children about brushing Happy VI-II's teeth.

"When I told him that horses don't need their teeth brushed, he wanted to know how the horse kept from getting cavities," Labrier laughed. "And the questions went on and on. The kid just couldn't believe that I didn't brush the horse's teeth for him!"[28]

Labrier reigned over the Masked Rider Program's thirtieth anniversary during the homecoming game against Baylor University in 1984. In honor of the anniversary, the homecoming theme was "Tradition Rides Again." A reception for former riders was held the night before the game in the University Room of the Holiday Inn–Civic Center with a Masked Rider display.[29] A pregame ceremony honored the riders. During the game, Jim Douglass presented the Ex-Students

Jerrell Key poses with Happy VI-II in front of the Will Rogers statue. (Courtesy the Southwest Collection)

Association Community Service Award to the Masked Rider Program, which Labrier accepted on its behalf.

After a year of firsts and a major reunion, Labrier transferred the reins of Happy VI-II to Jerrell Key, who had served as an assistant to Labrier, on a sunny Wednesday afternoon on March 6, 1985, at Jones AT&T Stadium. Key had bested ten other applicants to become the 1985–1986 Masked Rider.[30]

Key, a Lubbock native and Monterey High School graduate, became the third College of Business Administration student to serve as Masked Rider. He was a dual major in agricultural economics and real estate with a minor in finance. Key grew up going to Texas Tech games and watching the Masked Rider, but Coke Hopping, who groomed the horse in his parents' yard on game days, planted the seed in Key's mind. Key's family lived at 2516 56th Street while Hopping's parents lived on the opposite end of the same block at 2502 57th Street, right on the corner of 57th and University Avenue, a major Lubbock thoroughfare.

"I didn't really set my mind to it until Coke Hopping, who lived just around the corner from me, got it in 1979," Key told Texas Tech. "Then I realized it was something I wanted."[31]

Jerrell Key during a 1985 football game (Courtesy the Southwest Collection)

Key's father, Chuck, was a basketball standout who was a forward for Texas Tech from 1956 to 1959.[32] Key was not blessed with his father's college-level abilities. "I was a pretty good basketball player in high school, but I'm not really good enough to carry on my dad's tradition in college," he said. "Being the Masked Rider is my way of leaving my mark."[33]

Key's uncle was a team roper and brought him into roping. He received his first horse in the fifth grade and gave lessons at children's summer camps during college.[34]

Key began his term with an appearance at the American Business Club Rodeo (now ABC Rodeo) in Lubbock.[35] "Texas Tech has been a great part of my life," Key shared at Transfer of Reins, "and I am proud to wear the mask and cape which symbolize a great university.[36]

Jerrell Key shows his guns up aboard Happy VI-II during a 1985 football game at Jones AT&T Stadium. (Courtesy the Southwest Collection)

Daniel Jenkins and Happy VI-II pose for a photo with Texas Tech University President Lauro Cavazos (left) and Joe and Beverly Pevehouse at Jones AT&T Stadium in 1986. (Courtesy the Southwest Collection)

Daniel Jenkins was selected as the 1986–1987 Masked Rider and accepted the reins on March 5, 1986.[37] The senior animal production and pre-vet major grew up on his parents' Angus ranch in Higgins, Texas, an eastern Panhandle town near the Oklahoma border.[38]

Before and after his time as Masked Rider, Jenkins was a top student, a member of the horse and meat judging teams, and was named the outstanding sophomore of the Department of Animal Science at the first Animal Science Alumni Banquet (held in April 1984).[39]

Jenkins was inspired to try out for Masked Rider by his roommate and former rider Zurick Labrier. He had just finished his season with the meat judging team and was determining what to do his senior year with the help of his horse judging coach, Dr. Jim Heird. "I told him, 'I can either judge livestock or try out for Masked Rider. What do you think, Dr. Heird?'" Heird replied, "You've done meat judging. You've done horse judging. You've got as much out of judging as you can. This would branch you out to something else." Heird later went on to become president of the AQHA, a Texas Horse Racing Hall of Fame inductee, and an equine science faculty member at three universities for more than four decades.

Daniel Jenkins with Happy VI-II in 1986. (Courtesy the Southwest Collection)

During Jenkins's year, the Athletics Department shared the use of a Masked Rider–branded truck to pull the two-horse straight-load (or side-by-side) trailer. He spent the summer scheduling and managing his own appearances, which included plenty of rodeo grand entries (usually alongside rodeo queen candidates). He spent the fall at football games.

At home games, Jenkins was largely on his own to navigate the pregame and scoring runs—not only when to make them but also determining if it was safe to do so. He and Happy VI-II typically stood vigil in the southwest corner of the track on the field. The pair made runs up the west (home) side of the track, took the northwest curve, then slowed to a walk or trot down the visitor and student seating. Between runs, he took photos with fans and signed his full-page photo printed in the game programs. The pair traveled to two away games, the first of which was at Texas A&M. Jenkins was nervous to attend. The Masked Rider seemed to encounter issues when traveling to College Station or Austin, but he was treated well at the game. The second away game was the Independence Bowl in Shreveport, Louisiana. While Jenkins and Happy VI-II were unable to make the traditional pregame run or sideline runs, the pair "just darted around in the end zone before the game."

One of his most memorable appearances, though, took place at a Lubbock elementary school. Jenkins, in costume atop Happy VI-II, spoke to the schoolchildren. After their time concluded, teachers shepherded the children back inside. Jenkins took the horse back to the trailer to pack and load.

"I hadn't taken the saddle off yet, but I was putting up stuff and the bell rung," he recounted. "The kids came pouring out of that school building and made a beeline for me—70 kids with their coats flopping behind them because it was cool. I hopped back on, and they chased me out in the school yard until the teachers came out and rescued me."

He was also awarded Leader of the Year at the third-annual Student Organization Awards ceremony in 1987.[40]

Shortly after Jenkins finished his term, Texas Tech welcomed a new horse to the university.

Tonya Tinnin and Midnight Raider wait in front of a breakaway banner for their pregame run at a football game in 1988. (Courtesy the Southwest Collection)

# 6

# MIDNIGHT RAIDER

"I can remember having a solid black filly and telling Mother, 'I'm taking Yum Yum Fudge to Tech and ride around the football field like the Masked Rider.' Mother laughed, but she knew I was serious when she saw me riding like the wind with my Halloween mask and dish towel for a cape."

Kim Saunders hailed from Marfa, Texas, where she was an active rodeo competitor and named All-Around Cowgirl at Marfa High School. She received her real cape and mask on March 4, 1987, when she was announced as the 1987–1988 Masked Rider. Saunders, an animal production major and former member of the horse and livestock judging teams, beat out nine applicants during the initial screening process and three finalists at the final interviews.[1]

Just less than two months after she took the reins, the university announced a new horse would take over for Happy VI-II.[2]

Happy VI-II quietly retired and most likely returned to the 6666 Ranch.[3] The Animal Science Alumni Association (ASAA), led by President Alvin Davis and more than seventy alumni donors from twelve states,[4] donated a new nine-year-old black horse. The individuals who donated a new horse also provided its name—a name typically not changed just for the position. The ASAA had different ideas: a naming contest.[5]

The first-ever name-the-horse contest opened April 28, 1987, and remained open until September 3 of that year. Anyone could submit their entry in person or by mail.[6] By August 25, fans submitted more than 240 names.

"We have some really good names which have been submitted so far, but we still need names because we want the new horse to have the best name possible," said Andy Kean, chairman of the Masked Rider Committee. "We've had some really unique names which only one person has thought of as well as names of legendary horses, such as Black Beauty, which have been submitted by several people."[7]

A name selection committee narrowed the choices to allow the Texas Tech student body to vote on the winner September 10 in the north lobby of the University Center.[8] At the first Texas Tech home football game of the 1987 season on September 12 against Colorado State—Spike Dykes's first home game as the new coach of the Red Raiders—a pregame ceremony recognized Happy VI-II and welcomed the new horse.

Saunders took Happy VI-II on one last ride around the Jones AT&T Stadium track, at the end of which she joined dignitaries on the field. Alvin Davis and other members of the ASAA led the new horse onto the field and handed the reins of the new horse to President Lauro Cavazos, who then handed the horse

Kim Saunders with Midnight Raider in 1987. (Courtesy the Southwest Collection)

Young fans pet Midnight Raider, with Kim Saunders aboard, at a football game. (Courtesy the Southwest Collection)

to Saunders. To symbolize the end of his service, Saunders unsaddled Happy VI-II and saddled the new horse.

Midnight Raider's name was then announced. The contest winner joined the group on the field and received a bronze figurine of the new horse, sculpted by Davis and casted by House Bronze.[9] (Davis later had replicas made of the figurine. The proceeds from the sale of the figurines benefited the Red Raider Endowment Fund.)[10] Saunders then hopped aboard Midnight Raider and took him for his first ride around Jones AT&T Stadium as the newest horse of the program.[11]

Lea Whitehead, a junior from Sonora, Texas, took the reins as the 1988–1989 Masked Rider. She was the 1982 American Junior Rodeo Association (AJRA) all-around champion at the National Finals Rodeo and took home the 1986 AJRA world championship in pole bending. She became the first agricultural communications major in the Masked Rider Program, beating six other candidates to earn the position. Whitehead, who grew up on a ranch, was a seasoned rodeo rider. She first learned about the Masked Rider from her elementary school principal, Clay Cade—father of former rider Larry Cade—and began dreaming of serving.

Whitehead made an appearance no other rider before her had made: an officially sanctioned international trip. From 1977 to 1993, the Coca-Cola Classic (previously known as the Mirage Bowl hosted by Mitsubishi Motors) hosted a regular-season college football game in Tokyo, Japan. Texas Tech took on then-twelfth-ranked Oklahoma State University on December 3, 1988, at the

Saunders with Midnight Raider. (Courtesy the Southwest Collection)

Lea Whitehead and Midnight Raider during her 1988–1989 season. (Courtesy the Southwest Collection)

Lea Whitehead. (Courtesy the Southwest Collection)

Tokyo Dome in front of a crowd of 56,000 spectators. Whitehead traveled with the football team to appear at the game—sans horse. Japan's Olympic trainers gave Whitehead and the Texas Tech contingency a tour of the city. In Tokyo, she met Barry Sanders, who at the time was finishing his junior year at Oklahoma State. Before the start of the game that day, it was announced Sanders won the Heisman Trophy, and he accepted the award via satellite from Tokyo.

"For a West Texas ranch girl that was very sheltered, traveling to Tokyo was very enlightening," she later reminisced. "Being Masked Rider opened so many doors for me. It pulled me out of my shell. It got me to experience so many things I wouldn't have gotten to otherwise."[12]

Lea Whitehead presents Tonya Tinnin with her mask for the 1988–1989 season. (Courtesy the Southwest Collection)

Tonya Tinnin with Midnight Raider. (Courtesy the Southwest Collection)

Tonya Tinnin followed Whitehead as the 1989–1990 Masked Rider. Like Whitehead, Tinnin was a junior majoring in agricultural communications.[13] Tinnin was born and raised in Amarillo, and around the time she graduated from Amarillo High School, her father, Rusty, had become the general manager of the famous 290,000-acre Bell Ranch.[14]

A crane lifts the Joe Kirk Fulton statue to place it in the athletics building lobby in 1990. (Courtesy the Southwest Collection)

Tinnin faced only one obstacle during her term: the need for a trailer. The bumper-pull trailer originally donated in 1976 was no longer serviceable due to a bent frame and rust damage. Also, it was too small to accommodate Midnight Raider's large size.[15]

The program began renting a trailer in March 1989, and by the fall, it still didn't have its own trailer. While Brunken Chevrolet, Inc. loaned the program the use of a truck, no trailer manufacturers were willing to broker a sponsorship for use of a trailer. Alvin Davis, who had become vice president and general manager of the National Ranching Heritage Center, called sixty trailer manufacturers in search of promotional consideration. Facing a $5,000 cost, the Masked Rider Committee hoped for donations to purchase a new trailer. Campus recycling programs were also contributing to the endowment.[16]

"The trailer is a recruiting tool," Tinnin told the *University Daily*. "When I show up with the trailer, they know the Red Raider is there. . . . The truck and trailer follow immediately behind me in parades in case of problems and also serve to identify me from Tech, but now it appears like someone is just showing off their truck and trailer."[17]

Without a branded trailer, Tinnin was obligated to convince Baylor stadium personnel she was in fact the mascot and supposed to be at the game. With 5,000

A skylight had to be removed for the Joe Kirk Fulton statue to be lifted into place. (Courtesy the Southwest Collection)

miles and fifty appearances behind her, Tinnin finished her term in the leased trailer.[18]

The 1989 football season brought a short-lived—but memorable—brand promotion: Roof Raider. The Athletics Department dressed up an anonymous man like the Masked Rider and had him stand on the roof of the athletic offices at the north end of the stadium, holding a red flag when Texas Tech was on offense and black for defense.

Fans and alumni complained to the Masked Rider Program that Roof Raider's costume too closely resembled the Masked Rider's.

"There is a great amount of tradition attached to the Masked Rider, and it is an honor for a student to be selected to represent Tech," Cheryl Shubert, advisor for the Masked Rider Committee, told the *University Daily*. "The committee was set up to protect that tradition."

It unanimously voted to recommend a costume change for Roof Raider.[19]

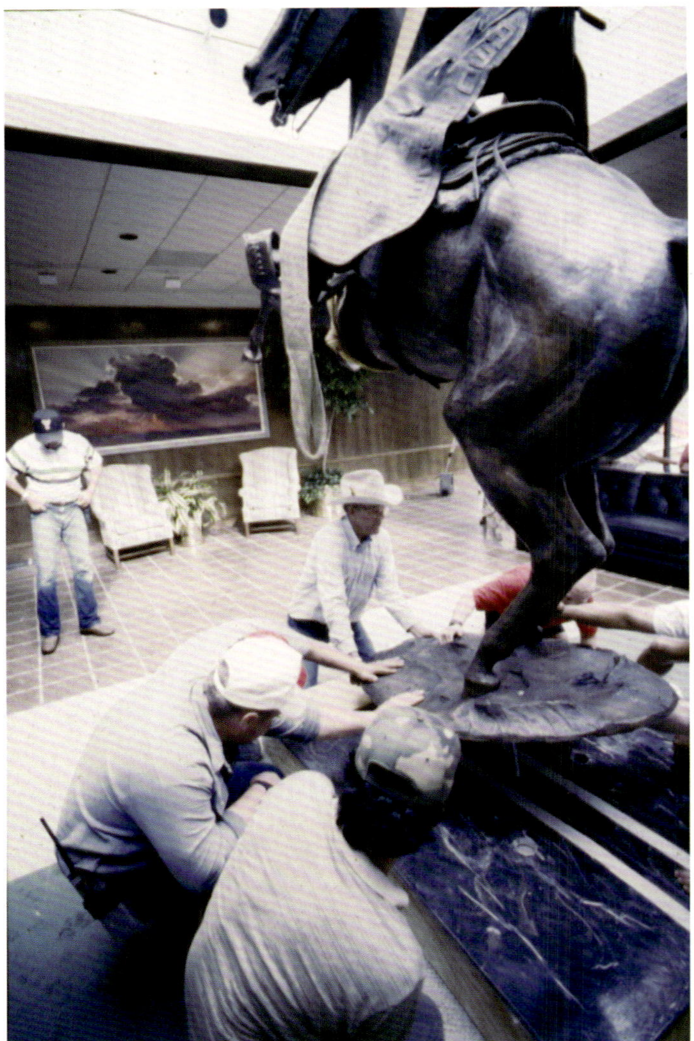

A crew places and installs the statue. (Courtesy the Southwest Collection)

In May 1990, word got out that a larger-than-life-sized bronze statue depicting Joe Kirk Fulton's first year as Masked Rider was in the works by Grant Speed, the sculptor of the Buddy Holly statue in Lubbock. The ten-foot-tall statue would show Fulton in his original Masked Rider gear—including his custom Red Raider chaps—atop a rearing horse—Blackie, Fulton's first mount—and reside in the lobby of the athletics offices at the south end of Jones AT&T Stadium.

Miniatures of the bronze would be sold to help fund the statue, and a mystery underwriter—suspected and later confirmed to be Fulton[20]—handled the rest. It had the blessing of Tech's president, its athletics director, and multiple regents. It seemed everyone was on board. But one lone dissenter made national news: longtime Tech supporter and alumnus Ralph Blodgett.

The skylight was reinstalled after placement. (Courtesy the Southwest Collection)

Blodgett served as president of the Ex-Students Association and contributed hundreds of thousands of dollars to athletics, the Goin' Band, and the College of Business Administration. The statue angered him so much he said he would pull his endowments from athletics if they proceeded to place the sculpture in the athletics offices.

"That's not intended as a threat," Blodgett told the Associated Press. "That will be an after-effect if they go through with it. I will withdraw my membership with the Red Raider Club, never attend another Tech football game, and make every attempt to get the lump sum money back from [the Athletics Department] and give it [to] some other school."

The source of his outrage? That the statue pictured Fulton in his original costume that resembled cowboy gear rather than the Spanish matador-style costume newer riders wore. He declared that Athletics Director T. Jones "made a helluva mistake" by deciding without any outside input that the statue should depict the original Masked Rider. Blodgett then alleged that Jones convinced Fulton to underwrite the statue. Jones conceded that he had the idea of the statue using the original costume but that he consulted other project stakeholders; university officials knew the project was in the works for months.

"I only anticipated joy from the friends and alumni of this university when they walked into our lobby and saw the statue of the original Masked Rider,"

Fulton with the statue at its official unveiling. (Courtesy the Southwest Collection)

Tonya Tinnin and Blaine Lemons with Midnight Raider as Lemons takes the reins in 1990. (Courtesy the Southwest Collection)

Jones said. "No one else has reacted negatively. . . . People who have seen it think it's marvelous. I'm thrilled to death with it. Everyone has the right to disagree; I have absolutely no problem with that. But the plan is to continue what was started months and months ago."

"We're not cowboys," Blodgett argued. "I've looked at pictures of Masked Riders through the years, and none of them looks like that. I think the work is fine; the workmanship is wonderful. My main objection is it doesn't depict the Masked Rider as he is today. That's why I'm so upset. There's no use having one bigger than Dallas if it's not going to depict the Masked Rider most people know. You'd have to be seventy years old to recognize that one. I'm going to do everything I can to stop it."

"They can melt [the statue] down or give it to Fulton and let him put it in his back yard," Blodgett continued. "What they ought to do is chisel the Texas Tech off the chaps and give it to Oklahoma State. They're Cowboys; we're not."[21]

Despite Blodgett's protests, the statue was unveiled in the Masked Rider Lobby of the athletics offices after it was lifted and placed by crane through the lobby's skylight. The public was invited to view the statue, and sculptor Grant Speed shared, "Being a part West Texas and a little part Texas Tech, I'm honored to be a part of this dedication."[22]

Bygones will be bygones, and the Red Raider Club inducted Blodgett into its Hall of Legacy in 2007.

Tryouts for Masked Rider in 1990 brought an extraordinarily large field of contestants—fifteen students applied. Although thirteen applicants competed in the horsemanship portion, only six made it to the interview stage with the Masked Rider Committee.

Blaine Lemons of Colorado City emerged from interviews as the 1990–1991 Masked Rider. The animal production major was revealed at the Changing of the Reins ceremony (the first time in the press it had been so named) on March 1, 1990.

"I would just like to thank you for giving me the opportunity to represent Texas Tech and allowing me the opportunity to fulfill this dream," Lemons told the crowd at the transfer ceremony. "I am looking forward to working with and getting to know the Masked Rider Committee and represent Texas Tech to its highest degree."[23]

After a summer filled with appearances at rodeos, parades, and Bob Wills Day, Lemons and Midnight Raider returned to Jones AT&T Stadium. In an interview with the *University Daily*, Lemons detailed what was involved with serving. "Even though being the Masked Rider is an honor, there is a lot of hard work that goes along with the title," he said. Midnight Raider continued to live at the New Deal farm, which Lemons visited three to four times per week to care for the horse. The horse center student manager took over feeding and care duties the remainder of the time. Lemons enlisted two assistants to help Midnight Raider travel.[24]

Exactly one year after becoming Masked Rider, Lemons took off his mask and cape for the last time as the university's twenty-ninth rider. "I know I'll remember this past year as the best 365 days of my life," he said in his farewell speech. Lemons set the record for Masked Rider duties, traveling more than 11,000 miles for appearances that year.[25]

His successor was Ralynn Key of Gail, Texas, one of the fifteen applicants from the year before.

Blaine Lemons with Midnight Raider during his 1990–1991 season as the Masked Rider. (Courtesy the Southwest Collection)

Blaine Lemons presents Ralynn Key with her mask during Transfer of Reins in 1991. (Courtesy the Southwest Collection)

Ralynn Key with Midnight Raider during her 1991–1992 season as the Masked Rider. (Courtesy the Southwest Collection)

Key, an office systems technology and business education major, competed in barrel racing as a young girl. Her mother graduated from Texas Tech and competed on the rodeo team. Key didn't have much of an interest in football or the game-day atmosphere except for one tradition she saw as a child, which inspired her lifelong dream to become the Masked Rider. Key followed in her mother's footsteps and also competed on the rodeo team. For her last two years of school, Key made the College National Finals Rodeo in barrel racing. Key even held the world record in pole bending with the American Quarter Horse Association.

"Ever since she was three years old, she's wanted to be the Masked Rider," Key's mother said. "She used to wear a cape and ride around on a stick horse when she was little."[26]

"It's a dream come true," Key told her hometown newspaper, which also contains the first reference to the name Transfer of Reins, the current name of the ceremony for transitioning the riders. It also marked the first time the incoming rider wore the black shirt and pants of the costume; previously, only the outgoing rider wore these costume pieces. "When I was younger, we would come to the football games and all my attention was focused on the Masked Rider. I[']d go home and ride my black horse, pretending I was the Masked Rider."[27]

As Masked Rider, Key's favorite memory was the light show and the infamous battery pack.

"I had a lighted costume," she told Texas Tech in 2011. "My hat was lit up, my cape was lit. We had a battery pack that we had to tie onto the saddle, under my cape—probably 35 or 40 pounds—and Midnight Raider hated that. It was real hard to get it tied on because he wouldn't stand still. . . . [Blaine Lemons] finally got it just in time as they started the fight song. I came down the ramp, and it was pitch dark. I couldn't see a thing other than just blurs. . . . I had the reins on the horse's neck, and I had my guns up—both hands out—and that was the scariest moment of my entire life. But I just kept thinking, 'The horse can see. I can't see, but he can see.' So I just trusted Midnight Raider."[28]

After a decade of fundraising, the Red Raider Endowment had reached $35,000. The Masked Rider, however, now cost about $17,000 annually—triple the amount from the early 1980s, with increased appearances and travel plus vehicle expenses.

The university held a press conference September 4, 1991, to announce an ambitious fundraising goal of raising $250,000 for the Masked Rider endowment.

Ralynn Key flips through a program as children pet Midnight Raider during a football game in 1991. (Courtesy the Southwest Collection)

Ralynn Key and Midnight Raider at a football game in 1991. (Courtesy the Southwest Collection)

"Tech is very fortunate to have the Masked Rider act as an official ambassador for future generations of Tech students to come," Athletics Director T. Jones said during the press conference. Lubbock Mayor B. C. "Peck" McMinn declared September 4 and 5, 1991, as Masked Rider Days.

Scott Hopping, assistant vice president for American State Bank and brother to former Masked Rider Coke Hopping, chaired the endowment committee and provided a voice to the public during fundraising efforts. These included mailing out 4,500 pledge cards and working with student organizations. Funding for the program was pledged from multiple sources.

"The animal sciences center is responsible for the care of the horse and the Athletics Department is responsible for the [liability] insurance of the Masked Rider," Tom McGinnity, assistant coordinator for student activities, said. "Student fees pay for the traveling expenses and the maintenance of the Masked Rider costume."

The quest for a self-sufficient program with a steady stream of funding continued.[29]

Ralynn Key places a cape on new Masked Rider Jason Spence at the Transfer of Reins ceremony in 1992. (Courtesy the Southwest Collection)

Jason Spence of Tahoka, Texas, took the reins in 1992. Spence, who knew he wanted to be an auctioneer since the age of ten, worked for Jack Aufill (father of former rider Jennifer Aufill) at the Lubbock Horse Auction from the year he was a freshman in high school through his graduation at Texas Tech.

"Tech was the only place I wanted to go," Spence told *The Agriculturist* magazine in 2018. "There were no other choices. Being the Masked Rider was another

Jason Spence high-fives young fans at a home football game in 1992. (Courtesy the Southwest Collection)

Jason Spence poses for the 1993 *La Ventana*. (Courtesy the Southwest Collection)

long-term goal of mine. I even had more tackles than the football team."[30]

During Texas Tech's home game against Wyoming on September 12, Spence collided with field judge Clair Gausman in the first quarter during an extra-point kick. While ROTC members guarded the west sideline and Saddle Tramps the east sideline for the clockwise pregame runs, the program's field safety members only lined the west sideline during scoring runs because riders were restricted to running down the west side and walking around the east side. Gausman was on the southeast corner of the field.[31] The hit laid out Gausman, rendering him unconscious, but he was able to resume his job in the second quarter. The thirteen-member Masked Rider Committee, chaired by Tom McGinnity, reviewed the incident over the following week.[32]

"I'm not sure what will be the outcome," Texas Tech Athletics Director T. Jones told the Associated Press the Monday after the collision. "He made a mistake. We ask them not to run on the back side of the stadium—the visitors' side—because [visitors] are unfamiliar with our tradition here."[33]

The committee met for forty-five minutes Wednesday, September 16 and prepared to release a statement that Friday. Committee spokesman Jim Barlow said, "The review process is lengthy. It is continuing. There has been no final determination. . . . This process must be thorough."[34]

The Friday statement said Spence violated approved safety procedures, but because there were no written disciplinary guidelines or policies for violations, they would not sanction Spence, despite some committee members advocating for removing him from his post. He returned to the saddle September 26 for Tech's game against Baylor.[35]

*Texas Monthly* covered the collision in the 1993 Bum Steer Awards under the heading "Horses and Zebras Don't Mix."[36] The committee implemented disciplinary and removal procedures for riders who fail to follow safety regulations.

Gausman continued to officiate college football games, and his son, Kevin, became a Major League Baseball pitcher after a successful career at Louisiana State University. In a 2008 interview with the *San Francisco Chronicle* about the unintended hazards of officiating (ranging from hospitalized knockouts to tripping over end-zone markers), Gausman recalled the incident. "I didn't know where I was. The first question they asked was: 'Where are you?' I knew I was in the end zone. They asked, 'What hit you?' I didn't know. They said it was a horse. If the next question was, 'What's your name?' I would have been afraid to answer."[37]

Spence faced one more challenge on the football field in 1992 in addition to referees: an influx of tortillas.

"A disturbing trend known as 'tortillas tossing' has surfaced during home football games," a heading in the *Daily Toreador* read, with pleas from student organization leaders, Spence, and even head football coach Spike Dykes.[38] The trend allegedly started in 1989, but by 1992, it had become a divisive issue on

Lisa Gilbreath during her 1993–1994 season as the Masked Rider. (Courtesy the Southwest Collection)

campus for students until the trend faded after penalties and tortillas laced with ketchup and mustard.[39]

After a year of service, a teary-eyed Spence transferred duties to Lisa Gilbreath during the Transfer of Reins ceremony on April 3, 1993. This was the first time the ceremony was held on a Saturday in April before the football team's Red and Black spring game.

"During those two weeks in September, I felt my world coming in on top of me," Spence recollected before the crowd. "But this has definitely been the best year of my life. Being the Masked Rider was one of my long-time goals. Now it's time to move on."

"I know that [Gilbreath]'ll get discouraged sometimes, but there's a hundredfold more good rewards than drawbacks," he continued. "Watch out for those referees."

Lisa Gilbreath, a pre-veterinary junior from Lewisville, Texas, started riding at nine years old and began showing horses at age twelve. The daughter of two Texas Tech alumni was a lifelong Masked Rider fan.

"I've been watching the Masked Rider since I was a kid," Gilbreath said. "I have pictures of myself as a three-year-old trying to lean over the rail and touch the horse. . . . It's one of the main reasons I came to Tech. A lot of the Masked Rider is PR for Tech. It was for me. It was great to see that black horse."[40]

Amy Smart with Double T during her 1994–1995 service as the Masked Rider. (Courtesy the Southwest Collection)

# 7

# DOUBLE T

In fall 1992, those close to Midnight Raider noticed some issues with the horse's legs. On a trip to College Station for the Texas A&M game, Spence and Midnight Raider went to a veterinarian who diagnosed the horse with a progressive bone disease—one without remedies at the time—and suggested searching for a new mascot. The Masked Rider Committee expected the horse would complete its appearances until his replacement was found, but his condition began worsening in the spring. With an impending heavy travel schedule on top of the progressing disease, Midnight Raider officially retired from service April 16, 1993, at the age of fifteen. He lived at the New Deal farm until his retirement home would be chosen.[1]

The endowment fund had reached just over $40,000, and the program ideally needed someone willing to gift the university a horse.

"We are hoping someone will donate a horse to the program," Masked Rider Committee Chair Tom McGinnity said, "but are checking all possible leads for black Quarter Horses in this area which will meet the qualifications for our mascot. . . . The horse has to be fairly gentle. The ability to perform around a large crowd is important. The closeness of the crowd in the stadium can be very demanding."[2]

The title of the article announcing the horse's retirement and lack of replacement—"Future of Masked Rider uncertain after retirement of Midnight Raider"—caused panic with some members of the public thinking that the program would be discontinued without a new horse.[3]

In the heart of summer rodeo season on July 22, 1993, Texas Tech held a press conference introducing the newest horse for the Masked Rider: Teriyaki Tiger, a four-year-old appendix Quarter Horse gelding from the Weaver Training Center in Canyon, Texas. Nicknamed Black Bart, the horse was solid black except for a small star on his forehead partially hidden by his forelock. He stood 15.2 hands, weighed 1,100 pounds, and had been showing in hunter under saddle classes for two years. After testing other horses and riding Teriyaki Tiger for fifteen days, the program chose him to be the next Masked Rider horse.[4]

"He's really gentle and he loves to be around people," Lisa Gilbreath shared.

The Texas Tech University Health Sciences Center (HSC) and Department of Orthopaedic Surgery jointly donated funds to purchase the horse for $3,700.[5]

"We at the Health Sciences Center thought it would be fun to participate in this joint venture with the university," Dr. Bernhard Mittemeyer, HSC executive vice president and provost, explained to the press gathered at the Transfer

Lisa Gilbreath with Double T in front of the Double T at Jones AT&T Stadium in 1993. (Courtesy the Southwest Collection)

of Reins ceremony. "We are very much a part of the Texas Tech family and wanted to show our support of Texas Tech Athletics. When we heard the Student Association was looking for a donor, we thought it would be a great opportunity for us."

Gilbreath and Teriyaki Tiger made their first appearance that night at the Brownfield rodeo.[6]

The next task for the Masked Rider Committee was to determine the horse's new Texas Tech name. The committee decided it had three options: the first was another public naming and student voting contest like the one held for Midnight Raider. Committee chair Tom McGinnity was not excited about that option because of the work involved. A second option was to name the horse themselves, and the third was to name the horse Midnight Raider II.[7]

Prior to the start of the September 4, 1993, home football game against Pacific University, Teriyaki Tiger was christened with his new Texas Tech name, Double T. "When Lisa was going through appearances," McGinnity said, "people would offer lots of suggestions. I recorded all of them and then we went through them and narrowed it down."

The three names they considered were Midnight Raider II, Black Bart, and Double T. The committee felt naming the horse Midnight Raider II was inappropriate because the horse came from a different ranch than Midnight Raider had. Black Bart, the second option, was simply the horse's barn name. After consulting with the donors, which harkened back to earlier days of naming, and then again with the committee, they decided on Double T—especially fitting as an abbreviation of the horse's registered name.

Dr. Mittemeyer of HSC and Dr. Eugene Dabezies, chair of the Department of Orthopaedic Surgery, presented Double T on the field to new Athletics Director Bob Bockrath, who then presented the horse to Gilbreath.

The ceremony also formally retired Midnight Raider to his former rider, Ralynn Key. Midnight Raider's former riders who were interested in providing his home in retirement had submitted application packets. The committee selected Key because they "knew that she'd care for the horse." Student Association president Mike Fietz led Midnight Raider onto the field and handed the lead to Texas Tech President Robert "Bob" Lawless, who then presented the horse to Key.

As Midnight Raider left Jones AT&T Stadium for the final time, fans gave him a standing ovation.[8]

After "a great life of retirement," Midnight Raider passed away at the age of twenty-six at the Borden County ranch belonging to Key's parents.[9]

Double T made a successful showing at his first football game after just two months on the job.

"I was cautious on the first run, so I didn't run him as fast," Gilbreath told the *Daily Toreador*. "But after that, I thought I ran him full speed. I was kind of nervous, but he did real good."[10] The pair finished their inaugural year and nine months together with about fifty appearances and 7,000 miles traveled.[11]

The following spring, the Masked Rider Committee selected Gilbreath to serve a second term as Masked Rider, making her the first to be selected for two

Ralynn Key receives the reins to Midnight Raider, at his retirement, from President Robert Lawless prior to the Red Raiders' home opener football game against Pacific University in 1993. (Courtesy the Southwest Collection)

Lisa Gilbreath is honored at halftime during the fall 1993 spring Red and Black game in lieu of a Transfer of Reins. Ron Dameron presents her with the traditional letter jacket. (Courtesy the Southwest Collection)

consecutive terms since Randy Jeffers had served from 1971 to 1973 and was the final rider to do so. She rode the horse at the Transfer of Reins ceremony on Thursday, March 31, 1994, and her selection was announced to the crowd two days later at the Red and Black game.[12]

However, good news for Gilbreath brought a change to the program. Less than a month later, the aspiring veterinarian found out she had been accepted to Texas A&M's College of Veterinary Medicine—a typical path where she would leave her undergraduate coursework a year early to begin vet school.[13]

Amy Smart of Richardson, Texas, was chosen to take over the position. Smart was a senior animal science major and the 1991 Texas State Horseman's Association Outstanding Horseman. She had also served on Texas Tech's horse judging team and equestrian team.

"I've rode and shown horses almost all my life, and I've always wanted to be the Masked Rider," Smart told the *University Daily*.[14] Smart began riding at two years old and showing at the age of thirteen. But after attending a Texas Tech football game with her parents as a five-year-old, she dreamed of becoming the Masked Rider.[15] "I went out with Lisa and I rode [Double T], and then last week I went out and rode him by myself," she said.[16]

The committee had a small reception for Gilbreath and Smart on Thursday, April 28, 1994, in the Athletics Department's south end zone building lobby, home of the Joe Kirk Fulton statue.[17]

Smart took the reins in time for the tradition's fortieth anniversary. After she completed sixty summer appearances aboard Double T—handing out general scholarship applications to Texas Tech students at each—Smart turned her attention to the football season and anniversary plans.[18]

The Masked Rider Committee planned the reunion, themed "Tradition Reins," for the first home football game of the year on September 3, 1994, against the University of New Mexico. The program was still using the saddle with large conchos donated by the Fulton family in 1955, and saddle design had changed immensely since the 1950s—not to mention the normal wear and tear a saddle receives over the years with extensive use. A new, more modern custom saddle and bridle for the program were commissioned and would debut at the game.

The sterling silver corner plates of the black saddle featured a ten-karat gold silhouette of the horse and rider that was also a part of the logo for the fortieth anniversary. The breast collar featured red tooled letters that read "TEXAS TECH" on one side and "RED RAIDERS" on the other. The new bridle featured sterling silver conchos with gold Double Ts on each side where the browband joined the cheekpieces. The braided gaming reins were made of red and black leather. (For safety, the Masked Rider horse always uses connected reins and not split reins.) The custom saddle cost $5,000, but with Alvin Davis's contacts and negotiating, the retailer cut the cost in half for the program.[19]

Snapshots by the *University Daily* of Smart in costume at the Livestock Arena with both saddles before the events of the anniversary picture her with a big smile.[20]

The goal of raising $250,000 for the Masked Rider endowment persisted. At the time of the anniversary, funds stood at $62,989.80. "The interest on this sum of money would cover the operations of Masked Rider Programs in the future," Cheryl Shubert, coordinator of Student Activities, told the *University Daily*. "This would free up student service fee money, and money in the Athletics Department budget. It would provide for the truck and travel expenses and the Masked Rider outfit. This would definitely guarantee the continuing of the Masked Rider in its current form."[21]

The anniversary kicked off at 8 p.m. Friday, September 2, 1994, with a reception for former riders and supporters at the Holiday Inn Civic Center featuring the Blue Denim Band. A ceremonial retirement of the thirty-nine-year-old saddle took place, which was later placed on display in the Masked Rider Room of the University Center, followed by the dedication of the new saddle. With a 1 p.m. kickoff versus the University of New Mexico the next day, a former rider reception was held at 10 a.m. in the courtyard of the University Center.

Like most early September days in Texas, the temperature reached above 90 degrees that afternoon. A total of seventeen riders came to the reunion and were recognized in a pregame ceremony. Double T was calm and debuted the saddle in the pregame run. In the third quarter, the Red Raiders scored a field goal to take the lead 20–17. Smart and Double T began their customary gallop on the track around the west side of the field, but as the pair reached the end of their run on the northwest corner of the track, the saddle slipped to the side, throwing off Smart.[22] Horses are prey animals and takes flight at perceived danger; a saddle slipping toward sensitive areas will scare them even when they are standing still, and they will attempt to evade the threat.

Double T turned back to return to the tunnel where he entered and exited the stadium. He cleared the players' benches, sprinting down the west side of the

Amy Smart, wearing a cast, looks over the wreath in honor of Double T during his memorial service. (Courtesy the Southwest Collection)

stadium, fortunately not hitting anyone. Multiple theories exist on what exactly caused his fall. Smart said in a 2014 interview his horseshoe nails snagged the turf, causing him to lose his footing. Others say he slipped on the metal drainage grate found where the southwest tunnel meets the field. Some believe he was simply going too fast to make the turn up the tunnel. Regardless of what caused his fall, Double T ran headfirst into the tunnel wall and died on impact.

An archived video allegedly shows Smart's fall and Double T's run back to the tunnel, but not his fatal crash. Only one photograph by the *University Daily* captures the chaotic scene. Police officers hold back a shell-shocked Smart sans bolero hat as she stares at Double T lying flat in the tunnel while she is being led to an ambulance. Program staffers are frantically removing his new saddle from his belly, and he still wears the new bridle. The scene is fully lit by a midday sun; the tunnels were not covered as they are now. Everyone—even the police officers—wears a look of panic and shock.[23]

Theories on why the saddle slipped in the first place continue to proliferate. More specifically, the theories deal with what caused the girth to fail. A saddle will slide if the girth is not tight, especially when the horse is rounding corners or riding in a circle. The girth, often called a cinch in Western tack, is a band that goes under the horse's belly behind its shoulders and elbows that attaches on both sides to a saddle's cinch straps on a Western saddle. These pieces keep the saddle on a horse. During saddling, horses hold their breath until after the girth is tightened, and they exhale to loosen the girth. Immediately before mounting, a rider re-tightens the girth. When riding, it is imperative that the girth is snug so the saddle—and thus the rider—do not slip.

Some believe that the cinch and cinch straps of the new saddle were not tightened up enough to the horse's belly and not readjusted before the saddle's debut. A more recent theory states that because the day was hot and Double T was sweating a considerable amount, the cinch gradually loosened. A final theory is that the cinch was loosened or unbuckled during halftime to let the horse relax—a common practice—but was not tightened again upon his return to the game. In Smart's 2014 interview, she generally confirmed something of this nature occurred.[24]

Even though no one had prepared for anything like this to happen, crews quickly covered the horse and found a way to remove him from the stadium and the view of onlookers.

Double T was buried that night at his home in New Deal at the Tech Farm. University veterinarian Dr. Mark Hellman told the press the next day that Double T suffered a blow to his head that crushed his skull, and he died from a severe concussion. Smart sustained a strained wrist and black eye.[25]

Double T's death left a cloud over Texas Tech and the Masked Rider Program. If the program ever had a defining moment up until that day, this was it. The event caused sympathy from many, outrage from some, and ridicule from others, including the University of New Mexico's costumed mascot, who allegedly mimicked the horse dying in front of the visitors' seating section at the game.[26]

In the aftermath of the tragedy, one fact became apparent: the Masked Rider was a tradition Red Raiders passionately wanted to continue.

Three days later on September 6, the Masked Rider Committee convened an emergency meeting. They first voted to continue the Masked Rider Program. The search was on for a new horse with calls already coming in from those

Amy Smart begins a pregame run aboard Hoot Owl at a football game in 1994. (Courtesy the Southwest Collection)

wanting to donate. The committee created two ad hoc committees: a horse search committee, and a Tech traditions committee to review safety procedures. The committee chose not to investigate the incident further, believing it was a freak accident and no one was close enough on the field to discern what exactly happened.[27]

"Our recommendation is that the tradition be continued in some form," Assistant Sports Information Director and committee member Kelly Robinson shared with the media. "Also, a search committee will be formed to find another horse. Whether or not that will be done this year, we don't know. But we have had a flood of calls and letters in support of continuing the tradition of having the Masked Rider inside the stadium."[28]

A moment of silence with guns up was held at the next home football game—a Thursday game against Nebraska two days after the committee meeting. Four football team members and two Saddle Tramps carried a horseshoe-shaped wreath onto the field, then Smart draped the new bridle Double T wore at his death on top of the wreath. The wreath was then carried to the southwest area of the track where the Masked Rider typically stands during games.[29] The Masked Rider Committee created a memorial fund to honor Double T and pay for a marker for his burial site. Within a week, fourteen donors had contributed $492.[30]

Smart went on to ride at more football games for the 1994 season after a trial of four interim horses.[31] For three games, including homecoming, she rode Hoot Owl, a horse owned by Gary Roland. Hoot Owl was sold during his interim period. For one home game and at the Cotton Bowl she rode Two Bar Boy, owned by Greg Collier.[32]

An initial analysis showed that official safety guidelines created by the Masked Rider Committee called for the pregame run to begin at the southwest corner of the stadium, gallop to the northwest corner, trot to the northeast corner, gallop to the southeast corner, and slow to a walk at the visitors' tunnel. If the field was not clear, the horse would not run. For scoring runs, the horse would gallop from the southwest corner to the northwest corner. Safety personnel included two additional handlers for the horse and ten ROTC members positioned along the path to clear the track for runs.[33]

The program then received renewed strength in three needed areas.

First, Sam Jackson, who first got to know the program as a high school student through twentieth Masked Rider Kurt Harris, finished his PhD in ruminant nutrition, and the Department of Animal and Food Sciences hired him as a full-time faculty member. Following the death of Double T, he joined the Masked Rider Committee.

"They asked me to help come up with a new plan and new ways of doing things," Jackson said. "The problem was that football game atmosphere changed, and it got a lot busier and a lot more people and a lot more involved, and we kept doing the same thing."[34]

Second, the horse search ad hoc committee found a horse up to the challenge of helping Red Raiders move forward past the tragic death of Double T.

Third, the Masked Rider Program finally reached its financial goals thanks to the initiative of Masked Rider Committee member Alvin Davis and a bank executive with horse sense.

Alvin Davis watched Will Rogers banter with the rodeo announcer at the 1934 Texas Cowboy Reunion in Stamford, Texas. When he was a young man, his parents, Glenn and Viva, had driven him from Post, Texas, over 100 miles to see a rodeo. Davis was hooked. But for a person weighing 140 pounds "soaking wet," throwing down a calf posed a problem, and team roping had yet to become the rodeo staple it is today. Instead, Alvin became an avid rider and champion of Western heritage.

After high school, Davis spent eighteen months in the US Army, after which he immediately enrolled at Texas Technological College in 1946. During his college years, he announced the annual Tech rodeo, which was held in Jones AT&T Stadium, the home of Red Raider football. He was named the 1948 Top 4-H Boy in the country, produced the World's Original All-Junior Rodeo, and formed the American Junior Rodeo Association.

Once he graduated with a bachelor's degree in animal husbandry in 1952, he served as the administrator of the National Intercollegiate Rodeo Association and had a stint working in banking. But his passion for the cowboy life never diminished.

Davis raised and showed horses competitively at the world and national level. He opened Western stores in Brownfield and Levelland and remained in the industry for twenty years. He returned to Lubbock to serve as the executive vice president and general manager of the National Ranching Heritage Center

(NRHC) for thirteen years. While working at the NRHC, he founded the National Cowboy Symposium and Celebration, the largest event of its kind in the country. It brought cowboy poets, musicians, performers, horse clinicians, storytellers, and a chuckwagon cook-off to Lubbock every September for more than thirty years.

While working for the NRHC in the late 1980s, Davis joined the Masked Rider Advisory Committee as the Animal and Food Sciences alumni representative. In 1994, he set out to gain funding for the tradition.

As usual, Davis approached Lubbock businesses and asked for donations for the Masked Rider Program in a piecemeal approach. He began by making an appointment with Gary Lawrence, the president of Norwest Bank in Lubbock.

Lawrence joined the bank in 1993 after spending more than twenty-five years in the banking industry. He also enjoyed working cattle on horseback on the weekends as a hobby.

Davis began his usual spiel. He shared how much it cost to run the program each year and asked for a contribution toward that amount. "Well, why don't we just pay the whole thing?" Lawrence responded. And a partnership was born.

In 1995, Norwest Bank established the Norwest Bank Masked Rider Endowment Fund and Scholarship, helping ensure the future of the tradition. Proceeds from the endowment covered the program's operating costs, and the Masked Rider received a larger scholarship. On June 9, 1998, Norwest Bank absorbed Wells Fargo, keeping the name of the smaller institution, and Wells Fargo became the program's premier sponsor. Wells Fargo retained the sponsorship and continued to increase the amount of the scholarship provided and set a goal for the endowment to reach $250,000 in 2004, the year of the program's fiftieth anniversary.

Financial limitations no longer posed a barrier for the Masked Rider Program.

JoLynn Self and High Red Bug begin a pregame run at Jones AT&T Stadium in 1995. (Courtesy the Southwest Collection)

# 8

# HIGH RED BUG

Most horsemen and horsewomen flinch at the thought of retraining an off-the-track retired racehorse. If they are unable—or not good enough—to retire to the breeding shed, many racehorses find second careers as show horses or recreational rides. But these horses often come off the track high-spirited and ill-mannered. They are not for the novice or faint of heart. Even though the Masked Rider makes a lot of runs, racehorses typically do not have the docile attitude needed to interact with the public. But High Red Bug was different.

B. F. Phillips Jr. was an oilman in the Dallas area. He started running cattle on his Frisco ranch, but after watching a cutting show, he sold his cattle in the late 1940s and bought show horses. He even hired famed horseman and 2001 American Quarter Horse Hall of Fame inductee Matlock Rose to run the ranch and train the horses in the early 1950s. But Phillips changed his preferences once again.

He sold all his show horses in 1966 and replaced them with racehorses. Phillips ended up breeding Dash For Cash, successfully campaigned for pari-mutuel betting in Texas, and served as the Texas Horse Racing Association's executive committee chair in 1987. He finished his horse career posthumously as an inductee into the American Quarter Horse Hall of Fame in 1989.

High Red Bug was foaled in 1986, the year before Phillips's death in 1987. His sire, On A High, had a speed index of 113 and earned over $1.1 million in his three-year racing career. (Speed indexes are used to gauge the fastest a Quarter Horse can run. Anything over 100 is considered extremely fast.) The son of Dash For Cash, On A High also won the All-American Futurity, the richest Quarter Horse race. High Red Bug's dam, Ida Red Bug, had a speed index of 80 and was sired by American Quarter Horse Hall of Fame inductee Lady Bug's Moon.

Cloyce Box bought High Red Bug as a yearling from Phillips's estate in July 1987. Box, a former Pro-Bowl tight end and quarterback for the Detroit Lions who had earned his law degree from Baylor University during off-seasons, became an oilman in his retirement and bred racehorses. In an article about the multimillion-dollar lawsuits he left in his wake after he passed away in 1993, David Pasztor wrote in the *Dallas Observer* that Box "was known, among other things, for not letting the law get in the way of a lucrative deal." One round of ongoing lawsuits involved J. R. Simplot, the Potato King of Idaho, who made a good deal of his fortune selling potatoes to McDonald's. Box also owned the Cloyce Box Ranch, the original location of the Southfork Ranch used in the first five episodes of the television series *Dallas*.

JoLynn Self and High Red Bug make the pregame run past Saddle Tramps at Jones AT&T Stadium in 1995. (Courtesy the Southwest Collection)

Self and High Red Bug make the pregame run at Jones AT&T Stadium in 1995. (Courtesy the Southwest Collection)

Box hired Jake Pletcher to run his Frisco, Texas, Quarter Horse farm in 1969. Pletcher then moved to Ocala, Florida, in 1985 to run Box's C. B. Farm. Pletcher remained with C. B. Farm until Box's death in 1993. According to the National Thoroughbred Racing Association, Pletcher helped start the careers of NTRA Hall of Fame jockeys Jerry Bailey and Mike Smith. Pletcher's son, Todd, is a four-time Eclipse Award winner.

High Red Bug raced only once on June 14, 1989, as a three-year-old. He recorded a speed index of 93, finished second, won $374, and earned a Register of Merit with the AQHA.

Craig Pelt of Collinsville, Texas, bought the horse as a five-year-old on September 20, 1991. Pelt performed with the Hella Shrine's Black Horse Patrol drill team. Originally called the Hella Mounted Patrol, two men created the group in September 1957 riding in a Fort Worth parade. The Hella Shrine's grand potentate approved the unit two months later. Now called the Black Horse Patrol, the group of men riding black horses has performed in the Tournament of Roses Parade and four presidential inauguration parades.

Riders in the patrol must buy their own horse and tack and are responsible for their equine partner's transportation to events. Since its creation, the Black Horse Patrol has won twelve national championships and twenty-eight Texas championships for its precision drill-team work.

High Red Bug spent four years as a member of the Black Horse Patrol with Pelt and a couple of years team roping and performing ranch work. But on April 1, 1995, High Red Bug—called "High Red" for short—became the eleventh Masked Rider horse.[1] Once again, the Texas Tech University Health Sciences Center stepped up to purchase a horse for the university.[2]

The horse—bearing the Lazy P freeze brand of B. F. Phillips's horses on his left hip, the same as his grandsire Dash For Cash—made his debut at the Red and Black game at Jones AT&T Stadium as Amy Smart handed the reins to his new rider. At 16.1 hands and 1,200 pounds, the sharp-looking black horse had floated to the top of a field of thirty-two prospective horses that was narrowed to nine serious contenders.[3]

JoLynn Self of Amarillo was announced as the next Masked Rider in a March 8, 1995, press release with an April 1, 1995, start date, likely because at the time of her selection, no horse had yet been named.[4] She began her new position at

JoLynn Self and High Red Bug at Jones AT&T Stadium in 1995. (Courtesy the Southwest Collection)

the same time as High Red at the Red and Black game on April 1.[5]

"I think he is the most awesome horse," Self said of High Red at his debut. "He has the best attitude, and he's the most experienced horse that we could have chosen."[6]

Self came to Texas Tech with a goal of serving as the Masked Rider. She spent her early years as an undergraduate preparing for the tryouts by taking equine science courses and joining the Horseman's Association to improve her riding skills.[7]

"I grew up in the area and saw the Masked Rider as a child," Self told the *Daily Toreador* in a 2004 interview. "I grew up taking care of horses, so it was kind of a dream to be the Masked Rider and represent Texas Tech while being a role model for the future. . . . It was a real honor and a privilege to be an ambassador for Tech. I got to spend time with the kids, and I hope to instill in them the feelings I felt about Tech."[8]

Self and High Red became the first team to appear at Raider Alley, the carnival-like area near Jones AT&T Stadium on home football game days that debuted the previous year.[9] Self and High Red also brought the return of—and still used—pregame field runs where the horse and rider lead the team from the south end zone to the north end zone.[10]

Martha Reed and High Red Bug lead a pregame run at Jones AT&T Stadium in 1996. (Courtesy the Southwest Collection)

The pair did not experience two game-day traditions. In the 1995 season, the Southwest Conference and NCAA threatened to enforce penalties for items thrown on the field during a game, namely tortillas.[11] Also suspended were scoring runs for the Masked Rider until safety procedures could be developed.[12]

Self and High Red finished the football season at the 1995 Copper Bowl.

"We led the team onto the field, and we jumped over the insignia in the center of the field and that left a really great feeling," Self said.[13] Because of the anatomy of horses' eyes, drastic changes in color like white and black make horses believe they are encountering a change in footing. What looks like a simple stadium logo midfield to humans appears to be a cliff or bottomless pit to a horse.

"The funniest thing," she continued, "was when I ran to the other side of the field where the parachuters were, and the horse left skid marks on the field from when we stopped."[14]

Martha Reed, a senior animal production major from Knickerbocker, Texas, a small community near San Angelo, took the reins for the 1996–1997 year. Reed also happened to be a cousin to Kelley Waggoner, the 1961–62 Masked Rider. For the second year in a row, the rider was announced on a date prior to the game—this time on March 15—and the transfer took place at the Red and Black Game on March 30, 1996. Self took her final ride as the Masked Rider, followed by Reed's first ride.[15]

For the first time, it was publicly shared that the Masked Rider would receive a $500 stipend per semester as remuneration for the twenty to thirty hours of work per week required by making an estimated eighty public appearances. Also for the first time, Luskey's Western Wear donated the black bolero hat for the costume.[16]

"My mom put me on a horse when I was real young," Reed said, noting that she broke her first colt when she was eight years old. "I exercise cutting horses and racehorses. I raise and break horses and sell them to make money for school."[17]

The summer of Reed's tenure brought a new face to the Masked Rider Program: Jenny Passow of El Paso. The two-time recent Texas Tech alumna had previously worked for the student affairs division, and she accepted the role as a new activities specialist advising the Masked Rider and Pom Squad and coordinating homecoming.[18]

With the fall football season approaching, Reed became the first Masked Rider in the Big 12 era. Weakened by the 1990 departure of the University of Arkansas for the Southeastern Conference and a string of NCAA suspensions including SMU's death penalty among other grievances, Texas Governor (and Texas Tech alumnus) Bob Bullock helped maneuver his alma mater, the University of Texas, Texas A&M University, and Baylor University into a merger with the Big 8, forming what would be called the Big 12. Although the announcement of plans to switch to the new conference occurred in early 1994, Big 12 athletic games began in fall 1996.[19]

Texas Tech Football and the Masked Rider have been intertwined since the ghost riders of the 1930s.

"The Masked Rider is by far the most visible and most popular spirit organization we have here at Tech," Sports Information Director Richard Kilwein told the *University Daily* at the beginning of the fall semester in 1996. "The Masked Rider is a wonderful ambassador for the university and is extremely valuable to the athletics department. . . . All the fans, young and old alike, love the Masked Rider."[20]

Following the death of Double T during a scoring run, the Masked Rider Committee's fifteen members comprising Texas Tech students, alumni, faculty, and staff suspended the sideline runs but retained the pregame run to lead out the football team.[21] The sideline, or scoring, runs marked where any Masked Rider incident in program history occurred.

On Thursday, October 3, 1996, leading up to homecoming weekend and the game against Baylor, John T. Montford, the first Texas Tech University System chancellor, who started his tenure just over a month earlier, met with Reed and Passow in his office. After Reed expressed confidence in making scoring runs, Montford said the horse would probably run "victory laps" at the homecoming game in two days and that he was disbanding the Masked Rider Committee effective immediately.[22] "Ultimately someone has to make the decision," Montfort added, regarding reinstating scoring runs.[23]

After the homecoming parade Saturday morning, Montford told Reed she would make a scoring run at the game later that day.[24] He next told the Saddle Tramps they would be assisting Reed at the game for the run, a job previously held by ROTC. Although happy to help, the Saddle Tramps weren't sure if they had enough members to clear the track or how long they would remain on the track, nor had they received any type of previous training.[25]

Reed safely made the traditional pregame run and one "victory lap," or scoring run, along the west track. One Texas Tech cheerleader said that while she enjoyed the scoring run, the cheer squad was unaware of the scoring run, giving them a scare.[26]

Because JoLynn Self and Martha Reed split the 1996–1997 year as Masked Rider, they both appeared for the Transfer of Reins to Becky McDougal. (Courtesy the Southwest Collection)

The news of the disbanding of the committee broke as the top story of the campus paper after the weekend, topping homecoming coverage and news of a $1 million donation to build the proposed United Spirit Arena.[27] The changes prompted a Monday, October 14 meeting of the Masked Rider Committee regarding safety issues and then a Tuesday, October 15 meeting with Montford and the committee.[28]

According to the *University Daily*, Montford reinstated the committee at the Tuesday meeting and acknowledged "in hindsight he probably should have visited with the committee first, but said he was not familiar with the committee's functions."[29]

Years later in 2016, Montford, who had become an impactful chancellor, the president of Southwestern Bell, and a successful business consultant, authored a book in which he offered an account of the events to illustrate how executives should put their shareholders first. He called the Masked Rider Committee "one of the most interesting committees" he had encountered. He wrote that he pleaded during a meeting with the Masked Rider Committee to allow the horse to make the pregame runs but compromised that the horse would not have to make every scoring run. He said the committee called an executive session and returned with a no. In thinking of his shareholders—students, alumni, and fans—he immediately disbanded the committee.[30]

The heart of the issue likely rested somewhere between what was reported by the campus paper and the book. While the Masked Rider never ceased pregame runs, fans missed the scoring runs. Based on the interviews given in 1996 after homecoming, the Masked Rider Committee was probably cautious in bringing them back for the safety of the horse, rider, and roughly 600 game-day personnel on the field—especially doing so for the first time in two years with about 48 hours' notice and it being the homecoming game. Reed and High Red Bug had practiced scoring runs during the summer, but game-day operations for them were not yet established.

The committee carried on and continued the work it began in August on updated safety procedures and new riding path proposals.

The scoring run path that ultimately prevailed took the horse from the southwest to northwest corner instead of the other proposed path that began slowly from the southeast corner to the southwest, followed by a faster run from the southwest to northwest corners. Additional safety measures included notification to visiting squads about the horse, a safety meeting thirty minutes before kickoff between on-field staff and game officials, and announcements stating when the horse will run. More full-game on-field safety personnel were added, including at least one Masked Rider assistant, thirteen Saddle Tramps, and five animal science assistants. The horse and rider would not make scoring runs six minutes before the half to allow band members to populate the track; neither would it make scoring runs four minutes before the end of the game to allow the horse and rider to exit before end-of-game sideline traffic.[31]

The October ordeal had finally settled, and Reed prepared to finish out the second half of the football season. She and High Red performed the updated runs for the Nebraska game.

Reed and High Red traveled to College Station for a rainy-day game against Texas A&M on October 26, 1996. As Reed rode the horse onto the concrete track, High Red began to slip. She returned to the trailer to outfit him with rubber boots over his hooves to give him greater traction. She rode the horse back and forth a few times to test them, but on the last turn, his feet slipped out from under him on the concrete. He fell on his side, pinning Reed's foot. High Red was unharmed, but Reed broke a bone in her foot, rendering her unable to put weight on it.[32]

Under the committee's direction led by chair Jenny Passow, the group determined a substitute was needed until Reed could return to the saddle. JoLynn Self, now a senior biology major, began riding High Red again and took Reed's

Becky McDougal poses with Caro, later known as Black Phantom Raider. (Courtesy the Southwest Collection)

place for football games.[33] But Reed called High Red "a good, reliable horse" when discussing the accident with the *Lubbock Avalanche-Journal*.

"Of course, he gets excited once in a while," she told the newspaper. "But he's real good for the situation he's put in."

Becky McDougal of Comanche, Texas, became the thirty-sixth Masked Rider

Joe Kirk Fulton with Black Phantom Raider at Jones AT&T Stadium in 1997. (Courtesy the Southwest Collection)

and served during the 1997–1998 year. Well into McDougal's term, she and Sam Jackson realized her childhood riding instructor was Jackson's sister.

At a rodeo in mid-August 1997 in Roby, Texas, with McDougal aboard, the eleven-year-old High Red suffered a cut below his knee on his front leg. A Roby veterinarian treated the wound, and High Red returned to his home at the Tech Farm in New Deal to recover.[34]

Program officials announced September 11, 1997—days before the football home opener—that High Red would have a replacement for the game. Chris Lawrence of Seymour, Texas, loaned Caro to stand in for High Red until he was well enough to make appearances.[35]

Caro did well in his initial football-game appearances with McDougal, and

Norwest Bank purchased the black gelding for Texas Tech for $7,500 and officially presented him at the Texas A&M game on October 27, 1997. Although High Red was still recuperating at the time, the purpose of purchasing Caro was to give the program the chance to alternate between the two horses.[36]

"We were proud to establish the Norwest Masked Rider Endowment Fund in 1995, and we are honored to continue our support for this time-honored symbol of pride for Texas Tech," Gary Lawrence, president of Norwest Bank, told Texas Tech. Lawrence presented the annual $25,000 check to the endowment while Mike Coomer, executive vice president for Norwest Bank, presented the $1,500 scholarship check.[37]

The seven-year-old solid black Quarter Horse gelding with a bit of a scraggly mane came from the Chris Lawrence Cattle Company, a working ranch in Seymour, Texas. Up to that point, Caro had spent his entire life working as a ranch horse.[38]

During the October 22, 1997, game against the University of Oklahoma, McDougal temporarily transferred duties so that the original Masked Rider, Joe Kirk Fulton, could make a special on-field appearance. Fulton rode Caro for the event, outfitted the horse with his own working saddle and the Masked Rider bridle, and wore his original costume.[39]

"It's not as big a deal to me as it is to some people," Fulton told the *Lubbock Avalanche-Journal* in an October 10, 1997, interview. "They came to me and asked me to do it, and I think it's an honor. . . . They asked me about a month ago. I told them I'd do whatever they wanted."

"I think Texas Tech has the best of all mascots in the Big 12 Conference," Fulton told Texas Tech in a news release leading up to the event. "Personally, I think the Masked Rider is the most colorful, and I wish I could take credit for the idea."[40]

High Red's injury would turn out to be career-ending. He received surgery on his injury in December 1997 and spent time recovering at the Tech Farm in New Deal. During a spring storm, thunder and lightning spooked High Red, and he ran head-on into a tall fence. Workers found him deceased in his paddock the morning of Sunday, March 15, 1998. A necropsy showed that the impact against the fence ruptured the horse's heart, and he died on impact in what McDougal called a freak accident.

"Obviously, everyone is pretty upset," Tech spokesman Michael Sommermeyer told the *Lubbock Avalanche-Journal*. "We honor these horses with high regard, so consequently the Masked Rider Committee is pretty upset, and the riders are all pretty upset."

High Red was laid to rest next to Double T in New Deal.

In March 1998, the Masked Rider Committee announced a naming contest for Caro, who became the next horse in the program on a full-time basis. Norwest Bank sponsored the contest, titled "Put Your Brand on Texas Tech." The committee opened entries at 11 a.m. on March 9 and closed them on March 25. Fans submitted more than 1,300 names, which were narrowed down by the committee along with Lubbock Mayor Windy Sitton, Norwest Bank President Gary Lawrence, Texas Tech President Donald Haragan, and outgoing Masked Rider Becky McDougal.

During halftime of the annual Red and Black football scrimmage on April 4, 1998, the committee named the winners of the horse-naming contest in five categories:

- Texas Tech student: Two Guns High submitted by Texas Tech student Danielle Lane.
- Texas Tech alumni: Gunzup submitted by Texas Tech alumnus Richard White.
- Lubbock ISD elementary school student: Black Phantom Raider submitted by Parsons Elementary School fourth grader KaSandra Hall.
- Lubbock ISD junior high student: Black Phantom submitted by Angelica Gutiérrez, a Wilson Junior High ninth grader.
- Other: Matadors Pride submitted by Nancy Reed, a Lubbock resident.

The name from the youngest submitter—and the group with the greatest number of submissions—was selected. KaSandra Hall won $300 and a statue of the horse made by Alvin Davis, and the remaining four finalists each won $50.

The day before Caro's name became Black Phantom Raider, his new rider for the 1998–1999 term, Michael "Dusty" Abney of Athens, was introduced to the public at the Transfer of Reins ceremony in the northwest corner of the field at Jones AT&T Stadium. Abney was awarded the Masked Rider scholarship, and supporters and sponsors of the Masked Rider Program were recognized.

Raider Red poses in Jones AT&T Stadium with Becky McDougal and Black Phantom Raider in 1997. (Courtesy the Southwest Collection)

Ten thousand miles and more than 100 appearances later, Becky McDougal took her final ride aboard Caro—now Black Phantom Raider—at the ABC Rodeo at the Lubbock Coliseum Saturday on the same day as the Red and Black scrimmage.[41]

"Becky is an outstanding leader and role model," Cheryl Shubert, who oversaw the Masked Rider Program, told the *University Daily*. "Her leadership went beyond the personal rewards she could gain. She really held dear the tradition and the institution, and she wanted to help guarantee the program's success in the future."

Dusty Abney, a red-haired and mustachioed animal science major and National Golden Key Honor Society inductee, had been riding since the age of nine and served as one of McDougal's assistants.

"Taking the reins is a little scary," Abney told the *University Daily* leading up to Transfer of Reins, "not from the standpoint of controlling the horse, but because you know 52,000 eyes are watching everything you do. It's a huge responsibility."[42] Throughout the year, Abney appeared at everything from a Cub Scouts ceremony to the Houston Livestock Show and Rodeo grand entry.

"Football games [are] a small part of what we do," Abney explained. While football games remain the most visible and publicized appearances, riders complete anywhere from five to nine games per year, which constitute roughly 2 to 5 percent of total appearances a rider will make that year. On top of appearances, Abney shared the rider "has to feed the mascot two times a day, clean the

Michael "Dusty" Abney and a Masked Rider assistant pose with Black Phantom Raider in front of the Administration Building in 1998. (Courtesy the Southwest Collection)

Becky McDougal and Black Phantom Raider make a pregame run at Jones AT&T Stadium in 1997. (Courtesy the Southwest Collection)

Abney and Black Phantom Raider make a pregame run at Jones AT&T Stadium in 1998. (Courtesy the Southwest Collection)

Dusty Abney masks Travis Thorne during the Transfer of Reins ceremony in 1999. (Courtesy the Southwest Collection)

Abney and Black Phantom Raider make a pregame run at Jones AT&T Stadium in 1998. (Courtesy the Southwest Collection)

stall daily, and exercise the mascot three to five times a week."[43]

It was during Abney's term as the Masked Raider that the horses from the Masked Rider Program were moved from the farm in New Deal to an oversized stall located on the north side of the Livestock Arena on Indiana Avenue and Main Street. The new location was significantly more convenient for riders to take care of the horse during the semester. The stalling and storage area was located along working pens and offered a wash rack with hot and cold water plus an indoor arena for riding and nightly turnout.

Thorne and Black Phantom Raider make a pregame run at Jones AT&T Stadium in 1999. (Courtesy the Southwest Collection)

Thorne makes friends with a young fan at a football game in Jones AT&T Stadium in 1999. (Courtesy the Southwest Collection)

Travis Thorne, a junior agribusiness major from Stanley, New Mexico, was announced as the thirty-eighth Masked Rider for the 1999–2000 year. He called it "the greatest privilege and honor one can achieve at Texas Tech." Thorne was often seen riding with his trademark black gloves.[44]

On Friday, March 26, 1999, Abney and Thorne completed the traditional Transfer of Reins ceremony at Jones AT&T Stadium. The next day, both riders made a unique appearance at the Red and Black spring football game, which also served as a small reunion weekend for former lettermen. Abney led the red team onto the field to open the game, and Thorne led the black team onto the field to open the second half.[45]

The year 1999 brought two very different types of art featuring the Masked Rider into the folds of Texas Tech traditions.

In the spring, the Texas Tech Ex-Students Association's Student Alumni Board revived the Texas Tech class ring and offered it in two styles: a traditional ring and smaller signet ring. The traditional class ring displays the Bell Tower on one shank and a rearing Masked Rider on the other. The popularity of the rings grew, and now, thousands of students wear them.

Beginning in 2011 with Christi Chadwell, the Texas Tech Alumni Association gifted the outgoing rider with a class ring of their choosing as a thank you for their year of service. Later, the ring would be gifted to incoming riders to allow them to wear it during their year.

Western sculptor Grant Speed of Lindon, Utah, created a bronze life-size replica of the saddle made for the program's fortieth anniversary. Former Saddle Tramps sent contributions for the Saddle Campaign to help raise money for the sculpture. The dedication and unveiling took place at noon in the southwest tunnel during the September 18, 1999, opening home football game against the University of North Texas. The sculpture's base bears a plaque that reads as follows:

> This saddle is dedicated to the memory of "Double T" and all the horses and riders who have exhibited dedication and pride as they represented Texas Tech Athletics.
>
> Strive for Honor
> Dedicated September 18, 1999
> Funded by Former Saddle Tramps

Travis Thorne and Chancellor John Montford share a conversation during Arbor Day 1999 in front of the Administration Building. (Courtesy the Southwest Collection)

The statue sat in the hallway to the Texas Tech locker room about thirty feet above the southwest tunnel from where Double T passed away. A tradition began for players to touch the saddle as they leave the locker room to play a game.

Speed possibly sculpted the saddle as a precursor to his next piece of Masked Rider art that was unveiled the following year. The program mailed him one of the saddles to use as a model, and the saddle sculpture is an exact replica, from the size of the seat down to the sheepskin lining on the bottom of the saddle.

Lesley Gilbreath, a senior finance major from Flower Mound, Texas, north of Fort Worth, took the reins as the 2000–2001 Masked Rider. Lesley and older sister Lisa became the second set of siblings in program history. "When I came to games as a kid, I loved the Masked Rider," Gilbreath told the *University Daily*. "It was my favorite part of the game. I think it's a great cause, and since not very many people get to do it, I'm . . . very honored."[46]

Fall 2000 came with a huge surge in popularity of the Masked Rider. Gilbreath's fall season received a kickstart on September 9: a gift of a new horse trailer donated by Wells Fargo Bank. The $8,900 two-horse-slant load trailer would provide ample space for Black Phantom Raider and his riders.[47]

Lesley Gilbreath poses at Jones AT&T Stadium in 2000. (Courtesy the Southwest Collection)

"The trailer we have is a lot older and we truly needed the extra space that the new one provides," Gilbreath told the *University Daily*. "This is just another generous offer from Wells Fargo Bank, and it truly shows their support of the Masked Rider Program."[48]

The Masked Rider scholarship also rose to $2,000. But the trailer wouldn't be the only unveiling that day.

At 2 p.m. on Saturday, September 9, 2000, just before the season's home opener, the Texas Tech Ex-Students Association (now the Texas Tech Alumni Association), unveiled the larger-than-life bronze statue of the Masked Rider and

Lesley Gilbreath and Black Phantom Raider make a pregame run at Jones AT&T Stadium in 2000. (Courtesy the Southwest Collection)

A crew places the Masked Rider statue near the Frazier Alumni Pavilion in September 2000. (Courtesy the Southwest Collection)

horse in a full gallop. Grant Speed, the Lindon, Utah, sculptor of the Joe Kirk Fulton Masked Rider statue and bronze Double T saddle memorial, created one of the most prominent and well-loved pieces of art on the Texas Tech campus.[49]

Standing ten and a half feet tall from base to the top of the rider's guns up, the one-and-a-quarter-sized $300,000 statue rests south of the Frazier Alumni Pavilion racing toward Jones AT&T Stadium. According to a September 11, 2000, issue of the *University Daily*, art dealer Bill Burford, a Texas Tech alumnus and former Red Raider football player, commissioned Speed to create the statue. James E. Sowell, then chairman of the Board of Regents, proposed the idea to the regents to commemorate the Masked Rider Program.

Chancellor John T. Montford opened the unveiling ceremony, and Texas Tech President David Schmidly and Ex-Students Association Executive Vice President and CEO Bill Dean gave their remarks. Alex "Ty" Cooke Jr., Lubbock mayor pro-tem, declared it "Texas Tech Masked Riders Day." Each Masked Rider at the unveiling received a copy of the proclamation.

Speed shared with the *Texas Techsan* he studied photos of a racehorse mare owned by Joe Kirk Fulton named "Dash's Dream" as she crossed the finish line to accurately depict a horse in a full, reaching gallop. Speed added a sheath to the sculpture to make the horse a gelding, the preferred sex of the program's mounts. He said he used program scrapbooks, photos, and newspaper clippings to get the look of the rider. Allegedly, Travis Thorne served as the primary model. Speed sought to create a composite sculpture of the different eras of Masked Riders. The saddle shows the best evidence. It combines the first and second official saddles used by riders; the oversized conchos of the first saddle dot the cantle, and the breast collar and custom silver corner plates featuring gold silhouetted Masked Riders found on the second saddle appear on the sculpture.

In a September 8, 2000, article in the *Lubbock Avalanche-Journal*, Speed acknowledged he "got a lot of help from a number of people." Metal Letters of Lehi, Utah, cast the statue, which arrived on campus by trailer a week before its unveiling. To raise funds for the project, the Ex-Students Association sold miniatures of the statue measuring two feet long by one and a half feet high for donations toward the project of $7,500 and above.

One other first for the season took place: The infamous Old West–style computer-animated video of the Masked Rider atop his mount, shooting eggs dressed as Big 12 conference foes played during the pregame.[50]

Gary Lawrence from Wells Fargo Bank presents Gilbreath with her scholarship check during a home football game in 2000. (Courtesy the Southwest Collection)

The year 2000 brought two more types of art commemorating the Masked Rider. Texas Tech revealed its new branding: a three-dimensional Double T—also known as the beveled Double T—along with secondary logos. Some featured the horse and rider from the side, and one showed the horse and rider galloping from a head-on view with cape flying, earning it the nickname of the "flying horse logo" within the program.

In November, the fourth installment of the Texas Tech University commemorative Christmas ornament series featured the Masked Rider. Based on the iconic pregame run photo of Dusty Abney and Black Phantom Raider, the horse and rider are framed by a gold horseshoe bearing "Texas Tech University" in red letters. The year 2000 takes the place of "Red Raiders" on the horse's breast collar. Sales of the $19.99 ornament benefited Campus Caregivers, a fund that provided financing for campus landscaping and public art projects, including the new Masked Rider statue.

"Not only does [the ornament] recognize the 39 men and women, to date, who have worn the famous mask, but it also commemorates the unveiling of Texas Tech's newest piece of outdoor sculpture, one of the projects of Campus Caregivers," Debbie Montford wrote in the November/December 2000 issue of the *Texas Techsan*. Montford, wife of then Chancellor John Montford, chaired the Campus Caregivers group and is responsible for reviving Texas Tech's Arbor Day into the campus-wide tradition it is now.

"The Masked Rider and horse in full gallop," she continued, "represent the very essence of Texas Tech—a determined spirit with sights set on victory, on and off the playing field."

With the newest piece of artwork on the Texas Tech campus featuring the Masked Rider, the 2001 Transfer of Reins took place in the Masked Rider Plaza south of the Frazier Alumni Pavilion surrounding the Grant Speed statue.[51]

Gilbreath finished a successful year and even represented Texas Tech in Washington, DC, in President George W. Bush's inauguration parade.[52] Her quote as the outgoing rider at Transfer of Reins reflected back upon what she shared a year earlier as she took on the role: "[Being the Masked Rider] is the greatest honor a student can hold."[53]

Gilbreath transferred the reins to Kathryn "Katie" Carruth of Lubbock. The daughter of former Masked Rider Johnny Bob Carruth, Katie's selection marked the first parent and child to serve as riders.

Katie Carruth and Black Phantom Raider make an appearance for the ribbon cutting of the new Broadway entrances to campus in 2001. Carruth is joined by Texas Tech Chancellor John T. Montford, Debbie Montford, Mozelle Rushing, and W. B. "Dub" Rushing. (Courtesy the Southwest Collection)

"This brings a whole other side of tradition to being a Masked Rider," Carruth shared in the days leading up to the April 20, 2001, Transfer of Reins ceremony.[54] As a child, Carruth would wear her father's mask, cape, and boots and gallop around their house pretending she was the Masked Rider.[55] "The Masked Rider is a vital part of Tech's history and future," she continued. "This is something I have always wanted to do."[56]

"I am extremely proud of my daughter," Johnny Bob said of Katie at Transfer of Reins. "It has been a goal of hers since she was young."

Katie Carruth rides in the Texas Tech homecoming parade in 2001. (Courtesy Texas Tech University Office of Communications and Marketing, hereafter Office of Communications and Marketing)

# 9

# "A BIG LOSS FOR TECH"

Katie Carruth, her assistant Mike Reynolds, and Black Phantom Raider traveled from a parade in Fredericksburg back to Lubbock the afternoon of Friday, August 24, 2001.[1] Classes would begin in three days, and the first home football for Carruth and the horse was in just two weeks.

About thirteen miles south of Mason on Highway 87, the driver of a 1996 GMC Sonoma pickup fell asleep at the wheel in the opposite lane and crossed the center line of the road.[2] Reynolds was able to veer the Masked Rider truck out of the path but not the trailer.

The GMC collided with the trailer, tearing off the trailer's hitch and axles and flipping it. Emergency responders spent three and a half hours removing a tranquilized Black Phantom Raider from the wreckage. The horse was taken to Hill Country Veterinary Hospital in Mason.[3]

The next day, he showed improvement and could stand for eight to twelve hours, but his health began declining Sunday morning. Black Phantom Raider could not stand, and the next day, the veterinarian found the horse was suffering from kidney failure. Paralysis began to set in. With a poor outlook and the horse in pain, the decision was made to humanely euthanize him on August 27, 2001.[4]

Black Phantom Raider was buried at the Texas Tech campus in Junction. His grave is covered in rock and topped with an iron silhouette of the Joe Kirk Fulton statue. A black granite monolith stands next to the site. Student Government Association Internal Vice President Kelli Stumbo planned a memorial service during the Student Senate retreat at the campus September 15, 2001.[5]

"I'm glad he's not in pain anymore," Carruth said.[6] "I've lost my boyfriend. I feed him twice a day, groom him, spend many, many hours a day with him. This is definitely a hard time—something that won't be easily cured."[7]

"It's going to be hard to replace him," Sam Jackson said. "We might be able to get a horse as good looking as him, but he had a great personality for his job."[8]

"We've lost a member of our campus community," Michael Shonrock, vice president of student affairs, shared with the *Lubbock Avalanche-Journal*. "This is a time when we've got to pull together as a campus community. We've been fortunate to have an unbelievable amount of prayer and compassion."[9]

Perhaps the most thoughtful words about Black Phantom Raider came from a statement from the editorial board of the *Lubbock Avalanche-Journal* titled "A Big Loss for Tech":

> THE TEXAS TECH RED Raiders will be taking the field this weekend for the opening football game of the season. Sadly, an old friend will not be sharing the field with them.
>
> Black Phantom Raider, a beautiful Quarter Horse that had been Tech's mascot for the past three football seasons, was euthanized last week after suffering massive trauma when a pickup truck hit a trailer occupied by the horse.
>
> The loss was a big one for Tech. Black Phantom Raider was one of the finest horses Tech has ever had. Nonetheless, the university is moving forward with a search for a new horse and will use a substitute at the game this week if a replacement has not been chosen by game time.
>
> The Masked Rider tradition at Tech is one of the most stirring college football traditions in the nation. The sight of the rider astride a black horse galloping around Jones SBC Stadium brings a thrill to young and old alike.
>
> It is a shame to lose such a fine animal. The Masked Rider tradition can and should go on, and it is good that the search for a replacement is under way. But Black Phantom Raider will be a hard act for another horse to follow.[10]

A search for the next horse immediately commenced. Gary Lawrence, president of Wells Fargo Bank, committed the bank to helping the program buy a new horse. "We bought the last horse, and we will buy the new horse," he told the press and expressed his sadness for the passing of Black Phantom Raider. "We are prepared to write some big checks for the program."[11]

Carruth and Jackson began systematically testing new horses. By the time of the first game on September 8, 2001, Carruth rode an eleven-year-old interim horse, Midnight, to a Rowdy Raider Rally pep rally, the very first Texas Tech student tailgate, RaiderGate,[12] and to the game.[13] For homecoming in October, another horse from a pool of six—a ten-year-old Quarter Horse gelding named Ace and owned by Melissa Brillhart from Slaton—took a turn as interim mascot.[14]

Due to game-day performance nerves, neither Midnight nor Ace was chosen for a permanent status. Jake, a fifteen-year-old horse in the Therapeutic Riding Program, filled in for the remainder of Carruth's appearances. The Spade Ranch donated Jake to Therapeutic Riding, and with his black coat and calm demeanor, he made an excellent stand-in mascot. Jake, though, had a habit of rearing for the pregame run, and this tendency, combined with his older age, meant he did not become a candidate for the full-time position.[15]

Carruth had limited appearances by horseback for the year and spent considerable time reading to children at schools and letting them try on her hat and mask.[16]

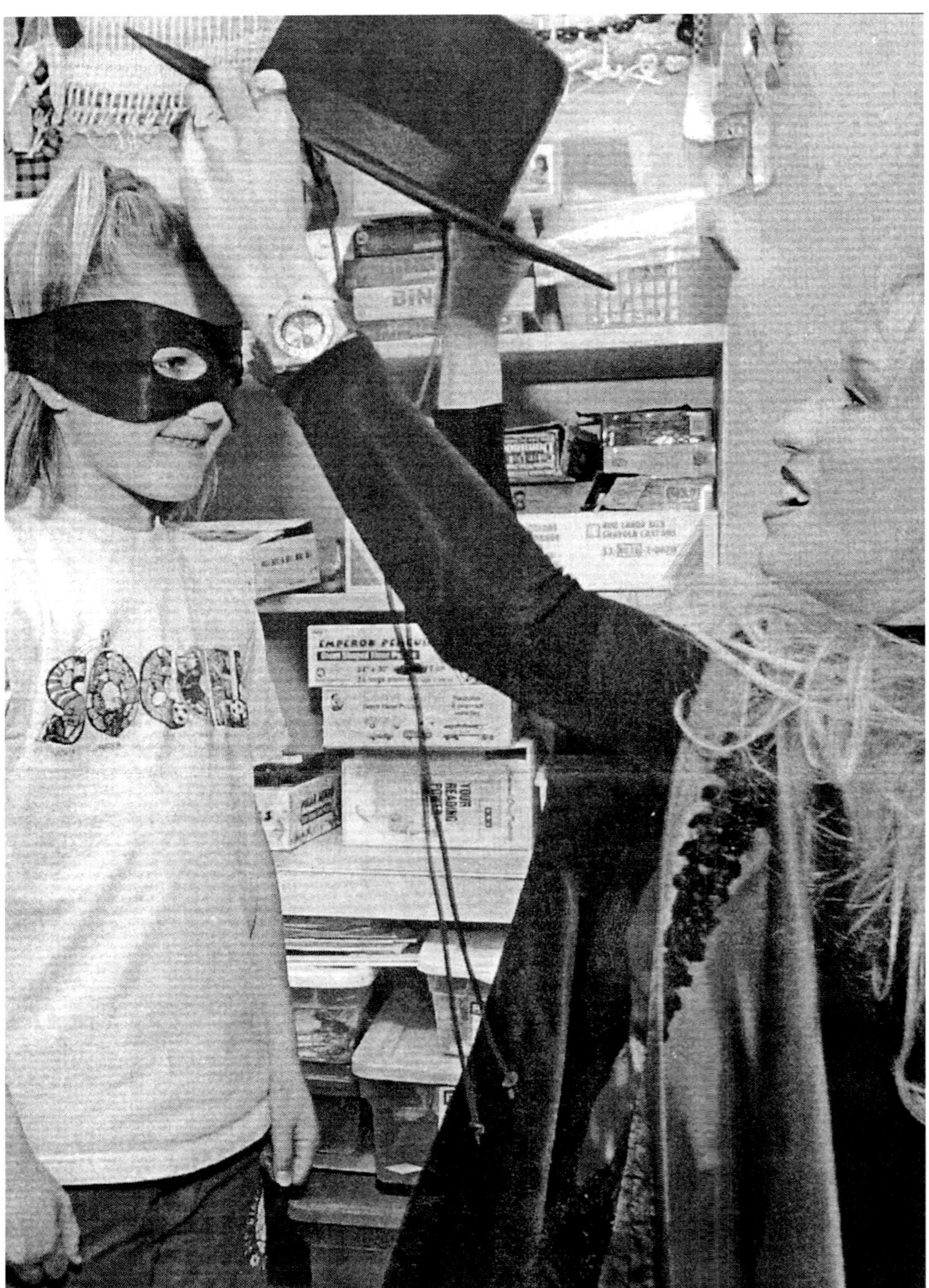

Katie Carruth helps a student try on her mask at Cooper Elementary School during her service as Masked Rider on March 5, 2002. (Courtesy the Southwest Collection)

"It's been an awesome, incredible year," Carruth told the *University Daily.*

"But it's also been a trying year. . . . I didn't have the experiences most Masked Riders have because of the horse. It was kind of disappointing. I always wondered how it could have been different."[17] She added, "You're the icon of the university," saying the great things she experienced outweighed the negative.[18]

Nine months and twenty-five horses later, Jackson still sought the perfect thirteenth horse for the Masked Rider Program.[19]

Jessica Melvin and Midnight Matador's official photo in front of the Administration Building in 2002. (Courtesy the Southwest Collection)

# 10

# ONE FAMOUS AMOS

Kim Lindsey saddled up her new gelding for a training ride. She and her friend Vicky Hoggett of Hoggett Ranch in Bluffdale, Texas, purchased him together and listed Hoggett Ranch as the owner. Amos, a big-hipped, solid-black Quarter Horse with ears just a bit too big for his head, wasn't supposed to be on a ranch.

Registered as A Famous Boon, the three-year-old should have been training for the National Reining Horse Association Futurity, the most famous and prestigious NRHA competition in the country. Despite his fifteen-foot-long sliding stop and American Quarter Horse Congress–winning sire, Primary Pine (also shown as A Famous Amos), he simply wasn't talented enough to win at a national level. Kim and Vicky bought the gelding from Amos's owner and breeder, successful NRHA amateur competitor and breeder David Waggoner, to repurpose him for Stock Horse of Texas (SHOT) shows.

SHOT prizes functionality in horses; class winners should ideally transition from ranch work to the show ring then back to ranch work. So Kim mounted up and took Amos for a ride across her Dickens, Texas, ranch as he moved from his career as a show horse to that of a ranch horse. Not long into the ride, the pair scared up a covey of quail. The birds exploded in every direction, including right into Amos's face. The show horse didn't flinch. The next day, Kim called Sam Jackson.

"Sam, I have a horse you need to look at."

Three-year-old horses are the equivalent of preteen children. They learn very quickly and are usually eager to please their teachers. But they occasionally become rebellious, have short attention spans, and are still learning how the world around them works. A three-year-old horse that takes parades, rodeos, and nationally televised football games not just in stride but enjoys them is like a 12-year-old child setting the curve in a university statistics class.

Three-year-old Amos began his trial at Texas Tech in April 2002. All potential Masked Rider horses must pass a series of tests that simulate game-day environments and community appearances. Prospective horses must arrive well trained and willingly and easily execute gaits and ground maneuvers to demonstrate that riders can control and guide them through crowds and during stressful situations.

Horses that show promise next attend a Goin' Band from Raiderland practice. This test separates the true contenders from the fearful. Most horses hate the sound of drumlines and do not know what to make of sousaphones. When

Jessica Melvin leads Midnight Matador on his first pregame run in Jones AT&T Stadium on September 14, 2002, against Ole Miss. (Courtesy the Southwest Collection)

a 300-piece marching band plays the Horse Music from fifty feet away, retreat is not the desired outcome. One horse tested in fall 2001 refused to even cross the street and enter the band practice lot. The horse ended up breaking away from his trainers and hiding behind the old Women's Gym where Talkington Residence Hall now sits. He bided his time eating the landscaping until his rescue. Another horse could not handle the band's loud music and was never unloaded from the trailer.

Prospective horses must show comfort navigating curbs, pavement, and inclines. These everyday occurrences for people are foreign to many horses. Horses in the program enjoy attention from fans and display a friendly nature. Masked Riders sign thousands of autographs each year while the horse stands patiently. People—especially young fans—enjoy petting and interacting with the horse at appearances. Above all, prospective horses must have a naturally relaxed demeanor. They must experience a football game environment before they are selected. This includes crowd noise, sideline reporters and photographers, cheer and pom squads, costumed mascots, marching bands, and loudspeakers in addition to the game itself. A poor showing at this stage automatically and irrevocably rules out the horse.

Some people have incorrectly speculated that the horses receive drugs to make them impervious to crowds of over 60,000 screaming fans. With proper selection of the horses and adequate riding before football games, poor attitude and fear are nonfactors. Galloping a sedated horse in this environment also poses danger not only to the rider but also to others on the field.

Amos received his on-field testing at the April 2002 Red and Black game. After a satisfactory appearance there, Dr. Jackson recommended his acquisition. Wells Fargo purchased Amos for the Masked Rider Program on May 21, 2002.

The next day, the Center for Campus Life opened a contest to give Amos his Texas Tech name. Entries closed on June 21, and the center announced the winning name and its submitter at the first home football game in 2002. Texas Tech alumnus Mike Meixner of San Antonio submitted the winning name. He received on-field recognition and a miniature version of the Masked Rider statue that sits near Jones AT&T Stadium.

The program's thirteenth and most publicized horse, Midnight Matador, began his reign.

•  •

Midnight Matador arrived during the Mike Leach era of Texas Tech. As campus became wrapped up in Leach's love of pirate history, Midnight Matador fit in perfectly with the pirate mentality. His stout build and 16 hands intimidated even some prospective riders who tried out. But he had a fierce personality to match his size. He read riders well during tryouts, and if they wavered or failed to focus for one second, he exposed it by breaking gait, trampling an obstacle, cutting off a corner or circle, or simply pushing them around. The well-trained horse could be easy to ride, but he had an active mind and needed mental stimulus during his exercising. He was responsive to riders who exuded confidence and adored riders who showed him affection.

One of Midnight Matador's few drawbacks was his mouthy nature. If anyone other than his rider ventured into his space around his head without his invitation, he would bite or grab what came into his air space. No one was safe from his precision. Miss Texas fell victim to a pinch on the behind, and the horse plucked straws from drinks during autograph signings. One football player ventured too close on a trip to the locker room, and Midnight Matador reached out teeth first and ears laid back an inch away from his jersey sleeve to scare him away. (It worked.) The horse was tall enough to nab errant candy bars and snacks left on the top of the sideline walls at Jones AT&T Stadium only to have assistants pry

Jessica Melvin won the title of Miss Rodeo South Dakota 2004. She came in fourth place for Miss Rodeo America 2005 and won the Raeana Wadhams Spirit Award at the pageant. (Courtesy the Southwest Collection)

the plunder from his mouth.

If Midnight Matador mirrored the pirate mindset, the pirate captain appreciated the Masked Rider tradition. Occasional complaints about female riders continue to roll in, but Leach favored a female in the saddle.

"I loved the Masked Rider tradition," he told SB Nation in a 2014 interview. "I loved the thing where he'd pop up and run down the center of the field. I thought that was a heck of a deal. And with all due respect to the male riders, I thought the female riders looked better doing it. In particular if they were blonde, because you had the contrast—first of all, you'd have this stallion [*sic*] that would be gigantic. . . . You had a smaller figure on the horse, so the horse looked even bigger and more surreal. And then you had the contrast of the blonde hair kind of streaming from this whole black image of horse and Masked Rider uniform."[1]

A close-up of Midnight Matador's Double T freeze brand. (Courtesy Stacy Stockard Caliva)

For the April 22, 2002, Transfer of Reins, two major decisions shaped all subsequent ceremonies. First, the Transfer of Reins was held indoors for the first time—this event at the Frazier Alumni Pavilion at the corner of Red Raider Avenue and Akron Avenue on the Texas Tech campus across from Jones AT&T Stadium. Second, the rider's identity was purposely held as a secret until revealed at the ceremony to build excitement.[2]

Jessica Melvin, a blonde Pierre, South Dakota, native, became Midnight Matador's first rider, the first graduate student Masked Rider, and the first current Texas Tech University Health Sciences Center student to serve. Melvin's mask followed a more streamlined design that rested higher on the cheekbone, and her cape featured a tie closure like that of older capes.

Melvin, who would go on to win Miss Rodeo South Dakota in 2004, was a talented roper and barrel racer who served on Texas Tech's rodeo team and pursued a physical therapy degree. She ran out of eligibility years to compete on the

A selection of portraits of Ben Holland in 2003 with Midnight Matador by photographer Artie Limmer. (Courtesy the Southwest Collection)

Rodeo Team and saw an advertisement for Masked Rider tryouts. "I was kind of looking for something I could do," Melvin told the *University Daily* toward the end of her term in March 2003. "This is a once-in-a-lifetime opportunity."[3]

"She had other people that knew her ability to handle horses," Melvin's father, Mark, said. "And she's always been a good speaker."[4]

Melvin had her doubts about riding a three-year-old at a football game. At one appearance, Midnight Matador refused to step onto asphalt. At another, he refused to load into the trailer. But the mischievous gelding found his niche in the world with the help of Melvin's training. She took the horse to her home in the country to train him and let him spend time with her rodeo horses. In the final months of her reign, she had him freeze-branded with a Double T on his left hip from a branding iron she had made for the occasion. Amos remains the only Masked Rider horse to wear the brand.

"It's such a tremendous responsibility," Melvin told the *University Daily*. "It's such an honor. You feel like a miniature celebrity. I'm excited to be an ambassador for Tech."[5]

After 15,000 miles aboard one of the youngest horses in program history, Melvin reminisced at the April 22, 2003, Transfer of Reins ceremony at the Merket Alumni Center: "In the end this was all priceless. The best thing I will remember is showing up and seeing the kids' faces."[6]

"I have seen a lot of Masked Riders," Interim President Donald Haragan said as he spoke to the crowd. "Certainly it is the greatest tradition in a university, in the nation."[7]

Among other items gifted to Melvin was the traditional Texas Tech letter jacket, which was still in transit. "Don't worry," Athletics Director Gerald Myers quipped to Melvin. "Our athletes don't get them on time either."[8]

On April 22, 2003, at the Merket Alumni Center, Melvin handed over the reins of Midnight Matador to Ben Holland, a senior animal science major from the far corner of the Texas Panhandle in Texline.

"I want to thank the committee and the university for giving me this honor to represent Texas Tech University next year," Holland shared during his address. "I am excited to do it. Since the first time I saw the rider I wanted to do it."[9]

Holland's first order of business: mastering the precarious mask—a trial for all new Masked Riders. "I hope I get a little more used to it," he laughed to the press at Transfer of Reins. "I am sure I will. I just have to find the best way to wear it." He joked, "Being able to see is the main key."[10]

The Masked Rider mosaic inside the lobby of the west side of Jones AT&T Stadium. (Courtesy the Southwest Collection)

Holland grew up riding working horses in the ranch country. He learned certain things about the feisty four-year-old Midnight Matador: He wouldn't turn or bend at a run, and the horse would run right through a snaffle bit at public appearances that involved a degree of speed. Holland also learned that if a gate was left unlatched, Midnight Matador would open it and escape. Occasionally, someone would not realize the horse was in the arena and fail to reclose a gate. In one of these instances, the Texas Tech Police Department found Midnight Matador grazing on campus early one morning.

Holland served as an assistant to Katie Carruth and tried out the previous

Stacy Stockard and Midnight Matador on the sidelines at a football game in 2004. (Courtesy Jaime Tomás Aguilar)

year, making it to the finals and picking up experience. For 2003, he beat out five other applicants.[11] Holland became the first man to serve since Travis Thorne in 1999–2000.

"A lot of people have asked, 'Why is it always a girl?'" Angie Labaj, coordinator for the Center for Campus Life, explained, citing an oft-asked question. "But it is not always a girl. The most qualified person always gets it."[12]

Holland spent the year riding in countless parades (including three on the Fourth of July weekend), appearing at Carol of Lights, and speaking to children in addition to fall game days.

"It's hard to beat football games," Holland remarked to the *University Daily*,[13] referring to sitting atop the horse as the best seat in the house.

During Holland's football season, Texas Tech revealed its new look of Jones AT&T Stadium: A facelift to its west (press box) side offered event spaces, luxury suites, a retail area, and a new press box, all encased in the Spanish Renaissance architecture. Housed inside its main entrance were four large-scale mosaics made of one-inch tiles. The most prominent one featured a two-story-tall mosaic of the Masked Rider.[14] A photo from the era of the corona-style breast collar and

Stacy Stockard and Midnight Matador make a pregame run at Jones stadium in 2004. (Courtesy Office of Communications and Marketing)

browband inspired the mosaic, but red lips and long blonde hair were added to the rider while the horse appears to be Charcoal Cody.

Another significant addition to the Masked Rider Program took place during Holland's year. Stephanie Rhode joined the Center for Campus Life and was placed in charge of overseeing spirit programs, including the Masked Rider along with Cheer, Pom, and, starting in 2005, Raider Red. Her daughter had been a member of the Tech Pom Squad, so she was familiar with the demands of spirit programs.

Rhode already loved the Masked Rider, but as she grew into her new role, she came to deeply treasure how much the mascot meant to Red Raiders and the high quality of students the program drew. The Masked Rider was a symbol of the university she has worked to protect and grow stronger with every year, ensuring the Masked Rider will always be held in the highest regard.

Rhode also began learning the intricacies of dealing with a live mascot. "The thing that I never really realized as a fan coming into this was how much goes into that ten-second run and how many people have to be doing their jobs just right for that to happen," she said.[15]

Rhode's warmth and spirit made her a mom-away-from-home for the Masked Riders she oversaw. Even as alumni, many make trips to visit her in her office when they come to town. She earned nicknames—as terms of endearment—from riders over the years.

"These students who serve as Masked Rider are the cream of the crop of this university," Rhode told the audience at the 2019 Transfer of Reins ceremony. "I believe that with my heart."

Stacy Stockard, a senior agricultural communications major and animal science minor from Sanger, Texas, served as the rider for the 2004–2005 year. Growing up in the heart of show-horse country, she showed appaloosas on the breed and open-show circuits in all-around events and had been showing and training in hunter-over-fences classes at the time of Masked Rider tryouts.

"It's an amazing feeling to be able to represent Tech at this level," she shared at the April 23, 2004, Transfer of Reins.[16]

Stockard found a few more of Amos's quirks. After a parade in Dickens where Amos trotted in place for its duration, she learned he needed to be loped before an event, even if it meant as few as four or five strides. She also discovered that without enough turnout for him to freely run and buck, it was impossible to get Amos to behave even with hours of exercise.

During road trips, Texas Tech fans waved to the branded truck and horse trailer. On one trip to her parents' farm where Stockard brought Midnight Matador during university holidays, a person flagged down the truck and trailer on a country road. Stockard feared something had gone wrong with the rig, but it turned out it was a Texas Tech alumnus who wanted to chat about his time at the university and the Masked Rider.

The 1994 saddle and bridle were still in use, but the headstall of the bridle (the portion of the bridle on the horse's head) was showing its age with wear and tear and a missing concho. It was replaced with a more modern headstall lined with silver rivets and conchos adorned with crossed pistols. The headstall was a double ear style but customized to add a throatlatch. While throatlatches appear only on headstalls with browbands, it was added as a safety precaution to prevent the horse or a fan from accidentally pulling off the bridle during an appearance or football game.

The year 2004 marked the 50th anniversary of the Masked Rider and Joe Kirk Fulton's first ride. Similar to the 40th anniversary, the logo for the event contained the tagline "Tradition Reins." The celebration took place during homecoming weekend and kicked off with a reception and exhibit in the Croslin Room of the Texas Tech Library. A formal dinner followed with a group photo of former riders at the Merket Alumni Center.

Each former rider, university dignitaries, and Masked Rider Committee members received a miniature saddle purchased at cost from Alvin Davis by the Center for Campus Life and a corresponding wooden saddle stand donated by Alvin Davis. Each stand had the 50th anniversary logo lasered on the front along with the recipient's name and, for riders, their year of service.

The next morning, the returning riders all served as grand marshals and rode in various vehicles for the homecoming parade. Also in the parade was a freshly wrapped campus bus with the anniversary logo and a photo of Lisa Gilbreath on the driver's side and an image of Stockard racing atop Midnight Matador (taken by Jaime Tomás Aguilar) on the curb side.

During pregame, riders lined up along the hash mark of the football field to be recognized.

The Masked Rider Committee also took a chance to recognize those who had been pivotal to the program as Honorary Masked Riders. With a unanimous vote, Alvin Davis, George Tate, and Gary Lawrence became the first Honorary Masked Riders and were presented at the game alongside former riders.

Former Masked Rider JoLynn Self summarized the feelings of many of the program's alumni in attendance: "You can see how much it means to the former riders. What's most important is that the tradition continues, and it seems that each year it grows, and I'm glad to see that. . . . The Masked Rider is Texas Tech."[17]

The excitement even carried over into the Lubbock community. The local corn maze's fall 2004 theme was the Masked Rider logo in celebration of the milestone.

The year 2004 brought another Masked Rider sculpture to campus—again controversial, but unlike the previous two highly realistic sculptures, this one took on a cartoonish, playful nature.

Texas Tech tapped Brooklyn-based sculptor Tom Otterness to create a series of bronze pieces in and around the Student Union Building (SUB). The largest piece is *Tornado of Ideas*, and pieces corresponding to it were tucked away into nooks in the SUB's main lobby. The Texas Tech University System Public Art Collection describes the energy and ideas behind the piece:

> At the base is a house splitting in two from the force of a tornado; books flying through the spiraling storm for the bulk of the piece. Titles on the books reflect conflicting ideologies; symbolically, these polar ideas fuel the tornado's energy. Seated inside the divided house is a plump prairie dog eating coins. Riding high atop the piece is the artist's rendering of the Masked Rider, kicking her feet triumphantly in the quest for truth. Otterness hopes this piece provokes discussion and discovery among viewers.[18]

And it did. Over the years, small factions of students would occasionally protest the statue and even campaign against it. Discourse ranged from the titles of books included in the tornado (all of which are actual book titles representing a broad spectrum of beliefs) to the exaggerated physical characteristics of the figures.

Otterness included three depictions of the Masked Rider, all female, with the artist's trademark round bellies and cartoon features. A small rider sat precariously atop the tornado. The second depiction was found at the base of the tornado astride the horse, who wears a shrunken bowler hat, a mask, pants, and

Midnight Matador and his riders began competing at ranch horse shows with the Texas Tech Ranch Horse Team during his off seasons in 2005, 2006, and 2007. He competed in a show at the Will Rogers Memorial Center in Fort Worth in 2005. (Courtesy Joe Stockard)

Mickey Mouse–style shoes. The rider carried a lance it poked at a cartoon police officer sprawled across Otterness's signature oversized coins. The horse and rider sat atop the book, *Thieves in High Places*, a *New York Times* best seller written by twice-elected Texas Agriculture Commissioner Jim Hightower. This small pair frequently became a lightning rod for criticism when the *Tornado of Ideas* was critiqued.

The third depiction, called *Horse and Rider*, was a substantially larger version of the pair from the base of the tornado and sat atop a stone pedestal inside the Student Union Building, surrounded by tiny bronze figures and oversized coins and surveying the three-story open lobby. The university and Otterness made five-inch resin versions of *Horse and Rider* available in solid black and solid

Masked Rider Justin Burgin in 2005. (Courtesy Office of Communications and Marketing)

white to sell to the public for $27.95. By request of Otterness, current students could purchase them at a discounted rate of $17.95. The Texas Tech Public Art Conservation Endowment received $1 from the purchase of each.[19]

In late 2004, PhD student and horse judging team coach Kris Wilson pitched an idea to the Department of Animal and Food Sciences. Based on his horse judging, showing, training, and industry knowledge, Wilson saw a burgeoning interest in his circles: competitive ranch horse events. He had joined the advisory board of a stock horse organization and envisioned a new collegiate competitive group: the Ranch Horse Team.

Students would compete at these ranch horse shows on behalf of their universities—eventually competing in their own collegiate division against other university teams for national champion team titles and individual awards.

With the green light to start training and traveling with his first team in spring 2005, Wilson set about recruiting current students for the inaugural team—the first of its kind in the country.[20] Riders ranged from those who grew up on ranches but never showed to those who grew up showing horses but never worked cattle. Just a few had experience with showing working ranch horses. Wilson also recruited his former student, Stockard, to ride Midnight Matador.

Midnight Matador led an exciting life in the summer and fall seasons, but colder weather in the winter and early spring meant fewer outdoor appearances. The Masked Rider Committee gave Stockard their blessing to ride the horse on the team to give him new activities to learn and sights to see for a more enriching slow season.

Stockard and the following two Masked Riders rode Midnight Matador on the Ranch Horse Team, and each year, he seemed to excel in the classes his rider was most adept at training. For Stockard, it was trail, where at his best outing he placed third in a class of more than sixty horses at the Stock Horse of Texas Fort Worth show at Will Rogers Equestrian Center. His next rider's roping experience helped him rediscover his sliding stop from his previous life for reining. For the third who grew up ranching, it was working cowhorse.

Decades later, the Texas Tech Ranch Horse Team is a frequent national champion team in the collegiate division. It draws prospective students from around the region and state, and former team members became top-level trainers and

Justin Burgin and Midnight Matador make a pregame run in Jones AT&T Stadium in 2005. (Office of Communications and Marketing)

exhibitors. Ranch horse classes and competitions have record numbers of entries and take place around the country.

The indoor arena at the Texas Tech Equestrian Center where Wilson first pulled together a motley team that became the foundation for a new industry is now named after him.

Stockard's year ended on April 22, 2005. With the newly completed Animal and Food Sciences Building on Indiana Avenue, the Transfer of Reins ceremony took place for the first and only time in its glass atrium.

Justin Burgin, a senior animal science major from Scurry, Texas, was revealed as the forty-fourth rider. Burgin was a newcomer to the program with no experience as an assistant or field safety team member, but his kind nature and outstanding horsemanship made him a quick study.

What began with a gift of a pony on his third birthday grew into roping and

Burgin and Midnight Matador make a pregame run in Jones AT&T Stadium in 2005. (Office of Communications and Marketing)

Amy Bell with Midnight Matador in 2006. (Courtesy Office of Communications and Marketing)

Amy Bell's custom spurs. (Courtesy Office of Communications and Marketing)

rodeoing as Burgin grew older.[21] He grew up in a family of professional calf ropers and was a member of the Texas Tech Rodeo Team. Burgin also served as an assistant director at the Texas Horseshoeing School.[22]

"The Masked Rider Program is able to give a face and personality to the university's greatest symbol of tradition," Burgin told Texas Tech.[23]

Justin's tall frame posed just one complication: The stirrups on the existing saddle could not extend far enough to accommodate his height. A new saddle was commissioned, and the saddle that had debuted at the 1994 game for the fortieth anniversary was retired. The 1994 saddle took the place of the original saddle with large conchos in the display case of the Masked Rider Room in the Student Union Building.

In the Animal Sciences Building, an enclosed glass display area had been set aside under the atrium's winding staircase for safety. The concho saddle found a new home atop a replica horse in that space.

The new saddle was again black with silver corner plates, and the wording on

A detailed view of the hand-tooled and hand-painted breast collar. (Office of Communications and Marketing)

Kevin Burns with Midnight Matador during a pregame run at Jones AT&T Stadium in 2007. (Courtesy Office of Communications and Marketing)

the breast collar, "TEXAS TECH RED RAIDERS," was retained. The fenders of the saddle bore large tooled and dyed Double Ts.

Another major—and necessary—equipment change also occurred: a new lighted hat and cape. The crowd favorite at Carol of Lights had become stained and bleached in places over the years—and it was still connected to an extremely heavy motorcycle battery, making mobility problematic at best and impossible at worst.

The Center for Campus Life commissioned a re-envisioned model with Enlighted Designs Inc., a lighted clothing company founded by artist Janet Hansen of Encinitas, California.[24]

Hansen's work with wearables included LED stage costumes—with both static and programmable lights—for Britney Spears's Femme Fatale tour, M.I.A.'s performance at Coachella, nationally televised performances of the Rockettes, and Daft Punk's world tour and Grammy performance. Her costumes for the latter now reside in the Grammy Museum in Los Angeles.[25]

With Hansen's expertise in "fabric-mounted lighting with miniature controls,"[26] the hat and cape now worked with LED lights. The hat and cap each had their own independent battery pack using 9V batteries—a vast improvement in comfort and safety for both horse and rider. Independence from a forty-pound battery introduced new opportunities for the rider with a lighted hat and cape.

Burgin became the first rider to debut in the new costume pieces for Red Raider and Lady Raider Basketball pregame activities.[27] At center court in a darkened United Spirit Arena, Burgin flipped on the switch on the hat and cape for a dramatic premiere. The tradition of having the Masked Rider appear on the court pregame in the lighted hat and cape continues, and the rider also travels with Spirit Squads to the Big 12 Tournament and March Madness.

Burgin hung up his hat, mask, and cape one last time on April 21, 2006, to graduate from Texas Tech and attend Texas A&M University College of Veterinary Medicine.

•  •

Amy Bell next took the reins as the 2006–2007 Masked Rider. "The Masked Rider is the emblem of Texas Tech University and embodies the principles of respect, honor and school spirit," Bell shared at Transfer of Reins.[28] The Kermit, Texas, native and senior animal and food sciences major had a goal of visiting

Sam Jackson and Ashley Hartzog with Midnight Matador at a football game in fall 2008. (Courtesy the Southwest Collection)

small towns like the one in which she grew up.[29] "The first time I saw the Masked Rider run across the field at a football game," Bell recalled to the *University Daily* of a childhood memory, "I knew it was my thing."[30]

Bell had previously taught lessons at the Grand Teton National Park in Wyoming. The sharp equestrienne also spent five semesters on the Dean's List.

In mid-September, Bell recounted the feeling of riding the pregame run surrounded by the energy of the crowd: "My heart is pumping. It's so fun and a huge adrenaline rush. I can feel [the horse's] heart pounding and his muscles twitching."[31]

On April 20, 2007, in the club-level event space on the west side of Jones AT&T Stadium, Kevin Burns of Clovis, New Mexico, fulfilled a childhood dream and became the 2007–2008 Masked Rider.

"I grew up watching the Masked Rider," Burns said. "I was a Texas Tech fan and I worked with horses. It was just something I wanted to do."[32]

Burns, a junior animal science major, grew up on a horse breeding farm and spent his time showing and training horses. As a Texas Tech student, he joined the Horse Judging Team and was a founding member of the Ranch Horse Team, even traveling with the team to teach horsemanship clinics in Germany and Austria.[33]

"This is going to be an exciting year," he continued. "I've been looking forward to doing this for a long time. The Masked Rider is a Texas Tech icon, and I can hardly believe I get to be a part of this tradition."[34]

Burns became known for the handlebar mustache he grew during his term. "He has a very unique style," Assistant Director for Spirit Programs Stephanie Rhode laughed to the *University Daily*, miming his mustache. "He has an adventurous spirit and polite style."[35]

Burns's promise of an exciting year rang true. The competitive Red Raider football team was invited to return to the Gator Bowl, the birthplace of the Masked Rider tradition. Despite an end-of-season safety violation for placing the reins in his teeth for a pregame run, Burns, Midnight Matador, and support staff traveled more than 1,300 miles to Jacksonville, Florida, for the historic pregame run.

Burns's year also started a gradual uptick in appearances. Previous riders had averaged 115 to 125 appearances per year, but the appearance numbers for Burns ended with just over 150.[36] "It was the biggest honor and a great year," the mustachioed rider told the crowd at Transfer of Reins as he bid farewell.[37]

Picking up the reins after Burns was Ashley Hartzog. The senior animal science and Spanish major came from Farwell, Texas, a town about an hour and a half northwest of Lubbock along the Texas-New Mexico border. The Hartzog family ran a cattle-ranching operation, in which Ashley took an active part. She saw the Masked Rider at a football game when she was five years old and was hooked. Once she arrived at Texas Tech, she spent years on the field safety team in addition to the Ranch Horse Team, Equestrian Team, and Horse Judging Team.[38]

Hartzog would prove to be not only an exceptional Masked Rider—traveling more than 13,000 miles to more than 155 appearances with a sparkling safety and care record[39]—but she would also be one who would help propel the Masked Rider Program further into the national spotlight.

Bradley Skinner and Midnight Matador watch a game from the sideline at Jones AT&T Stadium in 2011. (Courtesy Office of Communications and Marketing)

# 11

# VISION, TRADITION, AND NATIONAL COVERAGE

Texas Tech's outlook for the 2008 football season was promising. Coach Mike Leach entered his ninth season with two Heisman hopefuls: wide receiver Michael Crabtree and quarterback Graham Harrell. *Dave Campbell's Texas Football* featured the trio on its 2008 edition cover and picked the Red Raiders to win the Big 12 South.

Texas Tech won its home opener and its next three non-conference games. During one of those games, the coach discovered his new starting extra-point kicker thanks to a kick-for-rent promotional contest sponsored by a local housing complex. The team went on to win its first four conference games. Its biggest challenge came Saturday, November 1 against No. 1 University of Texas. ESPN picked Texas Tech to host *College Gameday* for the game, making it the first time for Lubbock to host. The fan base, already at a fever pitch, exploded.

Leading up to the game, Bud Light's Gameday Rivals YouTube series featured Ashley Hartzog and Midnight Matador, making it one of their most-watched videos.

The morning of the game, *College Gameday* set their stage at the south end of the Engineering Key with Memorial Circle and the Administration Building serving as their backdrop. The show kicked off with Hartzog and Midnight Matador making a run from the top of the key to near the stage—but with a little less speed due to the sidewalks crisscrossing the grassy area.

That night, the sellout crowd of 56,333 fans arrived dressed in black for the blackout game. The crowd noise was deafening on the field. The stadium was so loud, the Goin' Band's Horse Music, which provides the cue for the run, could barely be heard even on the field. Luckily, the cues were finally caught, and Hartzog and Midnight Matador's perfect pregame run was broadcast on ABC to roughly 8,590,000 households. The viewership made it ABC's most viewed college football game of the season up to that point.[1] The game's national coverage promoted a new surge of interest in the Masked Rider mascot from across the country.

A literal last-second catch by Crabtree from Harrell led the Red Raiders to a 39–33 victory over the Longhorns in a game many consider to be the greatest football game in Texas Tech history.

Fans rushed the field, but fortunately for the horse and rider, the pair always leaves football games with about six minutes left on the clock to keep them safe from rowdy fans, a jam-packed end-of-game sideline, and traffic leaving the stadium.

The following week, the Red Raiders claimed the No. 2 spot in the AP poll. Shortly after the end of the season, *60 Minutes* aired a segment by Scott Pelley on Texas Tech and Mike Leach, in which Hartzog and Midnight Matador made a prominent appearance.

Hartzog's spring season also held a surprise: the first Masked Rider run at a Red Raiders home baseball game. On Friday, April 3, 2009, before the first pitch of the series opener against Texas A&M University, Hartzog and Midnight Matador entered the outfield from a gate at left field and took off at a gallop. Their path tracked just inside the outfield wall and ended at the right-field gate.[2]

"On the football field, the rider does a straight run down the field and the horse does not even get to top speed, so the run is over in about seven seconds," Hartzog explained. "But for baseball, the run was about three times as long because I got to make the run all of the way out in the outfield. During my first run at the baseball game, I remember I was keeping a somewhat tight rein on Midnight to keep his speed in check. However, since the baseball run was so much longer than a football run, I gave him the reins and let him run as fast as he wanted to. Being the first Masked Rider to run at baseball games will always be one of my favorite Masked Rider appearances."[3]

Hartzog's historic year ended fittingly. She transferred the reins on April 17, 2009, to her best friend, Brianne Aucutt-Hight, for whom she had served as maid of honor during Hight's wedding the previous holiday season.

Brianne Hight, a senior animal science major with a production specialization, grew up in Clovis, New Mexico. She spent time ranching and rodeoing and had two rodeo queen titles under her belt. Hight served as a field safety team member to Hartzog and was the sixth consecutive Ranch Horse Team member to be named Masked Rider.

Ashley Hartzog poses with Midnight Matador in front of the Administration Building in 2008. (Courtesy Office of Communications and Marketing)

Her game-day-run photos aboard Midnight Matador are some of the most used game-day images of the Masked Rider. She made more appearances at basketball games than previous riders and continued with the runs at baseball games. Hight and Midnight Matador completed a game-day run at the Texas Tech–Baylor game on November 28, 2009, in the new Cowboys Stadium in Dallas in front of nearly 72,000 attendees. Midnight Matador appears to be the first horse to perform in the stadium, predating Professional Bull Riders events and The American Rodeo.[4]

Hight's most memorable role, however, was as the face of Texas Tech's new fundraising campaign.

In 2010, the university system publicly launched "Vision & Tradition: The Campaign for Texas Tech." The massive campaign had a goal to increase the Texas Tech University System endowment to $1 billion. The public phase of the campaign launched with an eight-minute video highlighting research and students across Texas Tech and the Texas Tech University Health Sciences Center.

System leaders picked the Masked Rider to symbolize the spirit of the university through the campaign. The narrative of the video tracks the journey of a girl—intended to be a young Hight—from watching the Masked Rider runs on television to being accepted at Texas Tech, culminating in her game-day run as Masked Rider as another young fan watches on television. The unforgettable video was used for various purposes for years after the conclusion of the campaign. Hight made a repeat appearance in the celebration video as a graduate student. The video's themes continue to resonate with generations of Red Raiders.

Hight and her husband attended the gala hosted in honor of the success of the campaign—a monumental financial goal that changed the trajectory of the university.

In spring 2009, former rider Gerald Nobles and his wife Debbie created the Masked Rider Scholarship Endowment through the College of Agricultural Sciences and Natural Resources to supplement the $2,600 Wells Fargo Masked Rider scholarship. Hight became its first recipient.

Four years later, Terry Fuller, chairman of the Texas Tech Foundation Board of Directors, and his wife Linda, an eight-year national board member of the Texas Tech Alumni Association, established the Linda and Terry Fuller Masked Rider Scholarship Endowment. Once fully funded, the scholarship provided $4,500 to the current Masked Rider.

Another public art collection piece featuring the Masked Rider was added to Jones AT&T Stadium in time for the 2010 football season. American artist

Brianne Aucutt-Hight's official Masked Rider portrait with Midnight Matador in 2009 at the Broadway entrance to campus. (Courtesy Office of Communications and Marketing)

Bradley Skinner and Midnight Matador make a pregame run at a fall 2011 football game. (Courtesy Robert Rhode)

Kenneth Pirtle created *Visions from the Matador Song*, a series of ceramic tile mosaics. Eight mosaics follow the lines of the school song, highlighting key moments of football through the years. The final line of the song, "Long live the Matadors," is accompanied by a mosaic of Midnight Matador and Stockard based on a pregame run photo taken by Norvelle Kennedy. The mosaic is found at the southernmost portion of the east concourse of the stadium.

Christi Chadwell of Garland, Texas, became the 2010–2011 Masked Rider. Chadwell, a sophomore agricultural communications major, grew up with two Red Raiders for parents. For her tenth birthday, her parents gifted her horseback riding lessons. Her father told her she could become the Masked Rider if she went to Texas Tech. Chadwell competed in barrel racing and goat tying at rodeos and, once at Texas Tech, joined the Masked Rider Field Safety Team.[5]

Sam Jackson referred to Chadwell as "a very much [pen]-to-business rider. You didn't have to wonder if she was going to show up on time or do what she was supposed to do. . . . All of the things we expect a successful rider to do she has fulfilled that role."[6]

Christi Chadwell rides Midnight Matador during a homecoming parade in 2010. (Courtesy Office of Communications and Marketing)

Bradley Skinner and Midnight Matador make a scoring run. (Courtesy Robert Rhode)

A close-up of the Masked Rider's belt buckle. The buckle was added to the uniform in 2011 with Bradley Skinner to commemorate the 50th rider in the program. (Courtesy Office of Communications and Marketing)

One of Chadwell's more memorable appearances was riding Midnight Matador in her lighted hat and cape into the sanctuary of her hometown church as part of one of their programs. It was a secret Chadwell revealed to only a few at the time and later divulged at a former-rider reunion. Chadwell's favorite appearance, though, was Farm Days at the Scottish Rite Hospital for Children in Dallas—a place where she had been a patient when she was a child.

"It was really rewarding to be able to go back to a place that meant so much to me as a child," she said. "It made everything worth the time to see the kids get excited to see the Masked Rider, pet Midnight Matador, and take pictures with us. It was a priceless feeling to provide kids with joy and a role model."[7]

Chadwell was also able to make a hometown appearance with two runs at Dallas's Cotton Bowl in the heart of Fair Park, once for the regular-season game against Baylor during the State Fair of Texas, and again for the New Year's Day TicketCity Bowl game against Northwestern University.

Chadwell's term saw the beginning of nationwide recognition of the program by fans and media outlets. In late August 2010 before the start of the football season, the Masked Rider came in ninth on the Associated Press's list of top twelve college football mascots.

Ashley Wenzel rides temporary horse Trey for a pregame run at AT&T Stadium in Arlington for the Baylor University game in 2013. (Courtesy Robert Rhode)

"This is a tremendous honor, and we would like to thank the many voters of the Associated Press for recognizing our Masked Rider Program," said Gerald Myers, the Texas Tech athletics director. "The AP recognizes something that we Red Raiders have known for a very long time, in that the Masked Rider is very special in college sports and represents the great strength of the students and alumni of Texas Tech University. Nobody makes a better entrance on Saturdays than the Masked Rider, and I would like to pay tribute to Christi Chadwell, our current rider, and all the former riders that have come before her. Their service and representation of Texas Tech University is unparalleled."[8]

The ranking became the first of many. Bleacher Report released their list of top mascots a couple of months later, on which the Masked Rider ranked fourteenth. The Masked Rider again made the AP's top-ten list in 2014. In 2015, the NFL named the duo one of their "15 for '15" favorite college mascots. The horse and rider duo ranked ninth on Barstool Sports's top-ten mascot list in 2020.

On April 15, 2011, Christi Chadwell presented the hat, mask, and cape to Bradley Skinner, a senior animal science major. He started riding at the age of five and got his first horse when he was eight. The 4-H member did horse judging then started breaking and training horses when he was in high school.[9] Skinner beat a pool of thirteen candidates, and while he thought he had a chance, he did not think he would win.[10] His hometown of Arvada, Colorado—a suburb just northwest of Denver—made him the first rider in the program from Colorado and also the first transfer student since Jess Wall in 1976.

Skinner began his collegiate career at Colorado State University but visited Texas Tech and attended the Southern Methodist University game where he saw Chadwell make her run. Skinner set his sights on Texas Tech and becoming the Masked Rider. "The second I started here I felt like a part of Texas Tech," he told a reporter. "I was included; everybody liked me. I felt it going here, and I really want to spread that to other kids. . . . I feel more at home here than anywhere else."[11]

Skinner also emphasized the amount of time and work it takes to be the Masked Rider. "It's a full-time-and-a-half job," he said, mentioning he spent four to five hours every day with Midnight Matador. Even stopping for gas took extra time due to fans and those who were simply curious coming up and talking.[12]

Skinner became Texas Tech's fiftieth Masked Rider, a milestone celebrated at the first football game of the season, against Texas State University on September 3. Former riders were invited to a pregame reception and reunion. To commemorate the occasion, the costume gained a new piece: a custom-made belt buckle to be passed from rider to rider. The silver buckle features a large gold Double T in the center, flanked on both sides by a gold star. "Texas Tech" arches across the top in gold with "Masked Rider" along the bottom.

Skinner and Chadwell also became part of a new tradition at the first baseball game following the Transfer of Reins ceremony. The outgoing and incoming riders along with the horse gathered around home plate. The outgoing rider would again retire their hat, mask, and cape and present the incoming rider with theirs. The incoming rider then ran the path in the outfield to start the game.

The *Lubbock Avalanche-Journal* videoed Skinner as he prepared for and attended the event.

"You're not going to find a better horse in the country for this job," Skinner said about Midnight Matador as he groomed and saddled the big black gelding. "This'll be his tenth year. He knows his job. He knows what he's supposed to do. I think he's about the brokest horse I've ever ridden. Nothing bothers him. He's good with kids. You can bring anything and everything up to him. He'll stand around all day and let you sign autographs on him."[13]

When Skinner's year wound down, he reflected on some of his favorite appearances: attending the Denver Texas Tech alumni fundraiser in July 2011 where he spoke about the Masked Rider Program to those from around his hometown and appearing at the Lone Star Lineman's Rodeo in Amarillo because his father was a lineman.

On April 20, 2012, Ashley Wenzel was revealed as the 51st Masked Rider.[14] Wenzel's hometown of Friendswood, Texas, made her the first rider from the Houston area. Wenzel was a sophomore education major who started riding at age five by taking lessons from a family friend. The horse she took lessons on became her first horse. Growing up, Wenzel rode in a variety of events: English, competitive trail, barrel racing, pole bending, goat tying, and breakaway roping.[15]

The 2012 football season became the first to introduce fireworks during the National Anthem and following scores. As Wenzel ran the first scoring run of the first game of the season, Midnight Matador—a football game veteran of a decade—lazily cantered down the sideline. As the fireworks went off from the video board, he visibly startled midstride at the change—not spooking, but now very awake, watching the fireworks, and realizing that wasn't a routine part of the game.

Wenzel's year started seamlessly, but a massive change loomed in the fall.

Ashley Wenzel and Midnight Matador during his on-field retirement ceremony in 2012.
(Courtesy Robert Rhode)

# 12

# A CAREER-ENDING INJURY

The vet moved the ultrasound down Midnight Matador's fetlock and pastern in his front left leg. The prognosis wasn't good.

That morning, only a few days before homecoming festivities would begin and the Red Raiders would take on No. 5 West Virginia, Ashley Wenzel found Midnight Matador lame after a night of turnout. She made an immediate visit to Dr. Bo Brock's vet practice an hour south of Lubbock in Lamesa. The scan showed a tear in the outside branch of his left suspensory tendon. The suspensory tendon runs down the back of a horse's leg then splits into two branches at the fetlock, or ankle, that run down the inside and outside of the pastern, or the area between the fetlock and the hoof. These tendons provide support to the lower leg.

Not only was the tear season-ending, it was also career-ending. Suspensory injuries are frequently seen in high-intensity performance horses like barrel racers and racehorses. Some tears happen in an instant, and others tend to develop over time; the vet wasn't sure which scenario had occurred. Midnight Matador was blessed with many gifts, but great structure in his front legs was not one of them. Very, very few horses have perfect bone structure, and what happens to most horses—and even humans—also happened to Midnight Matador: He got older, and his structural imperfections resulted in an injury. While this type of injury wouldn't necessarily end the careers of most horses, just simply sideline them for a year or two, the nature of the Masked Rider's horse's work would put too much stress on the injured leg even if it healed. Midnight Matador was only sound enough to ride in the homecoming parade and make his appearance at the bonfire.

For the first time in Texas Tech history, Raider Red (with Geoff Waller occupying the costume) surprised the crowd on Saturday, October 13, 2012, by riding unannounced on the back of a Harley-Davidson motorcycle driven by a Texas Tech staff member to lead the team out onto the field. For the first time in a decade, Midnight Matador missed a home football game. The Red Raiders upset West Virginia in a season that would end with the departure of head football coach Tommy Tuberville.

After homecoming weekend came to a close, program administrators decided to retire the horse and made the decision public on Wednesday, October 17. Midnight Matador's running days were over.

Midnight Matador received an outpouring of support from the community for his injury and retirement. Thousands of social media comments and interactions shared everything from how fans' first Texas Tech game was also Midnight Matador's first game to how they would remember him as the horse during their

Midnight Matador's former riders join him and current rider Ashley Wenzel on the field to honor his retirement in 2012. Also included are Alvin Davis (second from left), Stephanie Rhode (in front of group), and Dr. Sam Jackson (right). (Courtesy Robert Rhode)

time at the university. The hashtag "#ThanksMidnight" made the rounds on Twitter, and his news release was picked up statewide. A Lubbock store made commemorative shirts featuring him mid-run with Amy Bell aboard.

The Masked Rider Advisory Committee made plans for a retirement ceremony to be held during the November 3, 2012, football game versus the University of Texas. Committee members launched a massive effort to locate all of Midnight Matador's former riders and reunite them for his game-time ceremony. The committee spent weeks tracking down the ten alumni, who came from all corners of Texas and even deep in the remote ranch country of New Mexico.

Between the first and second quarters, Wenzel rode Midnight Matador off the sideline to the northwest hash mark on the 20-yard line with his former riders and Honorary Masked Riders Alvin Davis and Dr. Sam Jackson in tow.

At the conclusion of his ceremony, the 50,000 fans in attendance gave Midnight Matador a standing ovation. After eleven years, more than 100,000 miles, and over 1,500 public appearances, the failed show horse had become one of the most well-known and publicized horses in the country during his lifetime.

Just as with Midnight Raider, the Masked Rider Committee accepted applications from Midnight Matador's former riders to select his home for his retirement. A subcommittee comprised of four members developed application criteria. The applications included short-term and long-term care plans for the recovering horse. He had reinjured himself in December during routine turnout and had to undergo stall rest at the Texas Tech Equestrian Center under the watch of an old friend: his former owner, Kim Lindsey, whom Texas Tech had recently employed to manage the center.

Stephanie Rhode made the call to Stacy Stockard on Wednesday, January 23, 2013, telling her the subcommittee selected her proposal and that Midnight Matador would be her ward in his retirement. The official announcement came Friday, January 25, 2013. Ashley Wenzel took the horse for one last ride in the Masked Rider trailer wrapped with his images the next day to his new home with Stockard at Blarney Stone Equestrian Center in Lubbock. Amos spent his days in retirement racing his new equine friends along his paddock fence, taking daily mid-morning naps at the same time sprawled out on his side in the same corner of his pen, and getting treats every evening before bed.

With his active mind and because his career led to excitement nearly every day—new places, new people, performances with large crowds—Amos required mental stimulation during his near-daily exercise rides. Like most horses, being ridden in circles led to boredom and inattentiveness to his task at hand. Instead, every ride included trail obstacles or learning a new maneuver.

When they see new, scary things, most horses prefer to be led by hand as they approach obstacles, followed by carrying a rider through it once they get accustomed. But because Amos spent nearly his whole life approaching new obstacles while being ridden, he disliked learning new obstacles from the ground—he had to be ridden through or over them. Occasionally, his injuries resurfaced, especially in muddy paddock conditions. He perked up hearing cheers from the neighboring Little League fields thinking he might be missing work at Jones AT&T Stadium.

He had all the stall toys available on the market, primary care and sports medicine veterinarians, an equine chiropractor, a masseuse, more hair products than a stylist, and pricey specialized horseshoes.

Amos's curiosity and mischievousness continued in his retirement. One day, he fished out a hoof pick from a grooming bag. When a plastic bag floated into his paddock on a breezy day, he walked up to sniff it while the jumping horse in the next paddock ran away snorting. He chewed on the crossties during grooming and saddling, and his lead rope was perpetually wet with slobber. Amos could also untie himself using two different methods. Having Amos in a barn was like having a toddler; everything in his reach had to be Amos-proof.

Retirement did not diminish his cantankerous side. One day, he picked up a barn hand by the side of the man's leg and slung him across the stall. The bruise grew to the size of a football before it subsided. Sometimes he did not want to load in the trailer. Amos disliked being brushed and would pin his ears and try to sneak in a bite of the one doing the brushing—or really just anyone in the vicinity of his teeth. If he liked you enough, though, he would let you scratch his favorite spots on his belly, the front of his cannon bones on his back legs, and under his mane, especially with his favorite curry comb.

Despite his bold behavior, Amos adored people, especially children. He enjoyed being around people and being the center of attention. He allowed his favorite people in his personal space, particularly right in front of him where he could see them and rest his head in front of their chest. He was at his most gentle behavior around children, especially if they brought him a treat. His favorite was John Klein, a six-year-old who started taking lessons because he loved the Masked Rider. John was on his second pair of boots that looked just like the Masked Rider's and dressed up as the Masked Rider during Halloween. After every one of John's lessons, he went to visit "Midnight Matador" and take him a pocketful of treats. As a surprise during one of John's lessons, John got to ride Amos instead of his usual lesson horse, and he rode in his Masked Rider costume. Amos, who had never been ridden by a child, let alone led with a child in the saddle, was incredibly confused at what he was supposed to do.

At 6 a.m. on Monday, January 26, 2015, the barn owner arrived on site and found Amos in his stall with severe colic. Because of his high tolerance for pain, the on-site staff had not heard him rolling and pacing throughout the night in an effort to alleviate the pain.

After a poor prognosis at his general care veterinarian's office, Amos was hauled to Dr. Bo Brock's practice in Lamesa. Dr. Brock is known for his expertise in horse colic. A quick examination and blood draw showed Amos needed to go under colic surgery. By 8 a.m., he was in surgery. Dr. Peter Rakestraw, a former professor at the Texas A&M School of Veterinary Medicine who specialized in horses and taught colic care and surgery, happened to be in Dr. Brock's office that morning. Dr. Rakestraw floated between a racehorse barn in Dubai and, for fun, Dr. Brock's office following his time at Texas A&M.

Stockard and her family stayed by Amos's side during his anesthesia, surgery, and awakening from the anesthesia post-surgery. It turned out his last bite of hay got caught where the cecum attaches to the small intestine, causing a blockage. Amos passed through the surgery and anesthesia with flying colors, but equally tough would be the recovery. It became the only obstacle Amos couldn't tackle.

During his recovery, Amos went through gallons of fluid on an IV hanging six feet above his head in his recovery stall. Stockard sat with him in his stall every day from 8 a.m. to 8 p.m. for eight straight days. Ashley Hartzog, Clay Hight (the husband of rider Bri Hight), and even his farrier paid him visits in recovery.

Amos spent his last day outside in a grassy recovery paddock in warm sunshine. While the horse had begun drinking water again, he still refused to eat even his favorite foods and treats. He passed away at 2:30 a.m. on Wednesday, February 4, 2015, in the arms of Dr. Katie Bucks, the interning vet in residency at the clinic to whom Amos had taken a liking during his stay.

By that evening, Texas Tech issued a press release announcing Amos's passing. The story was on every television station. Amos had his own hashtag on Twitter. The Texas Tech Facebook post sharing the release became the page's most shared and most liked post up to that time. The story gained so much traction he was a Facebook trending topic.

The outpouring of condolences showed how many people cared for the mascot. Midnight Matador held a special place in many people's hearts. The caretakers of Tusk at the University of Arkansas sent flowers, which was the first of many flower arrangements their mascot program sent to spirit programs who lost a mascot. Another arrangement arrived from Amos's favorite visitor, John Klein.

Amos was cremated, and his remains await a final resting place that will be fitting for a Matador horse.

Corey Waggoner and Fearless Champion film a spot at Jones AT&T Stadium in 2013. (Courtesy Office of Communications and Marketing)

# 13

# FEARLESS CHAMPION

Replacing Midnight Matador was no easy task. The big, flashy horse that gave more than a decade of service to Texas Tech was the epitome of a professional. Thousands of fans had spent their entire student or professional careers knowing him as the Masked Rider horse.

Since taking the job eleven years earlier, the work environment of the horse evolved. Jones AT&T Stadium grew by more than 10,000 seats and was bowled in on three sides. When Midnight Matador started, the facility was undergoing a facelift that led to its current Spanish façade; the press box was shielded using tarps, and boxes on the east side didn't exist. Midnight Matador began his job with around fifty to sixty annual appearances and retired doing 200 per year due to the increased visibility and popularity of the Masked Rider.

Sam Jackson began the search. The first candidate was a tall, black gelding from New Mexico. He handled a stadium practice with the band and simulated crowd noise blasted through stadium speakers and was approved for testing at the University of Texas game on November 3, 2012. The first half of the raucous game featured Midnight Matador's on-field retirement ceremony. The new candidate was brought down for the second half. After an early Texas Tech drive at the south end zone, the crowd went wild. So did the horse. The on-field trial lasted less than two minutes, and the candidate didn't pass.

By the next home game on November 10, 2012, against the University of Kansas, another black Quarter Horse gelding, Trey, became a prospect. The small cutting horse from Lubbock stood about 14.2 hands and had a white sock, star, and snip—markings and stature similar to Charcoal Cody's. He was docile and easygoing—so easygoing that he trotted for a good portion of the pregame run. While his small size was a concern just for appearance's sake (and decried by some particularly vocal fans), his demeanor overshadowed the concern.

Trey passed the test of the game and received praise from Jackson, rider Ashley Wenzel, and fans. It became likely Trey would get another trial run at the Baylor University game at AT&T Stadium, home of the Dallas Cowboys.

"[The team is] going to need some help," Jackson joked with the *Lubbock Avalanche-Journal* on November 20, 2012. "I think it's important to have that mascot there. It just gives it a sense of completeness. A lot of fans come to see the horse and see him run. I think it's a positive." Jackson continued, "Obviously it's a test if he does poorly, but I don't know that there's anything he can do positively to make me any more likely to buy him. He could obviously do negative things to make us less interested in him."

Trey made the trip to Arlington and had another successful run down a football field. It seemed as though he would become the 14th horse of the program,

Fearless Champion stands underneath the Masked Rider mosaic based on a photo by Norvelle Kennedy in the east concourse of Jones AT&T Stadium. (Courtesy Office of Communications and Marketing)

Like most Masked Rider horses, Fearless Champion quickly took to Raider Red. (Courtesy Office of Communications and Marketing)

Ashley Wenzel with Woody, later Fearless Champion, with "guns up" at the Meineke Car Care Bowl in Houston in 2013. (Courtesy Robert Rhode)

Ashley Wenzel with Woody, later Fearless Champion, at the Meineke Car Care Bowl in Houston in 2012. (Courtesy Robert Rhode)

Woody, later Fearless Champion, makes his test run at the Meineke Car Care Bowl in Houston in 2013. (Photo by Norvelle Kennedy, courtesy Office of Communications and Marketing)

but negotiations on the horse faltered. The price for the talented cutting horse was just too great.

The program was back to the drawing board, but not for long.

In December, Jackson received a call from a group that included former rider Perry Church. The group branded cattle over the weekend near Tulia with someone riding an unflappable black horse named Woody. Jackson should take a look.[1]

The eight-year-old solid black Quarter Horse had a thick winter coat and was a bit scrappy-looking at 15.2 hands and 1,100 pounds.[2] It was obvious Woody was a working ranch horse. When Jackson hopped in the saddle for a test ride, the horse was friendly, supple, and responsive—good enough for a trip to Lubbock and a tryout for the bowl-bound Red Raiders.

After a couple weeks of riding Woody, Ashley Wenzel took the horse to the Meineke Car Care Bowl at (then) Reliant Stadium in Houston on December 28, 2012.[3] As soon as Ashley took off on Woody for the pregame run, fountain-style fireworks along the path of the run were lit. If the test horse could perform perfectly running between rows of fireworks in an NFL stadium immediately after coming off a cattle ranch, there was no stopping him.

"Through all of the testing he maintained the same calm demeanor and attitude that he expressed when I rode him the first time in an outdoor roping arena with no one around but cattle and horses," Sam Jackson told Texas Tech media. "After passing all of the behavioral tests, the final critical criteria that he met was that he was a big, stout, sound-structured, attractive black gelding that should be capable of carrying Masked Riders across the turf for many years to come."[4]

By mid-January 2013, Texas Tech completed Woody's purchase.[5] Woody, registered with the AQHA as BQH Hollywoodatdusk, became the 14th horse of the program.

Ashley Wenzel finished the year on Woody and reflected on her two favorite memories of her tenure at the April 19, 2013, Transfer of Reins ceremony, the first being her inaugural run as Masked Rider at the 2012 transfer ceremony at a Texas Tech baseball game.

"It was the first time I got to experience Midnight Matador's love for his job," Wenzel said. "Feeling his heart beating through the saddle was very intense! My second favorite memory was running at the Houston Livestock Show and Rodeo. Being from the Houston area, I grew up going to the HLSR as a kid and through high school. It was always a dream of mine to ride in the Reliant Stadium arena. Never did I think that I would get that opportunity."[6]

Many riders have fond memories of riding in their "hometown" arenas and traditions. Wenzel got to ride twice in what was then known as Reliant Stadium.

To properly christen Woody as a Masked Rider horse, he needed a new public name to fit his new role. The Masked Rider Committee reprised the naming contest that successfully found Midnight Matador his name. Nominations opened January 18, 2013, and by the contest's closing on March 1, the committee received 1,364 emails to namethehorse@ttu.edu containing more than 2,500 suggestions.[7]

At the Transfer of Reins ceremony on April 19, 2013, the public first heard Woody's new name: Fearless Champion. The program had received twenty-three submissions for Fearless Champion, but the one bearing the earliest time-stamped email came from Dr. Corey J. Haggard, a 1989 Texas Tech University Health Sciences Center graduate who now worked as an anesthesiologist.

The public was also introduced to the fifty-second Masked Rider: Corey Waggoner, a junior animal science major from Lubbock. The red-headed lifelong Red Raider fan had been around horses his entire life and started riding on his own at age 4. Waggoner especially excelled at timed events and at playdays.[8]

"During this time, I realized how special the Masked Rider is to Texas Tech and the community," Waggoner told the crowd during his speech at Transfer of Reins. "I will strive to embody what the Masked Rider stands for: character, high moral standards, perseverance, loyalty and respect."[9]

While 2013 brought a new horse and rider to the Masked Rider Program, it also had two major losses.

On May 2, 2013, Coke Hopping passed away after suffering a heart attack at a Professional Rodeo Cowboys Association rodeo in San Antonio. Hopping, who was finishing a PhD at Texas A&M University researching bareback riders, was in the saddle of a horse he had broken while serving as a pickup man during bareback riding. Brice Chapman, the son of Burney Chapman who was pictured in the first photo taken of Hopping and Happy VI-II, came up with the idea for Hopping's "last ride."[10] Two black draft horses pulled a buckboard wagon with Hopping's body in a traditional cowboy pine casket by the southwest tunnel to Jones AT&T Stadium.[11] Hopping's love for rodeo and Western heritage continues in his three children, including one who became known as the Western entertainer Dale Brisby.[12]

Nearly three months to the day of Hopping's passing, Joe Kirk Fulton passed away on August 1, 2013, at his Fulton Quien Sabe Ranch in Stonewall, Texas, near the LBJ Ranch. At his Lubbock service, a bugler played the Call to the Post to begin the ceremony. Waggoner made one of his most important appearances by standing dismounted with Fearless Champion outside the entrance to the chapel with Fulton's "Red Raider" chaps draped over the saddle's horn. Two massive floral Double Ts flanked the altar, and a longtime friend recounted Fulton's meeting with DeWitt Weaver.

Fulton had been inducted into the American Quarter Horse Association Hall of Fame and Texas Tech Athletic Hall of Honor. At the time of his passing, the horses he bred—including Dash's Dream and Special Leader—won more than $16 million on the track.[13] In Fulton's final days, Waggoner and Fearless Champion traveled to the Fulton Quien Sabe Ranch for a last goodbye.

The fall 2013 football season brought some changes to Jones AT&T Stadium. The Goin' Band's seating was moved to the south end zone, so for expediency, their pregame Double T formation—their last set in pregame—was moved from the northeast corner to the southeast corner of the field. The move provided the horse and rider an additional benefit of hearing their cue in the music, even over the loudest of crowds.

A new video board, sound system, and colonnade were added to the north end zone along with new loge boxes. Combined with the bowled-in seating and inner brick wall around the track that were added in 2006, Jones AT&T Stadium became an even more intense environment. A particular pinch point for the horse's sideline runs was a small stairway connecting the west sideline to the stands at the fifty-yard line near the players' benches. New media contracts to televise all games meant that television crews and large sideline television carts would be a staple instead of just at big games; a cart in the path of the touchdown run always meant the run could not happen. Bigger game-day atmospheres had resulted in more people on the sidelines. However, a horse new to the job meant a new opportunity.

Fearless Champion became the first horse to make scoring runs on field in the end zone opposite the score. The first runs caught the game-day crowd off guard, but they soon became routine. Because of the previous years' sideline congestion, some fans didn't even realize the horse still ran for scoring plays because they simply could not see the horse through the traffic.

Corey Waggoner poses with Fearless Champion at Jones AT&T Stadium in 2013. (Courtesy Office of Communications and Marketing)

Corey Waggoner and Fearless Champion make a pregame run at Jones AT&T Stadium in 2013. (Courtesy Office of Communications and Marketing)

Corey Waggoner presents Mackenzie White with her mask during the Transfer of Reins in 2014. (Courtesy Robert Rhode)

By the end of his term in 2014, Waggoner had carved out two new records for the program: 255 public appearances and 21,000 miles traveled in a calendar year.[14] At the 2014 Transfer of Reins ceremony, Waggoner looked back not at the high bar he had set, but at the relationships being Masked Rider afforded him.

"I will never forget the people I worked with in the program who have become like family to me," he said. "But most importantly I will never forget all of the Red Raider fans, alumni, and community. Every appearance I made, it was these people who made my year special."

Waggoner recalled a drive back to Lubbock from a very memorable run in AT&T Cowboy Stadium in Arlington, Texas, as proof that Texas Tech has one of the greatest fan bases.

"All the way back, driving along I-20 and Highway 84, I was constantly passed by enthusiastic Texas Tech fans and alumni waving as they passed by and holding their guns up," he said. "As the Masked Rider, I strived to leave an impact on everyone I met, but the truth is it was all these people that left an impact on me. I would like to say to all of Texas Tech University, thank you, and it has been an honor to serve as your Masked Rider."[15]

Mackenzie White, an agricultural and applied economics major with minors in Arabic and Spanish from Marble Falls, Texas, next took the reins. A competitive rider in horse shows, White had also racked up placings at horse judging contests and as a member of the Texas Tech Equestrian Team.

"The Masked Rider is the single-most recognized representative of Texas Tech," White shared, noting that she hoped her legacy would be "a hard-working horsewoman" dedicated to the position and Texas Tech.[16]

Texas Tech showcased the hard work that goes into preparing for the game-day run by following White the day of her first home football game. The video starts twelve hours prior to kickoff and concludes with a video of the run taken from a Go-Pro worn by White.

The season included the sixtieth anniversary celebration of the Masked Rider. Taking place the weekend of the September 13, 2014, rematch with Southwest Conference rival University of Arkansas, the reunion featured a dinner Friday night at the 50 Yard Line restaurant and a pregame breakfast tent near the Engineering Key.

Former riders had on-field recognition and watched White's pregame run from the field. The humid morning in the normally dry environment had an

Former riders, surviving family members of riders who passed away, and Honorary Masked Riders gather for a pregame photo during the 60th anniversary of the program on September 13, 2014. (Courtesy Robert Rhode)

unanticipated consequence: the fog machines used for the players' entrance created a large, thick cloud at the start of the run that refused to dissipate. The image of White and Fearless Champion breaking through the fog for their run remains one of the most dramatic photos of the pregame run, but White had to ride looking down to find the field markings and ensure she and the horse were in their correct path.

White's year was commemorated during the 2015 holiday season with the next installment of Texas Tech's Christmas ornaments. It featured a female

Mackenzie White and Fearless Champion ride through the unexpectedly thick pregame smoke with zero visibility during the 2014 60th anniversary by looking down for field markings. (Courtesy Robert Rhode)

White and Fearless Champion during the 2014 60th anniversary pregame run. (Courtesy Robert Rhode)

Future Masked Rider Charlie Snider, then an assistant, looks on as Rachel McLelland and Fearless Champion await the pregame run at Jones AT&T Stadium in 2015. (Courtesy Office of Communications and Marketing)

Masked Rider standing with guns up showing the Double T on the back of the cape. The character's long brown hair and boots appear to belong to White.

On April 17, 2015, White handed the reins over to Rachel McLelland, a junior pre-med and anthropology major. The 54th Masked Rider grew up in Tijeras, New Mexico, east of Albuquerque. McLelland had served as one of White's assistants, and the two even became roommates during White's term.

McLelland's mother, Betsy, was a horse person. Betsy and Rachel's father, Scot, bought her a horse named Flower Rose when she was three years old. At the age of five, Rachel was showing horses. By the time she graduated from high school, Rachel showed jumping horses nationally at the grand prix level, which requires horses to clear jumps at a height of over five feet with the fastest clean round winning. McLelland's game-day runs would be a piece of cake.

Betsy gave young Rachel the ill-mannered horses in their barn. Betsy believed Rachel had a gift for dealing with these problem horses and transforming them into competitive, confident mounts. Fearless Champion began anticipating his pregame and touchdown runs more so than expected for his job over the past

Rachel McLelland and Fearless Champion pose in Memorial Circle on the set of the 2015 Texas Tech television commercial. (Courtesy Office of Communications and Marketing)

Rachel McLelland and Fearless Champion make a pregame run in 2015. (Courtesy Office of Communications and Marketing)

couple years. Horses, like most animals, understand routines. Masked Rider horses know the succession of events that lead to the pregame run. Galloping is an exciting event for a horse, so they look forward to it. By the songs the Goin' Band plays and how people on the sidelines are arranged at certain times, the horse knows when his time to run grows near.

Unlike the way they train performance horses, the Masked Rider does not get the opportunity to correct a horse in a public setting. For a show horse that anticipates its job or acts up in a class, it attends schooling shows, or the rider audits a class at a show, allowing the rider to correct the horse's problem behavior in a show setting. Horses that need correction in speed events like barrel racing may attend playdays and races that slow down the horse through the patterns to help the horse regain focus and better listen to its rider. Horses also have bad days, much like when athletes have games where they cannot seem to catch a pass or consistently throw strikes. For the unlucky, flubs may occur during a horse show or a pivotal time when stakes are high. For the Masked Rider's horse, game days do not come often, and each performance is extremely important to the fans. Each run counts, and there is little to no room for on-the-job training for the horse.

Most pregame runs are aired live or at the beginning or end of breaks if the game is televised. Each run is photographed by local and national media and

Fearless Champion and Charlie Snider. (Courtesy Office of Communications and Marketing)

fans. The horse and rider may be filmed or photographed at any time inside or outside the stadium from the time the trailer leaves the barn until its return.

McLelland's skill in working with problematic jumping horses applied to Fearless Champion, and his anticipation diminished greatly. She gave him more space and independence while she prepared him for his runs. She kept him walking in small circles before his pregame run, which kept his mind calm and muscles warm. Fearless Champion's pregame run routine became the opposite of Midnight Matador's, who preferred to stand still with his right side against the field wall and chew his bit from the time the Goin' Band ran out of the tunnels until he rolled left to start his run.

When McLelland first met with Stephanie Rhode to start her year as Masked Rider, she determinedly stated her goal: "I'm going to beat Corey's appearance record." Rhode laughed. She hadn't thought Corey would reach his goal and never dreamed another rider could match Corey's record. Even during her last week on the job, McLelland continued scheduling appearances. On her busiest day, she made seven appearances.

At the Transfer of Reins on April 15, 2016, Rhode made McLelland's final tally public: 13,000 miles and 305 appearances, a new all-time program high. They included everything from football and baseball games to golf tournaments, birthday parties, and even a wedding.

"I didn't realize the impact I could make as the Masked Rider until I showed up at each event," McLelland said in her farewell speech. "Football games are very special as that is where the tradition started. There is nothing like running in front of 60,000 cheering Texas Tech fans." She told the crowd of attendees and reporters, "I knew if I were selected as the Masked Rider that it would be the ride of a lifetime, and it has been that and more."

McLelland also made fast friends with members of the Texas Tech Pom Squad after traveling with them to away games and basketball games. The aspiring doctor even shadowed Texas Tech Spirit Squad physician and University Medical Center emergency room physician, Dr. Eric Babb, on multiple occasions.

Following her record-breaking year, McLelland studied abroad as planned, became a counselor at Red Raider Camp in Brownwood, Texas, worked as a trainer for Lady Raider Basketball, finished her degree in December 2016, and attended medical school at Texas Tech's Health Sciences Center.

Charlie Snider. (Courtesy Office of Communications and Marketing)

Charlie Snider and Fearless Champion ride through pregame fog in Jones AT&T Stadium at a 2016 football game. (Courtesy Robert Rhode)

Charlie Snider and Fearless Champion make a pregame run in Jones AT&T Stadium in 2016. (Courtesy Robert Rhode)

Charlie Snider had big shoes to fill as the fifty-fifth Masked Rider for the 2016–2017 term. The junior animal science major with an equine science emphasis from Corinth, Texas, had served for two years as a Masked Rider assistant before taking the reins. Snider first started riding at the age of thirteen and worked horses at a local barn before he bought his first horse. At Texas Tech, Snider began showing horses with the Texas Tech Equestrian Team and took up jumping. At the time of his Transfer of Reins ceremony, he presided over the equestrian team, worked with esteemed riding clinicians, and had won numerous high placings at shows.

"It's a great honor to serve the university in this capacity," Snider said in his introductory speech at Transfer of Reins.

"I'm just excited to see where we will go, what we will do, and make sure everyone who comes in contact with the Masked Rider and Fearless Champion has the best experience possible," he shared in an interview after the ceremony.

One year later, at the April 21, 2017, Transfer of Reins, Snider reflected on his spotless record for the year. "I know for the first two or three weeks, even after Transfer, every time I put on the mask and cape, it still felt like a dream," he told Texas Tech.

"Not much that I can tell you about running down the field because it's a very short run," Snider recounted. "I remember Stephanie [Rhode] asked me how it felt running down the field, and I said, 'Well, when it started it was great, and when it ended it was great, but everything in between I can't really tell you because it's about a fifteen-second blur.'"

Snider also ended his reign as Masked Rider by completing more than 300 appearances, but he bested McLelland's record by seven more appearances, eventually settling at 312. "There's almost something about every single appearance you can say was very memorable," he said.[17]

Laurie Tolboom became the fifty-sixth Masked Rider in 2017. Tolboom was a December 2016 agricultural communications graduate and a master's student in mass communications. She was particularly skilled in photography.

Tolboom grew up in Dublin, Texas, and began riding at the age of five. She had a successful show career with the American Paint Horse Association, winning a youth world championship and open reserve world championship. Tolboom's father was from the Netherlands and her mother was from Wisconsin, so she was not exposed to Texas Tech until a visit to Lubbock.

"This was the only school where I felt at home," she said. "Then, when I went back home, one of my teachers, who'd attended Texas Tech and knew my

Laurie Tolboom and Fearless Champion walk through the streets of Austin in 2018. (Courtesy Laurie Tolboom Martin)

Laurie Tolboom and Fearless Champion lead the Red Raiders onto the field at Jones AT&T Stadium in 2017. (Courtesy Office of Communications and Marketing)

Laurie Tolboom and Fearless Champion in 2017. (Photo by Ashley Rodgers, courtesy Office of Communications and Marketing)

background with horses, said, 'You could be the Masked Rider.' I looked it up and knew it was something I could potentially be involved in."

Tolboom joined the field safety team her sophomore year then served as an assistant to both McLelland and Snider.[18]

In October of Tolboom's year, Texas Tech Police Officer Floyd East Jr. was killed inside the university's police department while questioning a suspect. The campus mourned his death, and Tolboom asked to attend his service in his hometown of El Paso with Fearless Champion as a representative of the university and its students. The request was immediately granted by the university. When interviewed about the subject, Tolboom explained her strong feelings:

> In my other appearances, I've come to realize the Masked Rider is a symbol for everybody—present, past, and even future Texas Tech alumni and students. With that situation, I knew that a lot of people would not be able to travel to the memorial service in El Paso. So I wanted to go and represent everybody who was there [on campus] who could not be there [at the service] because I knew it could potentially mean a lot to the family. . . . It was really an honor to be there.[19]

Laurie Tolboom and Fearless Champion make a scoring run at a football game in 2017. (Courtesy Office of Communications and Marketing)

Tolboom also became the second rider to make international appearances. Her sister lived in Germany and, during one visit, Tolboom took along her Masked Rider costume, making appearances in the area.

As Tolboom's year ended on April 20, 2018, she shared why the Masked Rider is so special to Red Raiders: "It was an experience of finding a new family, a second family, because Texas Tech and all the people in it are all so united in their love for Texas Tech. The Masked Rider Program is a symbol of that unity."[20]

Fearless Champion and Lyndi Starr pose in front of the Administration Building during a nighttime photo shoot in 2018. (Courtesy Office of Communications and Marketing)

# 14

# AN OLD HORSE AND NEW TRICKS

The 57th person to serve in the Masked Rider Program was Lyndi Starr, a senior agricultural communications major from Mount Vernon, Texas. Starr was initially recruited to North Central Texas College in Gainesville, Texas, to compete on its ranch horse team and Intercollegiate Horse Shows Association western horsemanship team. After earning an associate's degree in applied equine science, she transferred to Texas Tech.

As a Red Raider, Starr joined the Equestrian Team, Horse Judging Team, and Ranch Horse Team, where she won the Stock Horse of Texas Limited Non-Pro World Championship.

"I believe the Masked Rider is about far more than attending football games," she said at the Transfer of Reins ceremony. "I want to spread the school spirit that brings West Texans together as a family, and I want to inspire others to attend college, set goals, and go after them."[1]

The accomplished rider also shared how much she looked forward to bonding with Fearless Champion, and the two completed a summer together full of parades, rodeos, and Red Raider Orientations. They appeared at the Texas Tech Alumni Association's first Red Raiders at the Downs event, an alumni gathering held at the Ruidoso Downs racetrack in New Mexico. Starr and Fearless Champion led the post parade for the named Texas Tech race that day then took a group photo in the winner's circle with attendees.

Two weeks before the start of the 2018 football season, Fearless Champion slipped and fell off a curb following an on-campus appearance in what could only be described as a freak accident. The horse injured his patella—the equine equivalent of a kneecap on the back of the hock joint. Although he did eventually recover, he was unable to run for a while.

"The fan base and the alumni really like to have a horse on the field," Sam Jackson told AQHA's *America's Horse* magazine. "Now that we know we can't use [Fearless Champion], can we find another one that will be safe and effective in the stadium? Eight or nine days was the lead time we had."

A veterinarian examines Fearless Champion at the Brock Veterinary Clinic in Lamesa, Texas, during his recovery in 2018. (Courtesy Office of Communications and Marketing)

Lyndi Starr walks Cody past the Masked Rider truck at the Texas Tech Equestrian Center in 2018. (Courtesy Office of Communications and Marketing)

Sam Jackson rides Cody among the members of the Goin' Band as part of his testing in 2018. (Courtesy Office of Communications and Marketing)

Sam Jackson rides Cody during Goin' Band practice in 2018. (Courtesy Office of Communications and Marketing)

One of Starr's assistants and her ranch horse teammate, Sidney Dunkel, spoke up. Her grandparents had a twenty-one-year-old black Quarter Horse gelding in their pasture they used for ranch work, trail riding, and roping. They also happened to be traveling to Lubbock that day and could bring him.

Jackson said yes, and Dunkel made the call. Skip Cody Jay, whose barn name was "Cody," arrived that day. The black horse had a sprinkling of gray hairs over his hips and frosting his face. His right ear pointed crookedly to the left due to nerve damage caused by a bout with ticks. Dunkel's grandfather—Jim Jennings, who would be inducted into the AQHA Hall of Fame in 2019—purchased the horse as a yearling, and it was the last foal by a stallion his father owned. Cody was a special horse.

Jackson gave Cody a ride, liked him, and took him to a Goin' Band from Raiderland practice. Cody then experienced the shotguns fired by Raider Red and the cannon fired at the end of each quarter. Cody took each stage better than the last. He got the starting job with the Dunkel family's blessing.

Starr knew Cody for nine days and put in nine rides, one of them the pregame run-through practice with the band and spirit squads. Her tenth ride came on game day—just a hair over a week from the first time she met the horse.[2]

With Fearless Champion still on the mend, Cody and Starr finished out the full football season. The pair appeared on the cover of *America's Horse* magazine with a five-page feature story.

Lyndi Starr begins early-morning warm-ups at the Texas Tech Equestrian Center with Cody before his debut in 2018. (Courtesy Office of Communications and Marketing)

Cody awaits his debut at the Texas Tech Equestrian Center in 2018. (Courtesy Office of Communications and Marketing)

Lyndi Starr and Cody make their pregame run at Jones AT&T Stadium in 2018. (Courtesy Office of Communications and Marketing)

Starr uses Cody to pony Fearless Champion as part of his recovery at the Texas Tech Equestrian Center. (Courtesy Office of Communications and Marketing)

Cody's arrival and Fearless Champion's rehabilitation combined with Starr's employment at the Texas Tech Equestrian Center (TTEC) led to a new living arrangement for the two horses. Both horses were kept at the TTEC to allow for proper stalling, turnout, and monitoring. The horses could stay together, making it easier for Starr to care for and keep an eye on both. With plenty of paddocks and riding arenas with good footing available, Starr never had to compete for space like at the Livestock Arena, where events that took over the space became more frequent and parking lots now filled what was grassy areas previously used as additional riding space. The arrangement stuck, and the TTEC became a new home for the horses.

On November 25, 2018, the football season ended, and Cody's time as a celebrity came to a close. Starr drove Cody back to his home pasture in Archer City, returning him to his retirement after a thrilling chapter of his life.[3]

Starr continued to rehab Fearless Champion. He finally made his return to running at Texas Tech Night at the Houston Livestock Show and Rodeo and at a Texas Tech baseball game. Despite the sidelining of her equine counterpart, Starr made 323 appearances in her year.

In her emotional farewell speech at the April 22, 2019, Transfer of Reins, Starr said, "I experienced so much this past year. And looking back, this position has changed me so much from the person that was sitting in that chair last year.

Fearless Champion makes his return at a Texas Tech baseball game in 2019 with Lyndi Starr aboard. (Courtesy Office of Communications and Marketing)

Lyndi Starr helps Emily Brodbeck arrange her hat and mask during a pre-transfer photo shoot in 2019. (Courtesy Office of Communications and Marketing)

I will be forever grateful for this experience as the 57th Masked Rider and what it has taught me. And I want to thank each of you for making this the best year of my life."[4]

For the 2019–2020 year, Emily Brodbeck, a graduate student in wildlife, aquatic, and wildlands science and management, fulfilled a childhood dream when she became the 58th Masked Rider.

"Growing up in Lubbock, my dad, as a student, was able to get season tickets for not very [much]," Brodbeck said. "They wanted to get a little more involved with friends and people he got to work with, so we started going to football games. When I was little, the only thing I remembered about the games was actually the horse and the big entrance. That's the only thing I really remember about going. Ever since then, I've always had an interest in it. Getting to be the rider now, it's been a lot of fun, and it's cool to finally see it become a reality."[5]

Like many Masked Riders, Brodbeck started riding when she was five years old and became a seasoned competitor in AQHA western pleasure, horsemanship, and trail. With a great deal of success on Texas Tech's Equestrian Team as an undergraduate, she became a volunteer assistant coach as a graduate student.

Brodbeck and Fearless Champion progressed through the summer with the horse back in good health. The two had a successful game-day run-through practice and completed two home games in back-to-back weekends. With a three-week wait until the next home game, things were looking up for Fearless Champion, but as the game approached, his veterinarians found inflammation in his front legs during a routine check. To preserve his health, the horse would be sidelined again for runs. Cody returned to Texas Tech for the last four home football games of the season and performed perfectly, just as expected.[6]

At the end of the season, Cody went back to his life of leisure in Archer City, and Fearless Champion continued low-impact appearances. He and Brodbeck participated in the Carol of Lights and made an appearance at opening day of Red Raider Baseball in February 2020. Brodbeck attended basketball games, including the Red Raider basketball game at Madison Square Garden in December 2019 and Texas Tech Night at a Dallas Mavericks game in February 2020. The pair also made a trip around Texas to the Fort Worth and San Antonio stock shows and rodeos.

Emily Brodbeck and Fearless Champion in front of the Administration Building during a university photo shoot in 2019. (Courtesy Office of Communications and Marketing)

Under the shade of the trees in the Engineering Key, Emily Brodbeck transfers the reins to Cameron Hekkert in 2020. (Courtesy Office of Communications and Marketing)

A month after the pair returned from their busy spring season of travel, Texas Tech announced students and employees would not return to campus after spring break due to the COVID-19 virus. All activities were halted, and work and classes immediately moved all online. The Big 12 Basketball Tournament was completely stopped and canceled during warm-ups of the first round.

Masked Rider tryouts were in progress. Candidates turned in completed applications and letters of recommendation and took the written test in January. As usual, the riding tryouts, truck-and-trailer-driving test, and interviews were scheduled for the week after spring break. The university's total shutdown of in-person activities applied to the tryouts. The Masked Rider Committee was left scrambling.

Brodbeck agreed to stay aboard as Masked Rider and Fearless Champion's caretaker until a new rider could be safely selected. Masked Rider Committee members looked through those in the candidate pool who had passed the written test and advanced to the riding stage. Some had tried out the previous year and passed the equestrian and trailer-driving tests, and the others had been observed riding by various committee members. All were deemed safe, capable riders. After sharing that this year would look different from previous years and so much remained undetermined, candidates were asked if they wished to continue to the interview portion of the process. All three accepted. A core

Cameron Hekkert, Fearless Champion, and Emily Brodbeck after the Transfer of Reins ceremony in 2020. (Courtesy Office of Communications and Marketing)

Fearless Champion sneaks a bite of leaves while Cameron Hekkert is distracted. (Courtesy Office of Communications and Marketing)

Cameron Hekkert prepares for her new rider portraits in the Masked Rider trailer's dressing room. (Courtesy Office of Communications and Marketing)

group of longtime committee members assembled online for interviews via videoconferencing software.

On August 10, 2020, four months later than the customary timeline, the Masked Rider Program announced they had selected Cameron Hekkert as the fifty-ninth Masked Rider. Hekkert and Brodbeck made the official Transfer of Reins outdoors in the shade of the trees in the north end of the Engineering Key with just the two riders, Fearless Champion, Stephanie Rhode, and a photographer.[7]

Hekkert came from Highlands Ranch, Colorado, a suburb south of Denver. The second Masked Rider from Colorado, Hekkert was the program's first sport management major and its first Honors College student.[8]

Hekkert had begun her studies at Texas Tech as an animal science major. After taking a course in sports management and participating in High Riders, a student organization dedicated to promoting Lady Raider Athletics, she changed her major to sports management. She also joined Texas Tech Athletic Ambassadors, a group that assists fan engagement and promotions at Texas Tech home games. Hekkert, though, continued serving as a research assistant for an animal science professor with a focus on equine-assisted therapy.[9]

Hekkert spent her early school years in the Denver suburbs, but in the summers she and her family went to the nearby mountains, where she rode a mare named Dixie every summer beginning at the age of four. Summer riding led to riding lessons in Denver, which led to competitions in barrel racing and breakaway roping. She purchased her first horse, named Pickle, and founded her high school's rodeo team. After Hekkert's first year at Texas Tech, she worked that summer at a Montana ranch learning roping, cutting, and reining.[10]

The 2020–2021 school year brought uncertainties and challenges. Wells Fargo declined to continue their sponsorship of the Masked Rider Program, citing a change in the direction of their marketing plan.

In September 2020, the United Family happily and graciously stepped forward as the largest financial supporter of the program. United, a grocery store company with headquarters in Lubbock, provided a \$10,000 scholarship to Hekkert and future riders and funded operating expenses through 2023.

COVID-19 still gripped the country. No vaccine had been developed, and the world was struggling to understand and control the virus. The year would largely be spent in face coverings, and in-person appearances would be minimal. Texas Tech canceled its May and August in-person commencements and offered virtual and modified in-person options for the December 2020 commencement. Many classes were held virtually while in-person classes were offered with social

Texas Tech cheerleaders pet Fearless Champion during an event for a United Supermarkets store in 2020. (Courtesy Office of Communications and Marketing)

Cameron Hekkert and Fearless Champion make a pregame run at Jones AT&T Stadium. Due to COVID-19 regulations, limited seating gave fans plenty of space during the 2020 season. (Courtesy Robert Rhode)

distancing. Football games took place, but only at 25 percent the capacity of Jones AT&T Stadium.

Despite a very different year, high points surfaced. Hekkert and Fearless Champion were cleared to do the traditional pregame runs at all home games with the caveat that the two—along with their field-safety team and staff—would leave the stadium immediately afterward as a safety precaution, thus reducing the number of people on sidelines for the games.

Hekkert became the focal point of the College of Arts & Sciences campaign called Innovation Never Stops that launched in late September 2020.[11]

The lessened appearance and travel schedule for Fearless Champion would be a silver lining for the horse, who remained sound and healthy for the entirety of Hekkert's term, which lasted eight months.

As she closed out her tenure at the April 23, 2021, Transfer of Reins ceremony, Hekkert reflected on the unusual year:

> I just had to keep reminding myself I'm blessed to be able to do this. A lot of people are going through times a lot rougher than us. And I think also, that's what was so great about it is that we were able to bring joy and put smiles on people's faces when they were going through such a struggle during this pandemic. . . . Even though the landscape of what my appearances looked like

Ashley Adams and Fearless Champion take a selfie at the Texas Tech Livestock Arena in 2021. (Courtesy Office of Communications and Marketing)

Ashley Adams and Fearless Champion pose in front of the Texas Tech seal in 2021. (Courtesy Office of Communications and Marketing)

Fearless Champion's riders gather to celebrate his retirement on November 20, 2021. (Courtesy Office of Communications and Marketing)

Fearless Champion's riders show off their matching boots during his retirement celebration on November 20, 2021. (Courtesy Robert Rhode)

> were so much different than in recent years, I'm still so grateful to have made any at all. I remember this time last year, we were wondering if there would even be a 2020–2021 Masked Rider. And so, being able to stand up here today and say I've made 166 appearances is really impressive to me.[12]

Hekkert retired her hat, cape, and both types of masks she had donned that year, graduated, and enrolled at Texas Tech's School of Law.

The sixtieth Masked Rider picked up right where Hekkert left off.

Ashley Adams is a true lifetime fan of the Masked Rider. When she was a baby, Adams's parents left her with a sitter when they attended Texas Tech football games. The sitter fell through for one of the games, and Adams's mother took her at the age of six months to a game, expecting to have to leave at halftime. Adams was transfixed by the horse for the entire game. Adams dressed up for several years as the Masked Rider for Halloween. As a kindergartener, she saw Masked Rider Katie Carruth at so many appearances, Carruth began recognizing her at the games. When Adams was spotlighted as the student of the week of her class, she shared that when she grew up, she wanted to be the Masked Rider.

Adams rode on a horse for the first time at the age of four during a birthday party at a local stable. When the children dispersed for cake, Adams's mom found her with the horses. Riding lessons started shortly thereafter, but soon that was not enough for Adams. She wanted her own horse.

Adams's parents told her if she could save $1,000, she could buy a horse. The enterprising ten-year-old began a pet-sitting business and cleaned stalls for $5 for college students at the Texas Tech Equestrian Center where she took horse riding lessons. She soon bought her first horse.

Two horses later, Adams had helped the Texas Tech Ranch Horse Team win back-to-back national championships. She served as an assistant to both Brodbeck and Hekkert and previously assisted Starr. She graduated from Texas Tech with a bachelor's degree in animal science, but she continued to dream of serving as the Masked Rider.

As a graduate student in the Department of Agricultural Education & Communications, Adams won the role she waited a lifetime to fill.[13]

Like humans, horses largely experience the same physical and mental impacts of growing older. They need more rest, and minor health disturbances and injuries take longer to treat and may show a proclivity to resurface. Horses can also grow tired of a job just as their human counterparts can and display their discontent through signs of boredom, finding distractions, or overly anticipating the cues for their assignment.

Fearless Champion remained in good health, but he showed the effects of aging. The Masked Rider Committee decided it was time for him to retire. He would complete the football season and celebrate his last run at Jones AT&T Stadium. He could also remain the Masked Rider's horse until a new one was found, giving him a farewell tour with Red Raiders across the state and country for the remainder of the Masked Rider year.

On November 17, 2021, the Masked Rider Committee announced that Fearless Champion would retire by summer 2022 and that weekend's final home game would be his last run at Jones AT&T Stadium.

On Saturday, November 20, 2021, during the Red Raiders' football game against Oklahoma State University, the horse made his final pregame run before a home crowd. His ten riders gathered before the game for photo ops and autographs. They were all honored alongside Fearless Champion in a special presentation during the game. Fearless Champion faced one last obstacle in his final

Ashley Adams and Fearless Champion make a pregame run at Jones AT&T Stadium in 2021. (Courtesy Office of Communications and Marketing)

home run: the addition of flames by the entrance of the players' tunnel. It proved to be only a momentary concern for the seasoned performer.

Fearless Champion continued his final year with Adams, making a run at the rodeo at the Fort Worth Stock Show and Rodeo's first-ever Texas Tech Night—which unfortunately occurred during a winter storm that engulfed most of Texas. The pair also performed runs at Rodeo Houston's Texas Tech Night and the AutoZone Liberty Bowl football game in Memphis where the Red Raiders, led by interim coach Sonny Cumbie, defeated Mississippi State University led by Mike Leach.

"Everybody loves Fearless, and he truly is the best part about Texas Tech," Adams said in an interview at the end of her term, in which she made 460 appearances. "He represents what a fearless champion is. He represents Texas Tech, and he has raised the bar for all of us in so many aspects. He, hands down, without a doubt, is my favorite part about Texas Tech and being the Masked Rider."[14]

Caroline Hobbs became the sixty-first Masked Rider on April 29, 2022. Hobbs, a junior animal science major and American Sign Language minor, had spent the previous two years serving as a Masked Rider assistant.

Hobbs continued her family's tradition of working with a school mascot. Her grandfather had served as a handler for Peruna, Southern Methodist University's black pony mascot, in the 1950s.

Hobbs started riding at the age of three—a potty-training incentive set by her mother. She rode English and Western, and at ten years old, she began training for "eventing," a competition consisting of dressage, cross-country (a phase of competition in which the horse and rider gallop over terrain while negotiating jumps, water hazards, and ditches), and show jumping. Hobbs's bold equestrian background would be an asset in the coming year. With a short time left aboard Fearless Champion, Hobbs would be the one in the saddle helping train his successor.

"With Fearless Champion retiring," she said, "the new horse and I have big shoes to fill."

Hobbs looked to those who came before her in the program with her goals for the year:

> Being named the sixty-first Texas Tech Masked Rider is a dream I have always hoped for. Thinking about leaving behind a legacy feels a million miles away, as my year is just getting started, but I hope to make the public, my friends and my family proud. To know that I will be added to the list of sixty riders who I have looked up to for years now is an amazing feeling.
>
> Character, respect, integrity and honor are a few of the virtues I plan to uphold in my year. I hope to establish a strong foundation for the new horse as it carries on the legacy of Fearless Champion and the thirteen horses before him. Past riders have left a phenomenal legacy for this university, and I plan to continue to build the relationships this program has set forth.[15]

While Fearless Champion, Adams, and Hobbs carried on, Sam Jackson once again began screening black horses—dozens, in fact. Some were located only miles away from the Texas Tech campus, and others came from as far away as Colorado and Canada. As usual, prospective horses were submitted by anyone with interest in the program, but the true contenders came from those familiar with the Masked Rider Programs and its rigors.

Jackson's selection process for the Masked Rider's horse begins with learning the horses' backgrounds and viewing their photos or videos. Using those visual aids as a filter, he makes a personal visit with those that appear to have a naturally calm demeanor and a workable conformation. He will watch the owners ride

Caroline Hobbs and Centennial Champion make a pregame run at Jones AT&T Stadium in 2022. (Photo by Justin Rex, courtesy Office of Communications and Marketing)

Sam Jackson leads the Field Safety Team meeting the day of the pregame run-through practice at Jones AT&T Stadium in 2022. (Courtesy Office of Communications and Marketing)

Caroline Hobbs leads Centennial Champion through his first run-through with the Goin' Band and Spirit Squads. (Courtesy Office of Communications and Marketing)

their horses—if a horse is not agreeable or quiet with its owner in the saddle, then neither will it be agreeable or quiet for a stranger. Next, Jackson will ride the horse himself, testing for suppleness and responsiveness, keeping the needs of the program in mind. Three strong candidates made it to the final stage of the search for the fifteenth horse of the program: the 2022 spring football scrimmage at Jones AT&T Stadium. Each horse had twenty minutes to test in the environment, and Jackson found their first reaction to be very telling.

The first of the three prospects, which had been the frontrunner leading up to the scrimmage, did not take to the appearance at all. The horse reacted poorly to the fan noise, football team, and spirit squads. He refused to go near his costumed counterpart, Raider Red. The second prospect did very well. The third horse also turned in a promising performance. When he was not sure of the markings on the field in the end zone, he quickly adjusted after walking over them. He and Raider Red became fast friends. He was sleek and well-built with a refined head. A small star often hid by his long, thick forelock served as his only marking. His biggest advantage over the other two horses, though, was being nonreactive to noise stimuli and sound.

Despite Jackson's cross-country travels in search of the next Masked Rider's mount, the third horse and Jackson's first choice came from Lubbock, owned by Shannon Asgard. Shannon had purchased CL One N Only, a nine-year-old Quarter Horse gelding whose barn name was Buzz, to compete at ranch horse shows. Buzz, however, did not turn out to be the horse that matched her goals.

"Buzz is very similar in disposition to the past two mascots, Midnight Matador and Fearless Champion," Jackson told Texas Tech. "He is comfortable around people and noise and appears to be a quick learner. . . . He was utilized in a variety of ways by his previous owners. His past jobs included working cattle, roping events, and general recreational riding."

The university bought the horse with a gift from United Supermarkets, and Buzz became the fifteenth horse of the Masked Rider Program. Hobbs and Buzz soon set out on their next biggest appearance, Lubbock's 4th on Broadway Independence Day parade. The horse reacted well, and the two continued to attend parades, rodeos, and Red Raider Orientations through the summer.

Like so many Masked Rider horses before him, Buzz did not quite reach the caliber of performance needed to excel at his original job, but he found a new and greater purpose in becoming one of the most beloved equine public figures in Texas. Perhaps the destiny of failed show horse Buzz, like that of mediocre racehorse High Red Bug and lackluster reining horse Midnight Matador, was to serve as a mascot and have a role where they are the greatest in the world at their job.

The pregame sidelines at Jones AT&T Stadium are bustling in 2022, compared to the early days of the program. (Courtesy Office of Communications and Marketing)

On June 15, 2022, a naming contest opened for people to submit their proposed Texas Tech name for Buzz. United Supermarkets hosted the contest and offered a $500 gift card to the winner. Naming decisions came from the Masked Rider Committee and a select group of former riders and program stakeholders.

In the first twenty-four hours of the contest, fans submitted over 4,200 names. By the deadline of 12:01 a.m. on July 15, 2022, 5,814 fans submitted roughly 10,000 names, 3,426 of them unique. The name would be a closely guarded secret held by only a handful of people until its reveal in the fall.

At the same time Buzz was receiving a new name, Fearless Champion was finding a retirement home. The deadline for his former riders to submit a proposal to keep Fearless Champion in his retirement was also June 15, 2022—the same day Buzz's naming contest opened. The affectionate horse had many who wanted to provide for him. A subcommittee of the Masked Rider Committee reviewed the proposals and selected his second rider, Corey Waggoner, to take ownership of him.

This time, Jackson had the privilege of making the call to give Waggoner the good news. The university made the announcement on July 8, 2022. After ten years, ten riders, 150,000 miles, and more than 2,600 appearances, Fearless Champion, or "Woody," began a life of leisure.

"Fearless Champion has faithfully served Texas Tech in a way unlike any other horse in the history of the Masked Rider Program," Stephanie Rhode shared in the press release. "He has set a record with the number of appearances he has made and the people he has met during his ten years of service. He truly has lived up to his name."[16]

Waggoner had met his wife Katelyn, now a veterinarian, while riding Woody in costume as Masked Rider. The horse was a huge part of their lives from that point forward, and the two welcomed Woody to their home near Amarillo to live out his days.

Prior to the beginning of the 2022 football season, Texas Tech prepared for its centennial year. An announcement event at Texas Tech's Allen Theatre on August 25, 2022, prominently featured Hobbs in costume sharing the history of the Masked Rider Program.

Eight days later on Friday, September 2 at 5:30 p.m., the university and United Supermarkets held a media event under the east portico of Buddy Holly Hall in the Lubbock Arts District. Emceed by Nancy Sharp of United Supermarkets, Stephanie Rhode and Sam Jackson spoke to the crowd about Buzz and the naming contest. President Lawrence Schovanec had the honor of revealing Centennial Champion as Buzz's new Texas Tech name on the eve of the horse's first football game.

The name was submitted nine times in the first twenty-four hours of the naming contest, but Iris Baker had the earliest time stamp on her entry, 10:30 a.m., thus she won the contest the same morning it opened. Baker, a senior animal science major, happened to serve as one of Hobbs's Masked Rider assistants and became the first Texas Tech undergraduate student to have their submission selected as a horse's name.

The next evening at 7 p.m., Hobbs and Centennial Champion made their first football game appearance. Few realize the extent of the preparation involved. In the week leading up to a game, the horse is ridden extensively each day, and the truck and trailer are washed. The costume is freshly dry-cleaned, and tack is cleaned and polished. The Masked Rider and Sam Jackson attend a football safety coordination meeting. Field safety assistants—Texas Tech students who volunteer to provide on-field assistance of clearing the path of the horse—have attended a training on their responsibilities, receive their assigned placements for the pregame run and rest of the game, and prepare their own uniforms.

The morning of a game comes early—sometimes as early as 4 a.m.—and requires at least three hours of riding. The horse is given a bath after his ride, and as he dries, the rider cleans his stall. The horse's meal routines largely stay the same as on non-game days, and water and extra hay are packed in the trailer for his halftime break. Masked Rider assistants may help with the prep work while the rider focuses on preparing the horse.

The rider leaves for the stadium in time to allow for about an hour and a half of autographs on horseback at the Frazier Alumni Pavilion. Their assistants and field safety members provide crowd control. Thirty to forty minutes before kickoff, the pair leaves the autograph area along with their assistants and field safety team to head down the ramp and get in place outside the south end zone. This time period comes before players leave their pregame warm-ups and the Goin' Band fills the tunnels. When the time comes, the horse and rider make their pregame run then find their place on the sideline and prepare for what everyone hopes is many scoring runs.

Amidst fog and fire, Caroline Hobbs and Centennial Champion make their pregame run at Jones AT&T Stadium in 2022. (Courtesy Office of Communications and Marketing)

Caroline Hobbs and Centennial Champion on the sidelines at Jones AT&T Stadium in 2022. (Courtesy Office of Communications and Marketing)

Overcoming approximately 59,000 screaming fans, fireworks, and even a pregame flyover, Centennial Champion had a positive first game with Hobbs's work and diligence. He made a few errors that Hobbs corrected and adapted over the course of the game. As the game went on, Centennial Champion got better at his new job.

The next weekend, the two experienced their second football game. Centennial Champion's pregame run was smoother and faster, he had grown more patient on the sidelines, and he grew more confident in his scoring runs. As the football season continued, he faced more obstacles than any of his predecessors: the number of fireworks used at games tripled, fire cannons became an every-game occurrence, a large group of parachuters landed in the stadium, and he stood still during several Air Force and Navy flyovers, including one that was so loud, it seemed to rattle the stadium.

Hobbs and Centennial Champion finished their year with more than 300 appearances. As Hobbs noted:

> One of my favorite things I like to do during my year was sit with him in his stall and do homework. I would just sit on the ground and try—emphasis on try—to do my homework. Because every time he would stare me down, put his nose on my nose, my computer or put his head on my shoulder. It was very hard to write a paper. I can't thank Texas Tech enough for allowing me to do this job, but also allowing me to follow my dreams of being the Masked Rider while getting a college degree and furthering my knowledge in the horse industry.[17]

On April 22, 2023, Lauren Bloss, a senior animal science major from El Paso, accepted the reins to Centennial Champion as the sixty-second Masked Rider. Bloss learned to ride both English and Western but spent considerable time with hunters and jumpers. As a high school student, she and her family came to campus for Family Weekend while her brother played for Texas Tech Tennis. She saw the Masked Rider's run and decided she would apply to Texas Tech and try out one day.

"I have a list of things I want to accomplish," Bloss said in an interview with the university. "There's so many, I have to sort through them all. But really it comes down to making an impact in the community and maintaining the amazing and positive name on Texas Tech in the Spirit program."

Centennial Champion and Caroline Hobbs take part in a photo shoot on a snowy day in 2022. The sculpture of the number 100 is an outdoor installation commemorating Texas Tech's centennial year. (Photos by Ashley Rodgers, courtesy Office of Communications and Marketing)

Lauren Bloss poses with Centennial Champion at the Texas Tech Equestrian Center in advance of the April 21, 2023, Transfer of Reins ceremony. (Courtesy Office of Communications and Marketing)

Raider Red hugs Centennial Champion during a snowy 2022 photo shoot. (Photo by Ashley Rodgers, courtesy Office of Communications and Marketing)

Bloss and Centennial Champion will continue their year of service. In the spring, a new rider will be chosen to carry on the tradition. The horses and riders will change, but the feelings they inspire in Red Raiders will continue for generations.

During their year of service, the pair will be part of the most memorable moments Red Raiders experience—first visits to campus, athletic events, campus celebrations, proposals, weddings, and funerals. The horses grow more confident and bolder with each appearance. The riders come out of their year as better horsemen and horsewomen—stronger and more confident in not just their riding and care skills but as leaders, speakers, and students.

This immense growth was best captured by Lyndi Starr in her farewell speech: "This position will change you, push you, and mold you. It'll change you tremendously if you let it."

For sixty-two riders and counting, it has.

Fearless Champion tucked away for the night at the home of the Tolboom family in Dublin, Texas. (Photo by Laurie Tolboom Martin)

# APPENDIX A: HORSE BLOODLINES

These pedigrees and backgrounds were compiled using American Quarter Horse Association records and supplemented with the Pedigree Online All Breed Database available at allbreedpedigree.com. Some are fully traced while others have no information. "Unknown" indicates the horse in the lineage could not be identified.

All horses in the lineage are Quarter Horses unless noted "(TB)" for thoroughbred. Despite some being registered as a color other than black, all appeared black. Some horses may appear black but are actually deemed brown due to brown or tan hair around their muzzle or groin area.

Some have exact dates for birth (or foaling) and death, and others do not. The birthdate of all horses is considered January 1 of every year for consistency. Many older AQHA records do not include an exact birthday. AQHA relies on reporting from members for dates of death and, unless notified otherwise, presumes the horse is deceased at age 25. Some exact dates of death included in this appendix were found through news releases.

**Understanding the Pedigrees**

The top left of listing includes the following:

- The horse's Texas Tech name
- Its number in the program
- Time of service (as accurately as can be discerned by news releases)

The pedigrees are read as follows starting with the Masked Rider horse at left:

- Registered name
- Barn name (if identified)
- Registered color and sex
- AQHA registration number
- Breeder (if available) and breeder's location

Much like a family tree, the next levels indicate the sire (father) on the top branch and dam (mother) on the lower branch as well as their year of foaling when available. Notable sires of great-great-grandsires and great-great-granddams are included after the year of foaling.

Centennial Champion pictured shortly after his introduction into the Masked Rider Program. (Photo by Ashley Adams)

**Blackie**
1st Horse of the Program

Served January 1, 1954, through 1955 football season

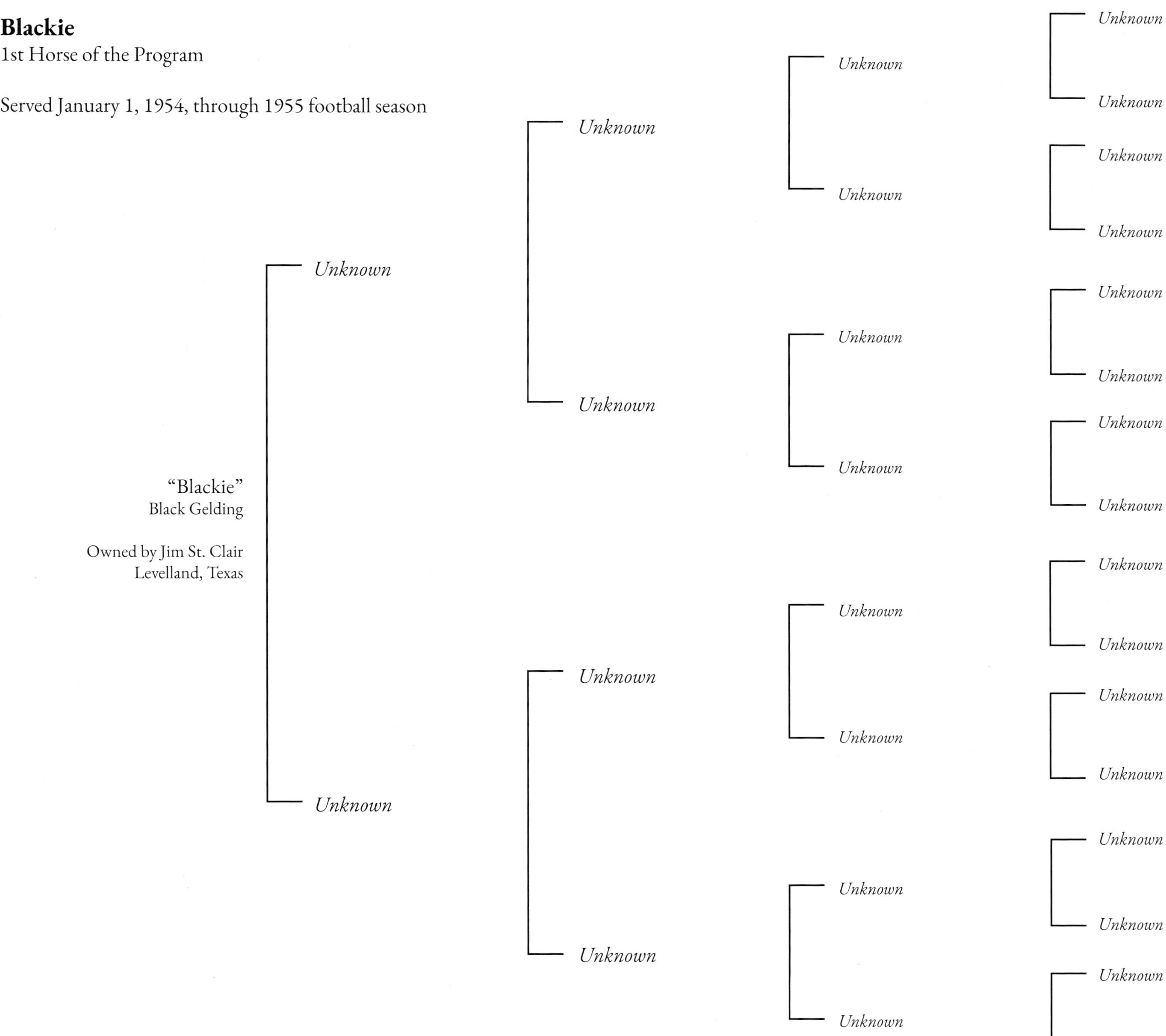

**Tech Beauty**
2nd Horse of the Program

Served 1956 to 1959 and
May 1961 to April 14, 1964

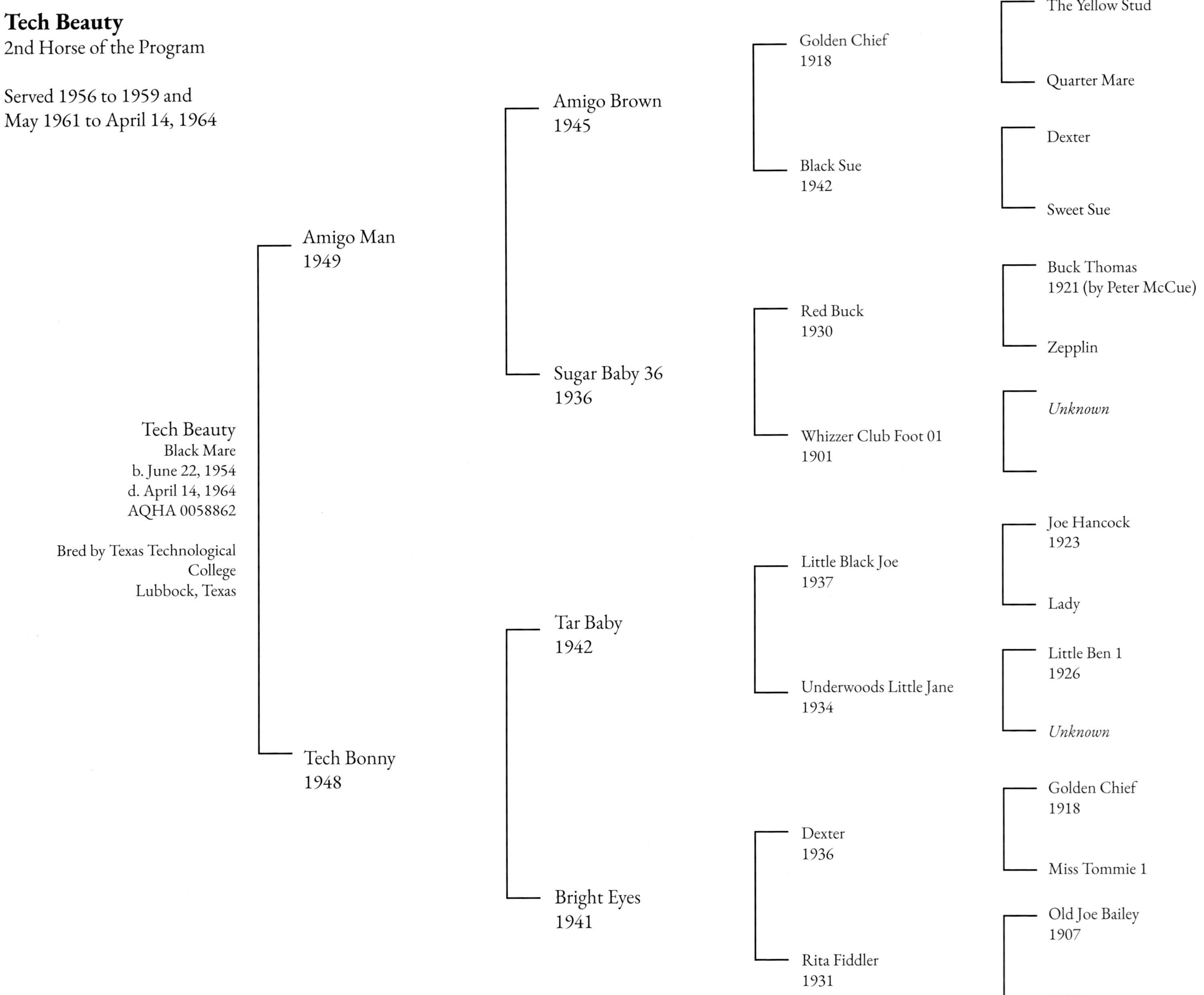

**Beau Black**
3rd Horse of the Program

Served September 1959 to May 1961

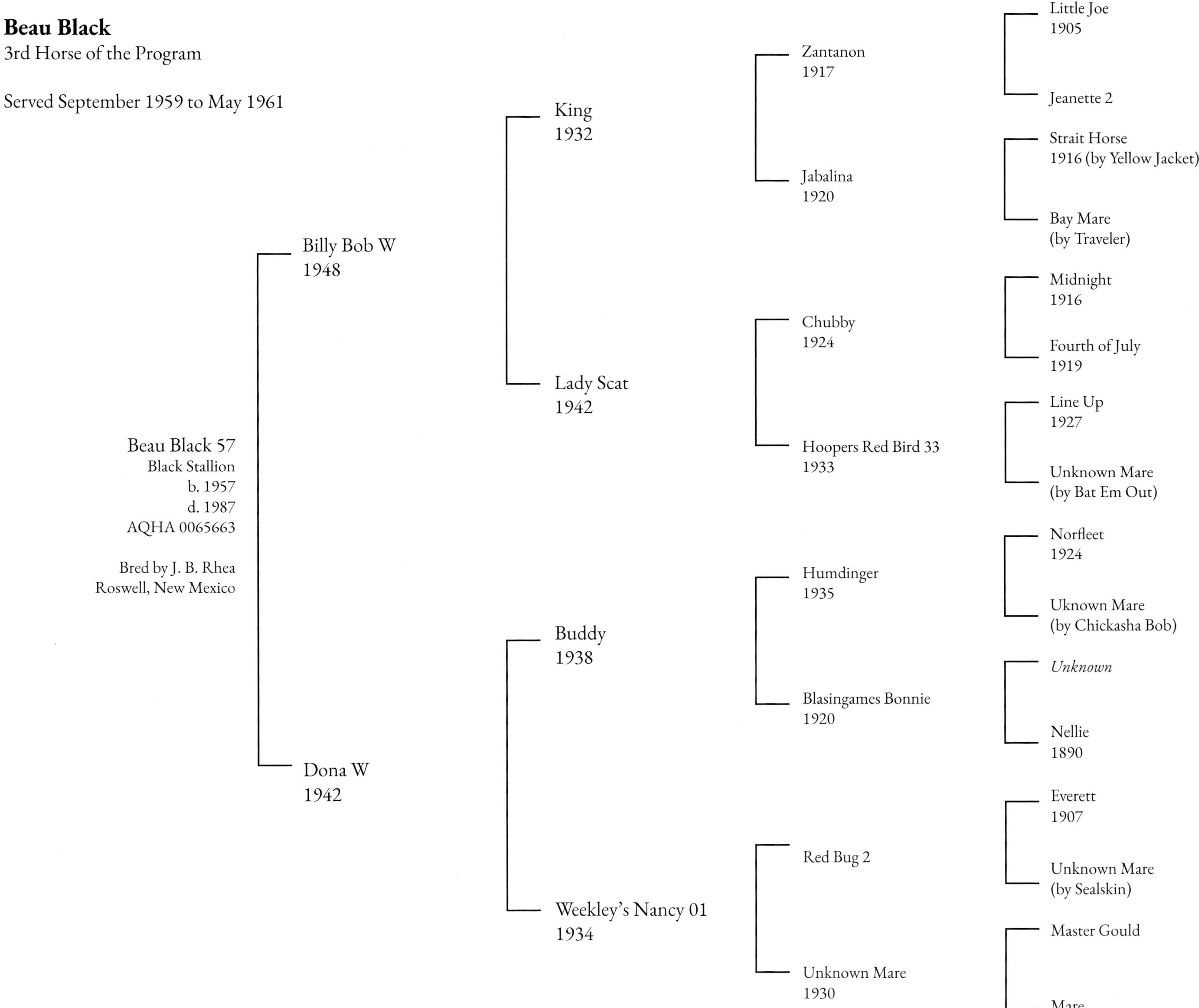

## Charcoal Cody

4th Horse of the Program

Served fall 1964 to 1972 and one game in fall 1963 during Tech Beauty's kidnapping

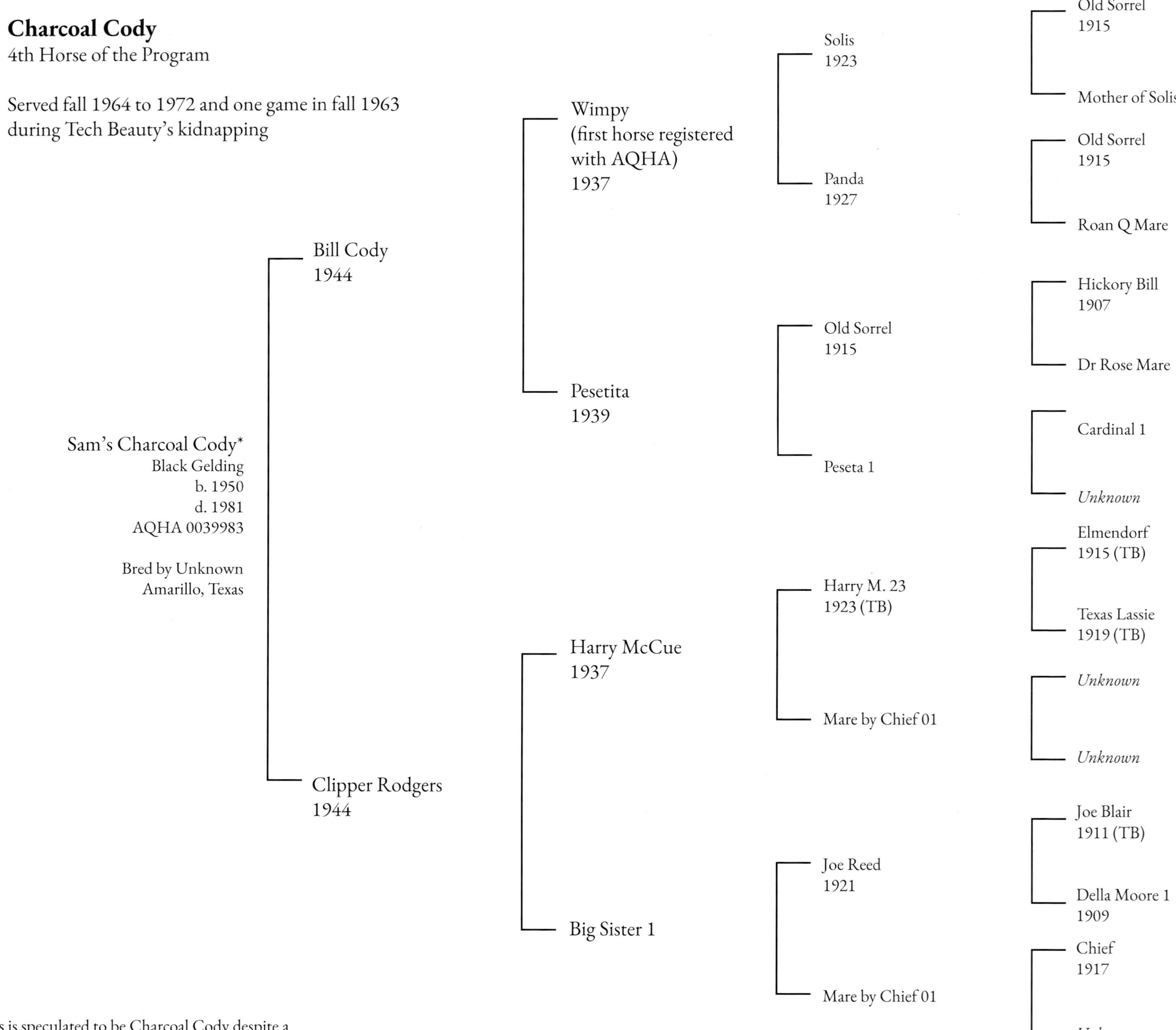


* This is speculated to be Charcoal Cody despite a one-year difference in age due to color, location of breeder, and closeness to registered name.

**Showboy Huffman**
5th Horse of the Program

Served 1971 to 1973
(1971 and 1972 made out-of-town appearances when Charcoal Cody was being used at home)

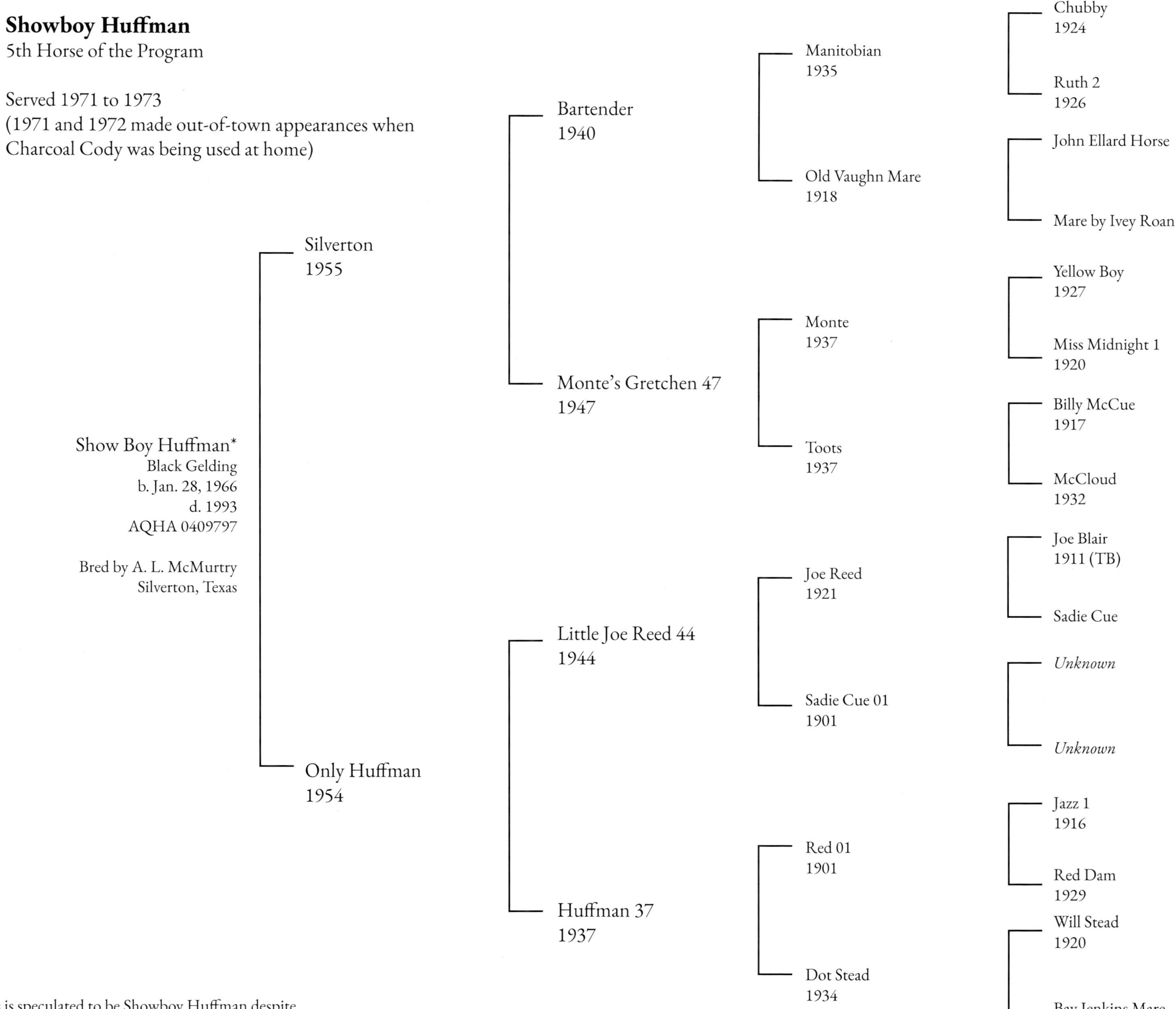


*This is speculated to be Showboy Huffman despite a two-year difference in age due to color, location of breeder, and closeness to registered name.

**Happy V**
6th Horse of the Program

Served 1973 to 1977

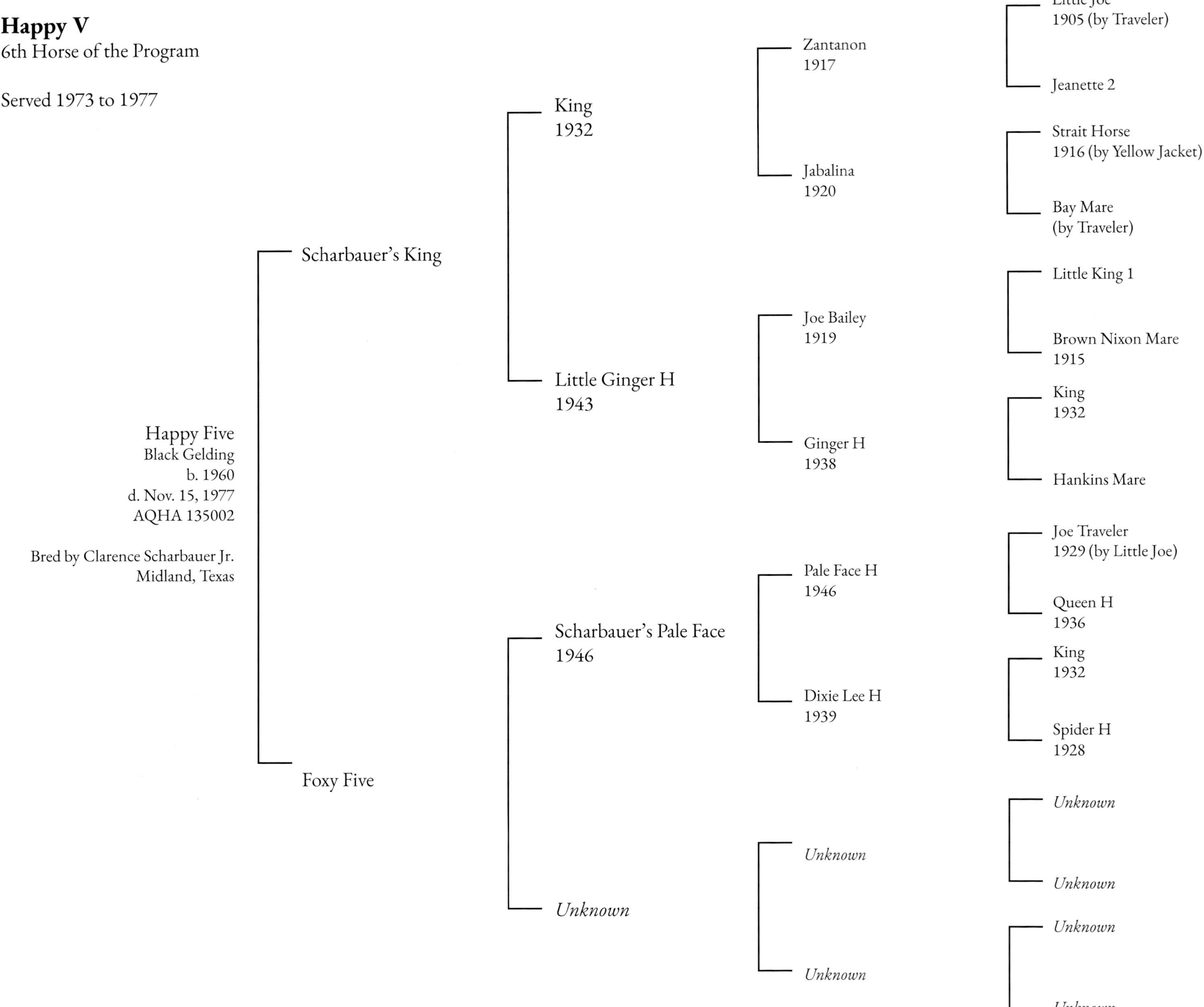

**Happy VI**
7th Horse of the Program

Served November 16, 1977, to October 11, 1979

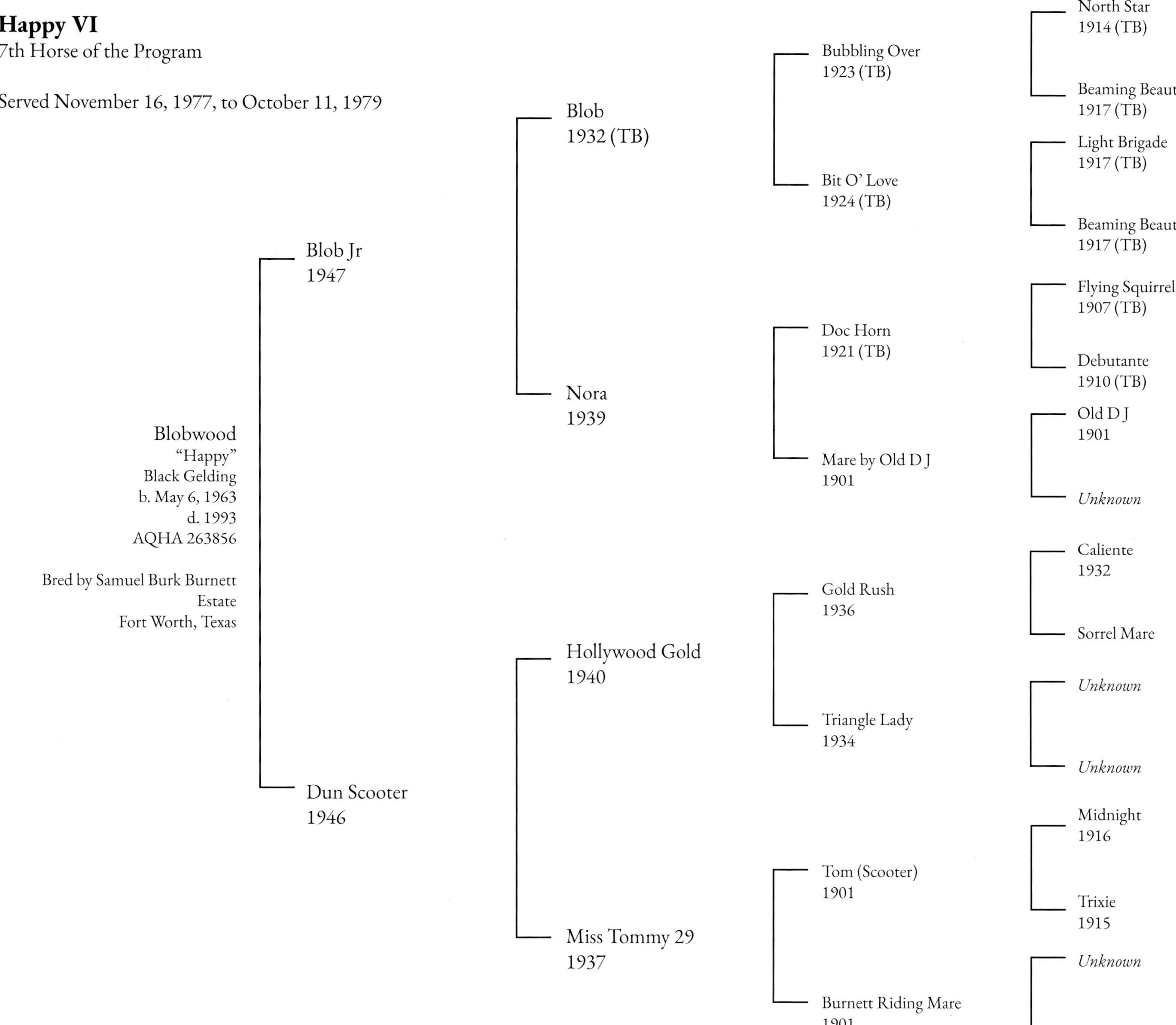

**Happy VI-II**
8th Horse of the Program

Served October 11, 1979, to April 1987

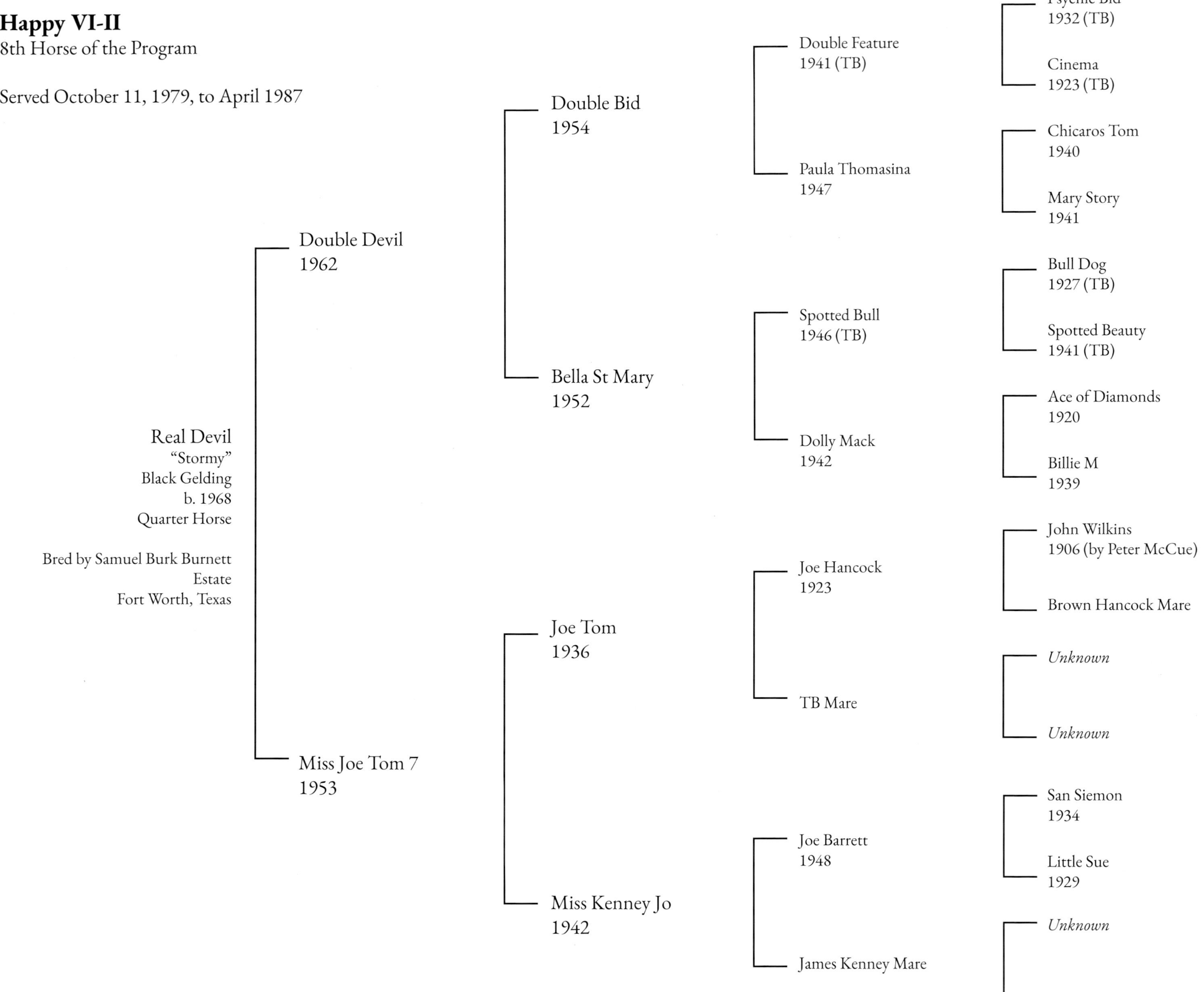

**Midnight Raider**
9th Horse of the Program

Served April 1987 to April 16, 1993

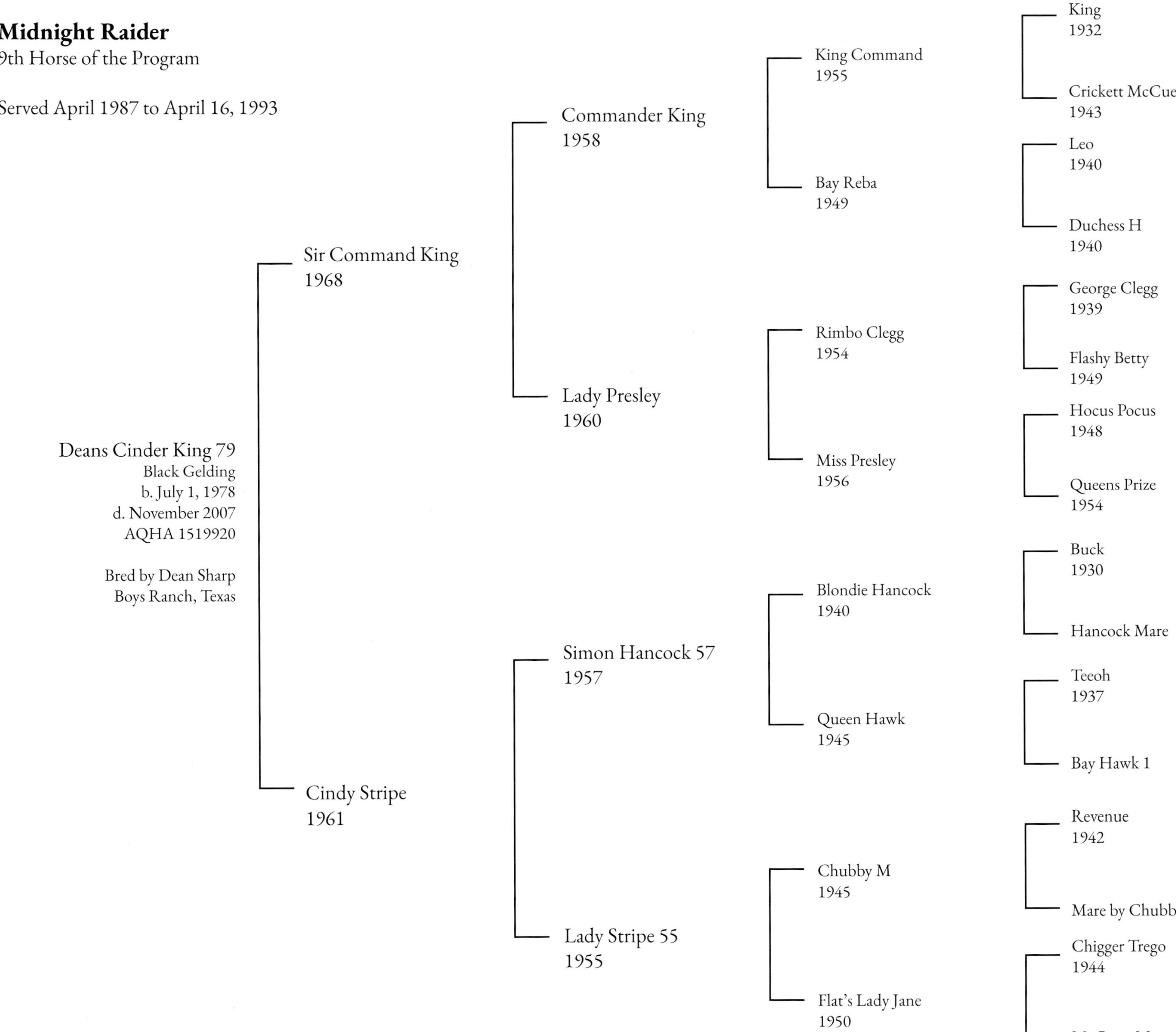

**Double T**
10th Horse of the Program

Served July 22, 1993, to September 3, 1994

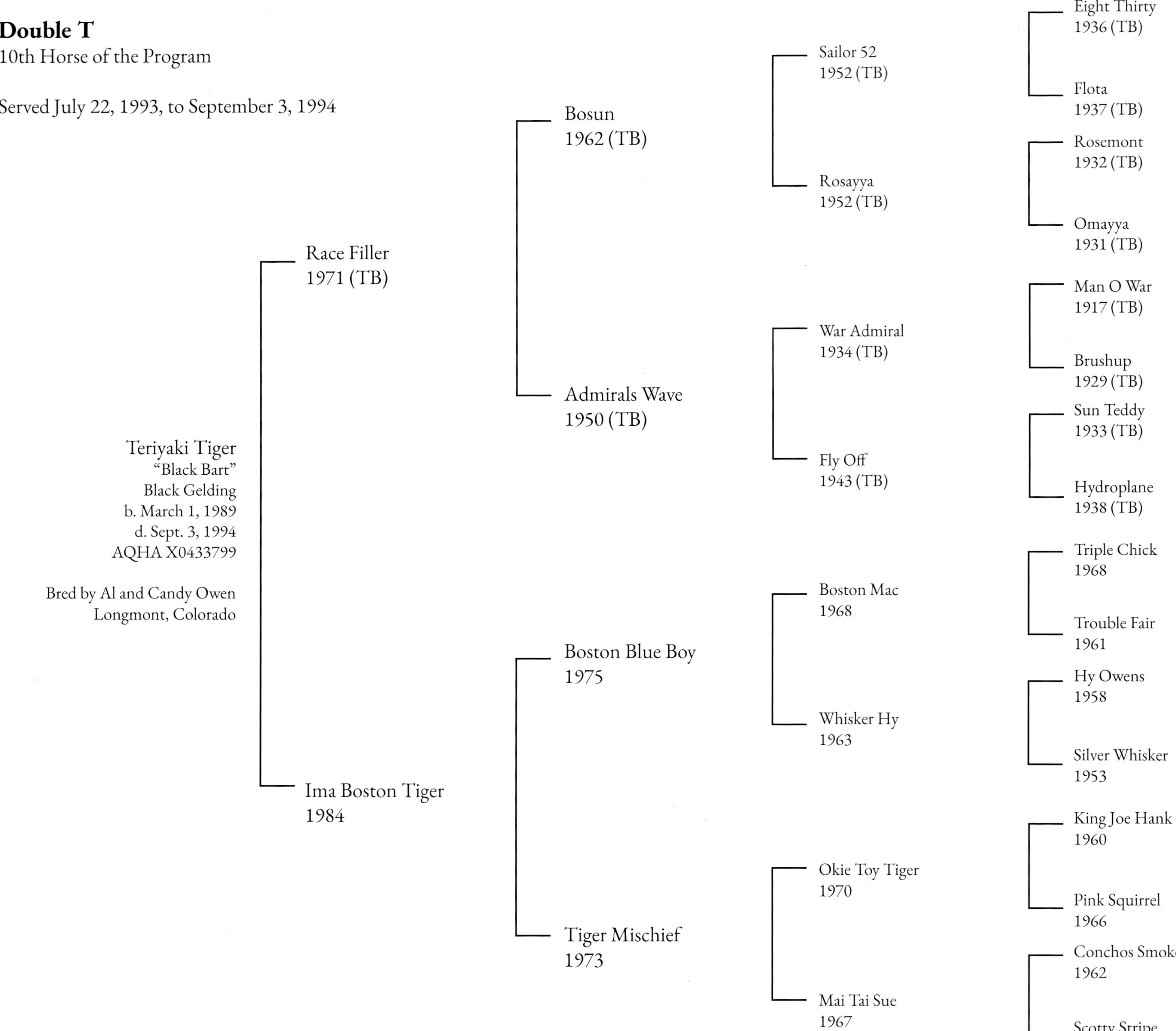

## High Red

11th Horse of the Program

Served April 1, 1995, to March 15, 1998
(Temporarily replaced due to injury and recovery starting September 11, 1997)

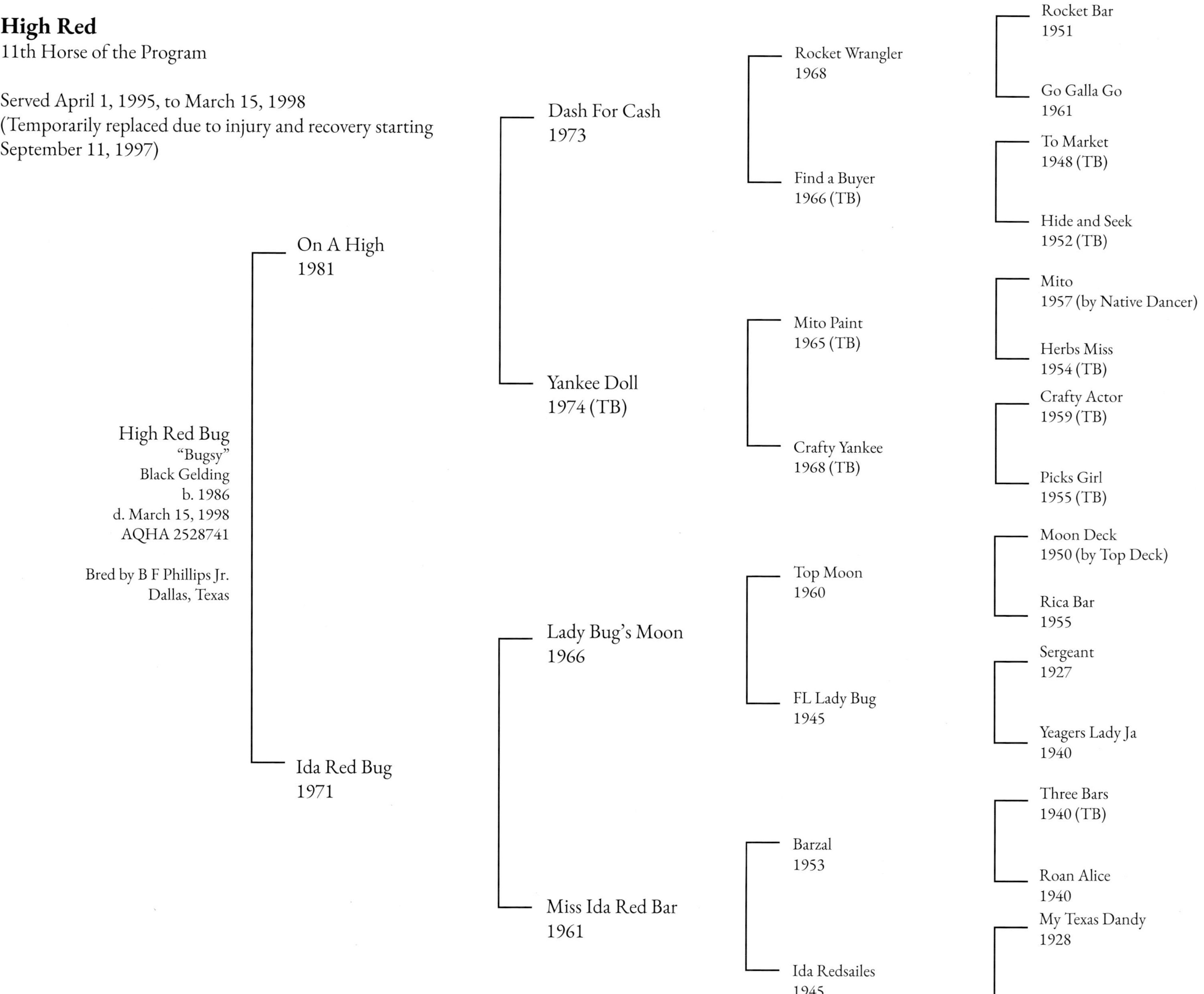

## Black Phantom Raider

12th Horse of the Program

Served October 27, 1997, to August 27, 2001

"Caro"
Black Gelding
b. 1990
d. August 27, 2001
Unregistered Quarter Horse

Previously owned by Chris Lawrence
Cattle Company
Seymour, Texas

*Unknown*

*Unknown*

*Unknown*

*Unknown*

*Unknown*

*Unknown*

*Unknown*

*Unknown*

*Unknown*

*Unknown*

*Unknown*

*Unknown*

*Unknown*

*Unknown*

*Unknown*

*Unknown*

*Unknown*

*Unknown*

*Unknown*

*Unknown*

*Unknown*

*Unknown*

*Unknown*

*Unknown*

*Unknown*

*Unknown*

*Unknown*

*Unknown*

*Unknown*

*Unknown*

**Midnight Matador**
13th Horse of the Program

Served May 21, 2002 to October 17, 2012

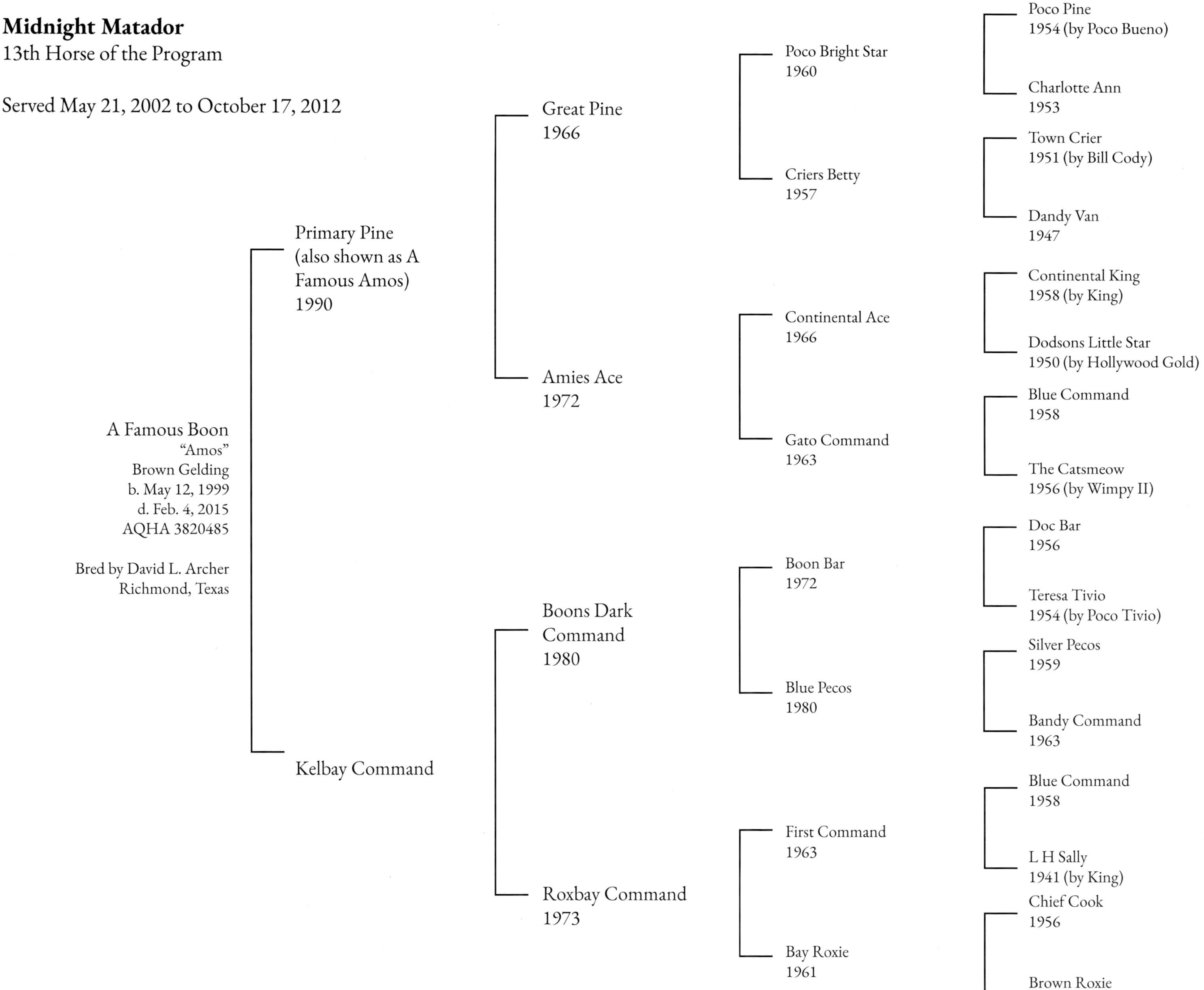

**Fearless Champion**

14th Horse of the Program

Served January 18, 2013, to June 15, 2022

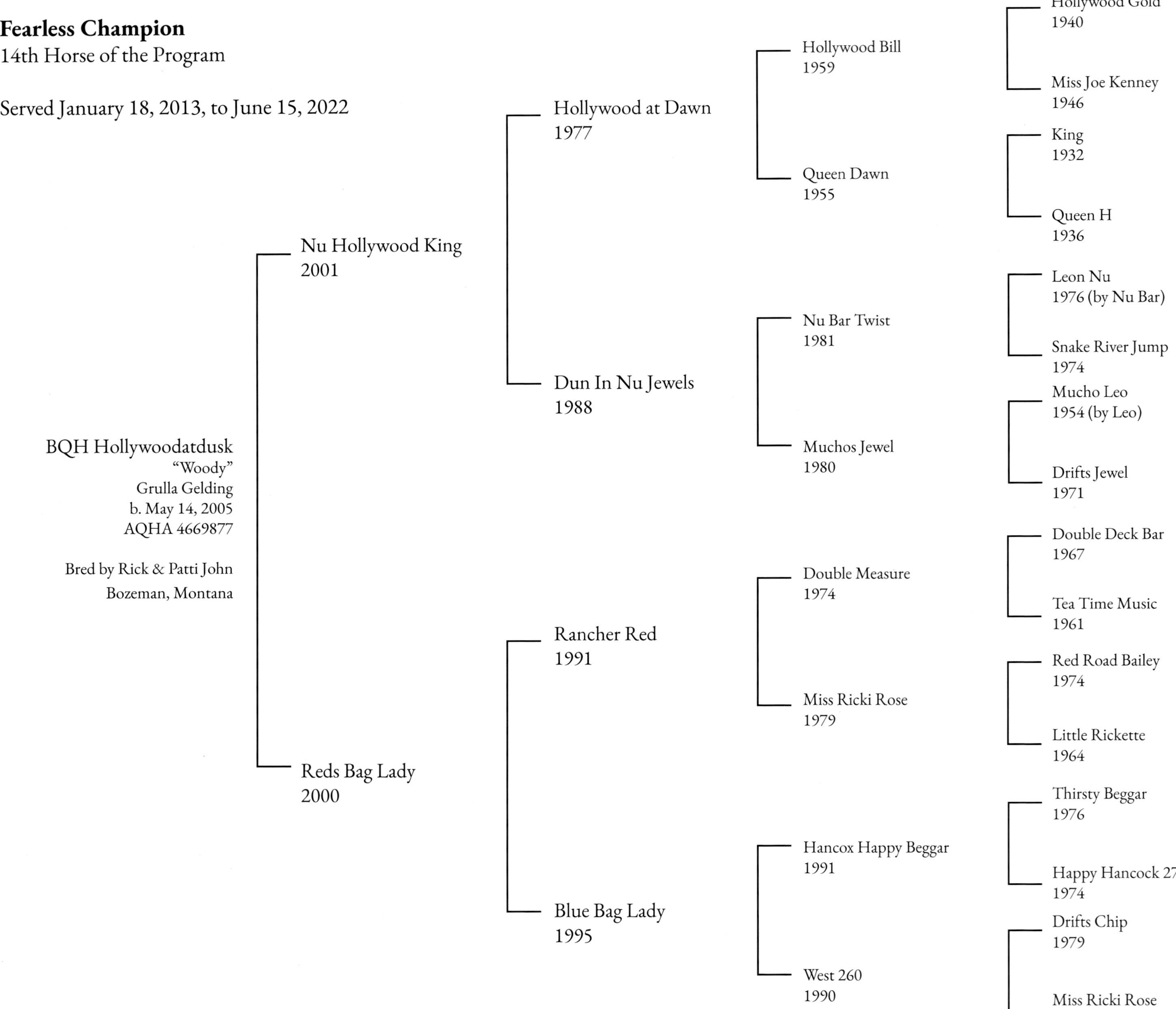

**Centennial Champion**
15th Horse of the Program

Served June 15, 2022, to Present

CL One N Only
"Buzz"
Black Gelding
b. March 25, 2013
AQHA 5573848

Bred by Lyle Lumax
Swan River, Manitoba,
Canada

CL First Choice
1994

CL Last Can Do
1999

Catch a Buzz
1981

My Miss Watergate
1984

This Black Can Do
1994

CL Last Skip
1994

Mito Paint
1965 (TB)

Tippsy Dippsy Do
1976

Watergate Leo
1977

Miss Chubby Cat
1976

Boston Can Do
1980

Sadiron Sue
1981

Bairds Big Un
1981

Miss Skipa Star
1971

Mito
1957

Herbs Miss
1954

Tippy Canoe
1969

Miss Vanny
1966

Sassy Leo Jack
1972

Pino Watergate
1973

Kansas Cat
1964

Chunkie Babe
1968

Boston Mac
1968

Tippy Can Do
1974

Iron Rebel
1969

Codys Jewel
1970

Will B Impressive
1976

Frona
1968

Skip a Mark
1967

Jewel Coffee
1962

# APPENDIX B: LIST OF RIDERS

| No. | Name | Years | Hometown* | Major | Horse |
|---|---|---|---|---|---|
| 1 | Joe Kirk Fulton | 54–55 | Lubbock, TX | Animal Husbandry | Blackie / Pretty Day |
| 2 | James "Jim" Cloyd | 55–57 | Canadian, TX | Animal Husbandry | Tech Beauty |
| 3 | Donald "Polly" Hollar | 57–59 | Guthrie, TX | Animal Husbandry | Tech Beauty |
| 4 | J. H. "Hud" Rhea | 59–61 | Lubbock, TX | Animal Husbandry | Beau Black |
| 5 | Kelley Waggoner | 61–62 | Henderson, TX | Veterinary Science | Tech Beauty |
| 6 | William "Bill" Durfey | 62–63 | Wellington, TX | Animal Husbandry | Tech Beauty |
| 7 | Douglas "Nubbin" Hollar | 63–64, 66–68 | Guthrie, TX | Animal Husbandry | Tech Beauty / Charcoal Cody |
| 8 | Douglas "Dink" Wilson | 64–66 | Matador, TX | Range Management | Charcoal Cody |
| 9 | Johnny Bob Carruth | 68–70 | De Leon, TX | Agricultural Education | Charcoal Cody |
| 10 | Tommy Martin | 70–71 | Throckmorton, TX | Animal Science | Charcoal Cody |
| 11 | Randy Jeffers | 71–73 | Amarillo, TX | Pre-law / Business Administration | Charcoal Cody / Showboy Huffman |
| 12 | Gerald Nobles | 73–74 | Midland, TX | Animal Business | Happy V |
| 13 | Anne Lynch | 74–75 | Dell City, TX | Animal Science | Happy V |
| 14 | Joe Kim King | 75–76 | Brady, TX | Animal Science | Happy V |
| 15 | Jess Wall | 76–77 | Perryton, TX | Agricultural Education | Happy V |
| 16 | Larry Cade | 77–78 | Sonora, TX | Geology | Happy V / Happy VI |
| 17 | Lee Puckitt | 78–79 | San Angelo, TX | Business | Happy VI |
| 18 | Vergil "Coke" Hopping | 79–80 | Memphis, TX | Agricultural Education | Happy VI / Happy VI-II |

* Does not necessarily indicate place of birth.

| 19 | Kathleen Campbell | 80–81 | Portland, TX | History / French | Happy VI-II |
|---|---|---|---|---|---|
| 20 | Kurt Harris | 81–82 | Stratford, TX | Animal Science | Happy VI-II |
| 21 | Perry Church | 82–83 | Friona, TX | Agricultural Finance | Happy VI-II |
| 22 | Jennifer Aufill | 83–84 | Lubbock, TX | Marketing | Happy VI-II |
| 23 | Zurick Labrier | 84–85 | Masterson, TX | Animal Production | Happy VI-II |
| 24 | Jerrell Key | 85–86 | Lubbock, TX | Agricultural Economics / Real Estate | Happy VI-II |
| 25 | Daniel Jenkins | 86–87 | Higgins, TX | Animal Production / Pre-vet | Happy VI-II |
| 26 | Kim Saunders | 87–88 | Marfa, TX | Animal Production | Happy VI-II / Midnight Raider |
| 27 | Lea Whitehead | 88–89 | Sonora, TX | Agricultural Communications | Midnight Raider |
| 28 | Tonya Tinnin | 89–90 | Amarillo, TX | Agricultural Communications | Midnight Raider |
| 29 | Blaine Lemons | 90–91 | Colorado City, TX | Animal Production | Midnight Raider |
| 30 | Ralynn Key | 91–92 | Gail, TX | Office Systems Technology / Business Education | Midnight Raider |
| 31 | Jason Spence | 92–93 | Tahoka, TX | Animal Science | Midnight Raider |
| 32 | Lisa Gilbreath | 93–94 | Lewisville, TX | Pre-vet | Double T |
| 33 | Amy Smart | 94–95 | Richardson, TX | Animal Science | Double T |
| 34 | JoLynn Self | 95–96 | Amarillo, TX | Biology | High Red |
| 35 | Martha Reed | 96–97 | Knickerbocker, TX | Animal Production | High Red |
| 36 | Becky McDougal | 97–98 | Comanche, TX | Agricultural Economics | High Red / Black Phantom Raider |
| 37 | Michael "Dusty" Abney | 98–99 | Athens, TX | Animal Science | Black Phantom Raider |
| 38 | Travis Thorne | 99–00 | Stanley, NM | Agribusiness / General Business | Black Phantom Raider |
| 39 | Lesley Gilbreath | 00–01 | Flower Mound, TX | Finance | Black Phantom Raider |
| 40 | Kathryn "Katie" Carruth | 01–02 | Lubbock, TX | Agricultural Communications | Black Phantom Raider |
| 41 | Jessica Melvin | 02–03 | Pierre, SD | Physical Therapy | Midnight Matador |
| 42 | Ben Holland | 03–04 | Texline, TX | Animal Science | Midnight Matador |
| 43 | Stacy Stockard | 04–05 | Sanger, TX | Agricultural Communications | Midnight Matador |
| 44 | Justin Burgin | 05–06 | Scurry, TX | Animal Science | Midnight Matador |

| 45 | Amy Bell | 06–07 | Kermit, TX | Animal & Food Science | Midnight Matador |
|---|---|---|---|---|---|
| 46 | Kevin Burns | 07–08 | Clovis, NM | Animal Science | Midnight Matador |
| 47 | Ashley Hartzog | 08–09 | Farwell, TX | Animal Science / Spanish | Midnight Matador |
| 48 | Brianne Aucutt-Hight | 09–10 | Clovis, NM | Animal Science | Midnight Matador |
| 49 | Christi Chadwell | 10–11 | Garland, TX | Agricultural Communications | Midnight Matador |
| 50 | Bradley Skinner | 11–12 | Arvada, CO | Animal Science | Midnight Matador |
| 51 | Ashley Wenzel | 12–13 | Friendswood, TX | Education | Midnight Matador / Fearless Champion |
| 52 | Corey Waggoner | 13–14 | Lubbock, TX | Animal Science | Fearless Champion |
| 53 | Mackenzie White | 14–15 | Marble Falls, TX | Agricultural & Applied Economics | Fearless Champion |
| 54 | Rachel McLelland | 15–16 | Tijeras, NM | Pre-med / Anthropology | Fearless Champion |
| 55 | Charlie Snider | 16–17 | Corinth, TX | Animal Science | Fearless Champion |
| 56 | Laurie Tolboom | 17–18 | Dublin, TX | Mass Communications | Fearless Champion |
| 57 | Lyndi Starr | 18–19 | Mount Vernon, TX | Agricultural Communications | Fearless Champion |
| 58 | Emily Brodbeck | 19–20 | Lubbock, TX | Wildlife, Aquatic, and Wildlands Science and Management | Fearless Champion |
| 59 | Cameron Hekkert | 20–21 | Highlands Ranch, CO | Sports Management / Honors College | Fearless Champion |
| 60 | Ashley Adams | 21–22 | Lubbock, TX | Agricultural Communications | Fearless Champion |
| 61 | Caroline Hobbs | 22–23 | Dallas, TX | Animal Science / American Sign Language | Fearless Champion / Centennial Champion |
| 62 | Lauren Bloss | 23–24 | El Paso, TX | Animal Science | Centennial Champion |

# NOTES

## CHAPTER 1

1. "City Population History from 1850–2000," *Texas Almanac*, accessed February 19, 2023, https://www.texasalmanac.com/drupal-backup/images/CityPopHist%20web.pdf.
2. Lacey Nobles, "A Rocky Road with a Triumphant Ending," Bullock Museum, January 8, 2015, accessed February 19, 2023, https://www.thestoryoftexas.com/discover/texas-story-project/texas-tech-lubbock; Sally Abbe, "Caprock Chronicles: William H. Bledsoe: Leading South Plains Citizen," *Lubbock Avalanche-Journal*, February 2, 2023, https://www.lubbockonline.com/story/news/history/ 2023/02/04/caprock-chronicles-william-h-bledsoe-leading-south-plains-citizen/69862942007/.
3. Abbe, "Caprock Chronicles: William H. Bledsoe."
4. Lawrence Graves, "Texas Tech University," *Texas State Historical Association Handbook of Texas*, accessed February 19, 2023, https://www.tshaonline.org/handbook/entries/texas-tech-university.
5. "City Population History," *Texas Almanac*; "Fall Enrollment Since 1925," Texas Tech Institutional Research, accessed February 19, 2023, https://www.depts.ttu.edu/irim/archive/enr/fallenrl.php; *First sidewalk construction, 1926*, print, 4″ x 5″, Southwest Collection/Special Collections Library, Texas Tech University, https://swco-ir.tdl.org/handle/10605/291254.
6. John Lee, "'Babe' Is Taken from the Streets; Has Sparkling Personality, Brown Eyes," *Toreador*, November 6, 1951.
7. J. S., letter to the editor, *Toreador*, February 18, 1947; Sue Holmes, "Where's the Mascot?" *Toreador*, November 15, 1950; Pat Johnson, "Homecoming Asks Techsans: UT's 'Bevo' or Army Mule?" *Toreador*, October 19, 1951; "Texas Tech Talk: Fireworks Planned for Homecoming," *Toreador*, October 23, 1951.
8. Jerry Stoltz, "Penny for Your Thoughts," *Toreador*, February 28, 1948.
9. "Matadors Take Clarendon Bulldogs into Camp, 13 to 7," *Toreador*, October 31, 1925; Marsha Gustafson, "In the Beginning . . . West Texas Pioneers That Time Refuses to Forget," *Texas Techsan*, May/June 1992, https://issuu.com/texastechalumniassociation/docs/1992_mayjune.
10. "Baby Bull to Boost Tech with Bellows an' Bawls," *Toreador*, October 26, 1951.
11. "Texas Tech Talk," *Toreador*, October 23, 1951.
12. Dick Brooks, "Owls Stop Raiders at Goal as Techsans Outgain Rice," *Toreador*, November 8, 1950.
13. "Members of Matador Football Team Capture Wildcat on Ranch; Expect to Make Feline Mascot," *Toreador*, January 11, 1936.
14. "Football Fans Boo When Bear Attacks Coach's New Pants," *Toreador*, October 20, 1948.
15. George Tate, 1984, interview by Richard Mason, October 11, 1984, cassette tape, Texas Tech University Southwest Collection/Special Collections Library, Texas Tech University, http://oralhistory.swco.ttu.edu/index.php?title=Tate,_George_M_1984,_1990.
16. George Tate, 1990, interview by Robert Clark, March 29, 1990, cassette tape, Southwest Collection/Special Collections Library, Texas Tech University, http://oralhistory.swco.ttu.edu/index.php?title=Tate,_George_M_1984,_1990.
17. Tate interview, 1984.
18. Ibid.; Jan Horn, "Masked Raider Thrills Fans with Stadium Rides," *University Daily*, October 31, 1969.
19. Lynn Whitfield, "Origins of the Ghost Rider," *Caprock Chronicles*, *Lubbock Avalanche-Journal*, November 10, 2018, https://www.lubbockonline.com/

news/20181110/caprock-chronicles-origins-of-texas-techs-ghost-rider.
20. Tate interview, 1990.
21. Ibid.
22. Texas Tech University press release, September 1936, https://swco-ir.tdl.org/handle/10605/281839.
23. Tate interview, 1984.
24. Ibid.
25. Ibid.
26. Ibid.
27. Ibid.; Tate interview, 1990.
28. Preston Lewis, "Ghost Riders," *Texas Techsan*, November–December 1984, 11.
29. Tate interview, 1984.
30. "Black Bull Proposed as College Mascot," *Toreador*, October 21, 1952.
31. "Techsans to Hold Pep Rally on Denton Square Saturday," *Toreador*, November 5, 1952.
32. "Mystery Clipper Rated as Expert," *Toreador*, November 14, 1952; "NT Plays Delilah," *Toreador*, November 12, 1952.
33. Ibid.
34. "SC Finishes Plans on Eve of Election," *Toreador*, November 25, 1952.
35. "Bull Session," *Toreador*, October 24, 1952; Ralph Shelton, "TECHnicalities," *Toreador*, October 28, 1952; Dick Shockley, letter to the editor, *Toreador*, October 28, 1952.
36. "Voters Choose Speakman, Preston in Major Races for Student Council," *Toreador*, April 10, 1953.
37. "Demand Is Down for Tech Mascot," *Toreador*, January 14, 1954.

## CHAPTER 2

1. Matthew Conner, "Interesting Facts You May Not Know About Texas Tech Football," Wreck 'Em Red, 2016, accessed February 19, 2023, https://wreckemred.com/2015/07/27/interesting-facts-you-may-not-know-about-texas-tech-football/7/.
2. Jennifer Ritz, "A Fine Tradition," *Texas Techsan*, July/August 2000, 30.
3. Bill Dean, "For Your Information: Be Proud of Texas Tech," *Texas Techsan*, March/April 2008, 6.
4. Blake Ursch, "Friends Remember Tech's First Masked Rider," *Lubbock Avalanche-Journal*, August 2, 2013, https://www.lubbockonline.com/story/news/education/2013/08/02/friends-remember-techs-first-masked-rider/15080744007/.
5. "Army Mules," Army West Point, accessed February 19, 2023, https://goarmywestpoint.com/sports/2015/3/6/GEN_2014010171.aspx.
6. Kimberly Smith, "The History of the Kansas City Chiefs' Original Mascot, Warpaint," *Grunge*, February 6, 2023, https://www.grunge.com/1189732/the-history-of-the-kansas-city-chiefs-original-mascot-warpaint/; "Text Page–American Indian Heritage Chiefs Name," Kansas City Chiefs, January 1, 2020, https://www.chiefs.com/news/text-page-american-indian-heritage-chiefs-name.
7. "Texas Tech Masked Rider," *Texas Tech Football '70 Magazine: The TULANE Game*, September 12, 1970, https://digitallibrary.tulane.edu/islandora/object/tulane%3A80086/datastream/PDF/view.
8. Early Scudday, "The Sports Scene," *Lubbock Avalanche-Journal*, May 15, 1967; David Murrah, "Tech's First Red Raider," Texas Tech in Retrospect, *Texas Techsan*, October/November 1980.
9. Ibid.
10. "Jill Hinckley and Joe Kirk Fulton," *A Dash of West Texas!* (LGH TTUHSC MedPlex Impressions, Fall 1984), 2.
11. Preston Lewis, "Ghost Riders," *Texas Techsan*, November/December 1984, 11.
12. Janet Moore, "Jim Cloyd Is Probably Tech's Most Proficient Horseman . . . But He Has Never Owned a Horse," *Texas Techsan*, October 1956.
13. Ibid.
14. Tara McQueen, "Masked Rider Receives Anniversary Saddle," *University Daily*, September 2, 1994, http://collections2.swco.ttu.edu/handle/20.500.12255/193072.
15. Moore, "Jim Cloyd."
16. Dailey Fuller, "Texas Tech's Southwest Conference Circle to be Preserved," Texas Tech University System, October 22, 2012, https://www.texastech.edu/stories/12-10-swc-circle-to-be-preserved.php.
17. Sandra Lee Wireman, "Town and Country," *La Ventana*, 1963, 25.
18. Jim Cloyd to the Special Feature Department, *Sundial* newspaper, El Paso, Texas, February 11, 1965, U114.1, Box 1, Folder 12, Jim Cloyd Collection, Southwest Collection/Special Collections Library, Texas Tech University.
19. Photocopy of message Cloyd wrote on his RSVP for the New Masked

Rider Horse Ceremony, September 12, 1987, U114.1, Box 1, Folder 12, Southwest Collection/Special Collections Library, Texas Tech University, https://txarchives.org/ttusw/finding_aids/20089.xml.

20. Jim Cloyd to the Special Feature Department.
21. David Bowser, "Brand Inspector: Just One Stop on Jim Cloyd's Winding Trail," *Livestock Weekly*, July 9, 1998, https://web.archive.org/web/20050123131210/https://www.livestockweekly.com/papers/98/07/09/whlbowl.asp.
22. Bowser, "Brand Inspector."
23. Wireman, "Town and Country."
24. "Vera Hollar Honored by the Paducah Lions Club as a Woman of the Year," *Wichita Falls Times*, March 2, 1958, https://newspaperarchive.com/wichita-falls-times-mar-02-1958-p-1/.
25. "Who? What? & Where? Polly Hollar Dies at 72," *All About Cutting*, accessed February 20, 2023, https://web.archive.org/web/20090916234423/http://allaboutcutting.com/who-what.html.
26. James Hamm, "A Little Bit," *Toreador*, October 9, 1958.
27. Adrian Vaughan, "Texas Tech Press Releases, September–October 1959," Department of Public Information, Texas Technological College, September 26, 1959, https://swco-ir.tdl.org/handle/10605/358334.
28. "Richard Earl Tolley," *Prabook*, accessed February 20, 2023, https://prabook.com/web/richard_earl.tolley/381374; Raider Ranch Independent Living, "GUNS UP! Football season has arrived at Texas Tech! We here at Raider Ranch wanted to share with you that our very own resident, Dick Tolley, wrote the Red Raider Fanfare 'Ride Raider, Ride' song!" Facebook, September 11, 2020, https://www.facebook.com/RaiderRanchRetirement/videos/641178233498791/.
29. Keith Bearden, "Oral History," interview by Lynn Whitfield, February 7, 2019, Southwest Collection/Special Collections Library, Texas Tech University, https://swco-ir.tdl.org/handle/10605/362057; "1926: Tech Band Takes Historic Trip to Become Goin' Band from Raiderland," Texas Tech Centennial 100 Impactful Moments, https://100.ttu.edu/moments/.
30. Pat Nickell, "New Masked Rider Takes Reins," *University Daily*, August 31, 1970, http://collections2.swco.ttu.edu/handle/20.500.12255/129255.
31. Bill G. Tompkins, "Borrowing Bevo," *Spirit: The Texas A&M Foundation Magazine*, Summer 2017, https://www.txamfoundation.com/Summer-2017/Time-Capsule.aspx.
32. "The Bears," *Baylor Magazine*, Spring 2014, https://www.baylor.edu/alumni/magazine/1203/news.php?action=story&story=142733.
33. "Peruna V (1950–1965)," Peruna, *SMU Student Affairs Spirit Squads*, January 10, 2023, https://www.smu.edu/StudentAffairs/CampusRecreation/Spirit/Spirit-Squads/Peruna.
34. "Committee Directs Blast at SWC Mascot Thieves," *Daily Toreador*, January 5, 1965; Everett Robertson, "Texas Tech Again Named 'Best Sport,'" *Baylor Lariat*, January 5, 1965; "SWC Sportsmanship Committee Considers Vandalism, Dissolution," *Rice Thresher*, January 7, 1965.
35. *La Ventana*, 1964, *View* section cover, Southwest Collection/Special Collections Library, Texas Tech University, accessed January 24, 2023, https://ttu-ir.tdl.org/handle/2346/48704.
36. Nubbin Hollar, Dale Zinn, Pat Roney, and Su Finley with Sugar Loaf, February 1, 1968, image, 5″ x 7″ SWCO DSpace Home, Southwest Collection/Special Collections Library, Texas Tech University, https://swco-ir.tdl.org/handle/10605/1217?show=full.
37. Red Raider Memorial at Jones AT&T Stadium, May 16, 2017, image, 120 mm. SWCO DSpace Home, Southwest Collection/Special Collections Library, Texas Tech University, https://swco-ir.tdl.org/handle/10605/316530?show=full.

## CHAPTER 3

1. *Toreador*, October 7, 1964, http://collections2.swco.ttu.edu/handle/20.500.12255/127351.
2. "The Texas Tech Masked Rider: A Tradition Reins," TTU News & Publications, 2000. These videos are only available to watch in person at the library. Reference number U185.853 (box 28, item 941). Some details are available at https://txarchives.org/ttusw/finding_aids_20093.xml.
3. "Masked Rider Means Pageantry," Unknown Publication, Southwest Collection/Special Collections Library, Texas Tech University, Archive U114.1, box 1, folder 11.
4. "Tech Fans Salute 'Masked Riders,'" *University Daily*, November 22, 1968.
5. Pat Nickell, "New Masked Rider Takes Reins," *University Daily*, August 31, 1970, http://collections2.swco.ttu.edu/handle/20.500.12255/129255.
6. "Texas Tech Masked Rider," *Texas Tech Football '70 Magazine: The TULANE Game*, September 12, 1970, https://digitallibrary.tulane.edu/

islandora/object/tulane%3A80086/datastream/PDF/view.

7. Bill Dean, "Who Is That Masked Man?" For Your Information, *Texas Techsan,* January/February 2003, accessed August 3, 2023, https://ttu-ir.tdl.org/bitstream/handle/2346/49319/ttu_aa0001_000305.pdf.
8. "'Guns Up' gesture began as reaction to UT horns," KCBD, October 28, 2014, https://www.kcbd.com/story/27147589/guns-up-gesture-began-as-reaction-to-ut-horns/.
9. "Masked Rider Interviews, item 2," undated, Southwest Collection/Special Collections Library, Texas Tech University, Reference number U185.9-836 (box 26, item 836), https://txarchives.org/ttusw/finding_aids/20093.xml.

## CHAPTER 4

1. Mary Rampellini, "Catching Up with Clarence Scharbauer," *Daily Racing Form*, July 11, 2013, https://www.drf.com/news/catching-clarence-scharbauer.
2. Lenny Shulman, "Alysheba Arrives at Kentucky Horse Park," *Bloodhorse*, October 31, 2008, https://www.bloodhorse.com/horse-racing/articles/151425/alysheba-arrives-at-kentucky-horse-park.
3. Rampellini, "Catching Up with Clarence Scharbauer."
4. "Masked Rider Interviews item 2."
5. Tom Scott, "Happy '5' Becomes Tech's Fifth Mascot," *Texas Techsan*, October 1973, 3, accessed September 15, 2022, https://ttu-ir.tdl.org/bitstream/handle/2346/49143/ttu_aa0001_000129.pdf.
6. Ibid.
7. "Masked Rider Interviews item 2."
8. Norman Martin, "CASNR Launches New Masked Rider Scholarship Endowment," Davis College NewsCenter, Texas Tech University Davis College of Agricultural Sciences & Natural Resources, April 2009, https://www.depts.ttu.edu/agriculturalsciences/news/oldPosts/2009/04/casnr-launches-new-masked-rider-scholarship-endowment.php.
9. Leslie Cranford, "Masked Rider No. 13 Wouldn't Take 'No' for an Answer," *Texas Tech Today*, October 14, 2011, https://today.ttu.edu/posts/2016/03/anne-lynch-13th-masked-rider.
10. Ibid.
11. "Committee to Pick New Red Raider," *University Daily*, February 14, 1975, http://collections2.swco.ttu.edu/handle/20.500.12255/125897.
12. "The New Red Raider," *University Daily*, April 2, 1975, http://collections2.swco.ttu.edu/handle/20.500.12255/125926.
13. Ibid.
14. "Kim King Named Tech's Masked Red Raider," *Brady Standard*, April 4, 1975, https://newspaperarchive.com/brady-standard-apr-04-1975-p-1/.
15. "The New Red Raider."
16. Jeff Klotzman, "Everyone Happy about Happy V," *University Daily*, September 29, 1975, http://collections2.swco.ttu.edu/handle/20.500.12255/125990.
17. "Ready to Go . . ." *University Daily*, October 9, 1975, http://collections2.swco.ttu.edu/handle/20.500.12255/126046.
18. Kim Cobb, "Wall Accepts Red Raider Reins," *University Daily*, April 9, 1976, http://collections2.swco.ttu.edu/handle/20.500.12255/127310.
19. Ibid.
20. Worth Wren, "Red Raider," *Texas Tech News*, Texas Tech University Office of Information Services, April 8, 1976, https://swco-ir.tdl.org/handle/10605/352933.
21. Ibid.
22. Ibid.
23. Cobb, "Wall Accepts Red Raider Reins."
24. Regina Smylie, "New Mascot Named," *University Daily*, April 4, 1977, http://collections2.swco.ttu.edu/handle/20.500.12255/126199.
25. Ibid.
26. Ibid.
27. Ibid.
28. Keith Mulkey, "Happy V Left Behind Unanswered Questions," *University Daily*, November 18, 1977, http://collections2.swco.ttu.edu/handle/20.500.12255/126432.
29. Keith Mulkey, "Mascot Absence at UT Result of Interpretation," *University Daily*, November 4, 1977, http://collections2.swco.ttu.edu/handle/20.500.12255/127589.
30. Keith Mulkey, "King Stables Mascot," *University Daily*, November 10, 1977.
31. Mulkey, "Mascot Absence at UT."
32. Mulkey, "Happy V."
33. Barbara Pogue, "Happy VI New Raider Mascot," *University Daily*, November 17, 1977, http://collections2.swco.ttu.edu/handle/20.500.12255/126446.
34. Mulkey, "Mascot Absence at UT."

35. Pogue, "Happy VI."
36. Concerned Raiders, "Letter to the Editor: On Horse, Deserves Much More," *University Daily*, November 29, 1977, http://collections2.swco.ttu.edu/handle/20.500.12255/126472; Debra Holt, Donna Palmentera, Kenneth Holt, "Letter to the Editor: On Happy V, 'We Too Are Upset,'" *University Daily*, December 1, 1977.
37. Concerned Raiders, "Letter to the Editor."
38. Brian H. Griggs, *Opus in Brick and Stone* (Lubbock: Texas Tech University Press, 2020), 224, 234–39.
39. "About," Texas Tech University Health Sciences Center, April 12, 2022, https://www.ttuhsc.edu/medicine/about.aspx.
40. Donald E. Green, *Fifty Years of Service to West Texas Agriculture: A History of Texas Tech University's College of Agricultural Sciences, 1925–1975* (Lubbock: Texas Tech Press, 1977), 134.
41. Texas Tech University Board of Regents, "Minutes of the Board of Regents Meeting, August 1, 1975," (motion 185), 4, https://swco-ir.tdl.org/handle/10605/358421.
42. "Facilities," Texas Tech University Department of Animal & Food Sciences, January 13, 2020, https://www.depts.ttu.edu/afs/thedepartmentfacilities.php.
43. "Rodeo Queen to Circle Jones AT&T Stadium as Tech Red Raider," *Lubbock Avalanche-Journal*, Saturday morning edition, March 15, 1980.
44. "American Quarter Horse Hall of Fame Human Inductees: Anne Burnett Tandy," January 12, 2023, https://www.aqha.com/hall-of-fame-human-inductees/-/asset_publisher/kz1Wsqd1xkSs/content/anne-burnett-tan-1.
45. Anne W. Marion, "2005 Cowgirl Honoree-Texas," National Cowgirl Museum and Hall of Fame, accessed January 12, 2023, https://www.cowgirl.net/portfolios/anne-w-marion/; "American Quarter Horse Hall of Fame Human Inductees Anne Windfohr Marion," accessed January 12, 2023, https://www.aqha.com/hall-of-fame-human-inductees/-/asset_publisher/kz1Wsqd1xkSs/content/anne-windfohr-marion.
46. B. Zeeck, *Texas Tech News*, Texas Tech University News and Publications, October 11, 1979, https://swco-ir.tdl.org/handle/10605/353186.
47. Ashley Pettiet Branch, "Chronicles: Bigun Bradley First Real Marlboro Man Cowboy," *Lubbock Avalanche-Journal*, July 1, 2017, https://www.lubbockonline.com/story/lifestyle/columns/2017/07/01/chronicles-bigun-bradley-first-real-marlboro-man-cowboy/14825495007/.
48. Pogue, "Happy VI."
49. B. Zeeck, *Texas Tech News*, Texas Tech University News and Publications, November 22, 1977, https://swco-ir.tdl.org/handle/10605/358748.
50. "Tech's Masked Rider," Texas Tech University Athletics Department, 1978 Football Media Guide.
51. *Tall in the Saddle* (photo and caption), *Lubbock Avalanche-Journal*, Thursday morning, April 27, 1978.
52. Carla McKeown, "Masked Riders Promote Tech Spirit Since 1936," *University Daily*, March 7, 1986, 4, http://collections2.swco.ttu.edu/handle/20.500.12255/190548.
53. B. Zeeck, "Lubbock—Happy VI-II," *Texas Tech News*, Texas Tech University News and Publications, October 11, 1979, https://swco-ir.tdl.org/handle/10605/353186.
54. Brittany Hoover, "Former Masked Rider Goes on 'Last Ride' Before Being Laid to Rest," *Lubbock Avalanche-Journal*, May 31, 2013, https://www.lubbockonline.com/local-news/2013-05-31/former-masked-rider-goes-last-ride-being-laid-rest?v=.
55. Ibid.
56. Brenda Malone, "New Red Raider Selected," *University Daily*, March 14, 1980, http://collections2.swco.ttu.edu/handle/20.500.12255/127948.
57. Ibid.

## CHAPTER 5

1. B. Zeeck, *Texas Tech News*, Texas Tech University News and Publications, March 11, 1981, https://swco-ir.tdl.org/handle/10605/359045.
2. Ibid.
3. Harvey Landers, *Texas Tech News*, Texas Tech University News and Publications, June 25, 1981, https://swco-ir.tdl.org/bitstream/handle/10605/359118/TTU%20Press%20Releases%2c%20June%2022-26%2c%201981.pdf.
4. B. Zeeck, *Texas Tech News*, Texas Tech University News and Publications, March 11, 1981.
5. B. Zeeck, "Attention: Agricultural Editors," *Texas Tech News*, Texas Tech University News and Publications, January 16, 1980, https://swco-ir.tdl.org/handle/10605/352932.

6. B. Zeeck, *Texas Tech News*, Texas Tech University News and Publications, March 11, 1981.
7. Harvey Landers, *Texas Tech News*, Texas Tech University News and Publications, June 25, 1981.
8. Carrie White, "LUBBOCK—The Texas Tech University Student Foundation," *Texas Tech News*, Texas Tech University News and Publications, March 1, 1982, https://swco-ir.tdl.org/bitstream/handle/10605/359132/TTU%20Press%20Releases%2c%20March%201-5%2c%201982.pdf.
9. Ibid.
10. Ibid.
11. Patrick Gonzales, "Masked Rider No. 21 Remembers Tradition of Pride," *Texas Tech Today*, October 7, 2011, https://today.ttu.edu/posts/2011/10/masked-rider-no-21-remembers-tradition-of-pride.
12. Ibid.
13. B. Zeeck, *Texas Tech News*, Texas Tech University News and Publications, March 10, 1982, Perry Joe Church of Friona has been named the 1982–83 Red Raider, https://swco-ir.tdl.org/bitstream/handle/10605/359133/TTU%20Press%20Releases%2c%20March%208-12%2c%201982.pdf.
14. "Masked Rider Suit Transferred," *Lubbock Avalanche-Journal Evening Journal*, February 13, 1987.
15. Gonzales, "Masked Rider No. 21."
16. "1982–83 Red Raider," *The Greater Llano Estacado Southwest Heritage*, Fall 1982, Southwest Collection/Special Collections Library, Texas Tech University, University Archive U114.1, box 1, folder 11.
17. "Rainbo Announces Program Actively Aiding '82 Texas Tech Athletics," *Lubbock Avalanche-Journal*, August 30, 1982, 10-A.
18. Glenys Young, "'Red Raider Coming at You': A Tale of Success, Recession and Resurgence," *Texas Tech Today*, February 16, 2018, https://today.ttu.edu/posts/2018/02/red-raider-coming-at-you.
19. "Jack and Twila Aufill Endowed Scholarship," Texas Tech University College of Agricultural Sciences & Natural Resources, accessed January 24, 2021, https://www.depts.ttu.edu/agriculturalsciences/Students/scholarships/afs/aufill.php.
20. "Masked Rider Interviews, item 2."
21. Heila Rogers, "Get Your Guns Up!" *Abilene Living Magazine* (Fall 2014), 86, https://s3.amazonaws.com/wyim-publications/AbileneFall2014/files/assets/common/downloads/AbileneLivingFall2014.pdf.
22. B. Zeeck, "Attention: Sports Writers," *Texas Tech News*, Texas Tech University News and Publications, March 7, 1984, https://swco-ir.tdl.org/bitstream/handle/10605/359197/TTU%20Press%20Releases%2c%20March%205-9%2c%201984.pdf.
23. Terri Lloyd, "LUBBOCK—The 1984–1985 Texas Tech University Red Raider," *Texas Tech News*, Texas Tech University News and Publications, April 2, 1984, https://swco-ir.tdl.org/bitstream/handle/10605/359238/TTU%20Press%20Releases%2c%20April%202-6%2c%201984.pdf.
24. Damon Pearce, "New Rider Named for Happy VI-II," *University Daily*, March 8, 1984, http://collections2.swco.ttu.edu/handle/20.500.12255/127183.
25. B. Zeeck, "Attention: Sports Writers."
26. Pearce, "New Rider Named for Happy VI-II."
27. B. Zeeck, "Attention: Sports Writers."
28. Lloyd, "LUBBOCK—The 1984–1985 Texas Tech University Red Raider."
29. "Media Advisory," Texas Tech University News and Publications, September 26, 1984, https://swco-ir.tdl.org/bitstream/handle/10605/359322/TTU%20Press%20Releases%2c%20September%2024-28%2c%201984.pdf.
30. "Continuing Tradition," *University Daily*, March 7, 1985, http://collections2.swco.ttu.edu/handle/20.500.12255/190401.
31. Preston Lewis, "LUBBOCK—Texas Tech University Senior Jerrell K. Key," *Texas Tech News*, Texas Tech University News and Publications, March 6, 1985, https://swco-ir.tdl.org/bitstream/handle/10605/359314/TTU%20Press%20Releases%2c%20March%204-8%2c%201985.pdf.
32. "Chuck Key," *Sports Reference College Basketball*, accessed January 24, 2021, https://www.sports-reference.com/cbb/players/chuck-key-1.html.
33. Pearce, "New Rider Named for Happy VI-II."
34. Lewis, "LUBBOCK—Texas Tech University Senior Jerrell K. Key."
35. Pearce, "New Rider Named for Happy VI-II."
36. Lewis, "LUBBOCK—Texas Tech University Senior Jerrell K. Key."
37. "New Masked Rider," *Daily Toreador*, March 6, 1986, 6, http://collections2.swco.ttu.edu/handle/20.500.12255/190547.
38. "New Masked Rider," *Texas Techsan*, May–June 1986.
39. Clifford Cain, "LUBBOCK—Texas Tech University's Department of Animal Science," *Texas Tech News*, Texas Tech University News and Publications, April 23, 1984, https://swco-ir.tdl.org/bitstream/handle/10605/359245/TTU%20Press%20Releases%2c%20April%2023-27%2c%201984.pdf.

40. "Tech Leaders Gain Student Organization Awards," *Daily Toreador*, April 15, 1987, 4, http://collections2.swco.ttu.edu/handle/20.500.12255/190710; Daniel Jenkins interview with author, August 5, 2023.

## CHAPTER 6

1. Preston Lewis, "LUBBOCK—Texas Tech University Junior Kimberly J. 'Kim' Saunders," *Texas Tech News*, Texas Tech University News and Publications, March 4, 1987, https://swco-ir.tdl.org/bitstream/handle/10605/359430/TTU%20Press%20Releases%2c%20March%202-6%2c%201987.pdf.
2. Beverly Taylor, "LUBBOCK—The Texas Tech University Masked Rider," *Texas Tech News*, Texas Tech University News and Publications, April 28, 1987, https://swco-ir.tdl.org/bitstream/handle/10605/359438/TTU%20Press%20Releases%2c%20April%2027-%20May%201%2c%201987.pdf.
3. Whitney Wyatt, "Texas Tech Mascots Make up Large Part of Raider Tradition," *University Daily*, August 28, 2001, http://www.dailytoreador.com/archives/texas-tech-mascots-make-up-large-part-of-raider-tradition/article_d38c355c-3948-5159-949e-e15355ba8829.html.
4. Beverly Taylor, "LUBBOCK—The Name of Texas Tech's New Masked Rider," *Texas Tech News*, Texas Tech University News and Publications, August 25, 1987, https://swco-ir.tdl.org/bitstream/handle/10605/359485/TTU%20Press%20Releases%2c%20August%2024-28%2c%201987.pdf, https://swco-ir.tdl.org/handle/10605/359485.
5. Taylor, "LUBBOCK—The Texas Tech University Masked Rider."
6. Ibid.
7. Taylor, "LUBBOCK—The Name of Texas Tech's New Masked Rider."
8. Ibid.
9. Ibid.
10. Taylor, "LUBBOCK—The Texas Tech University Masked Rider."
11. Taylor, "LUBBOCK—The Name of Texas Tech's New Masked Rider."
12. Beverly Taylor, "LUBBOCK—Lea Whitehead of Sonora," *Texas Tech News*, Texas Tech University News and Publications, March 3, 1988, https://swco-ir.tdl.org/bitstream/handle/10605/359593/TTU%20Press%20Releases%2c%20February%2029-%20March%204%2c%201988.pdf; personal interview with Lea Whitehead by phone on August 5.
13. "New Rider," *Daily Toreador*, March 2, 1989, http://collections2.swco.ttu.edu/handle/20.500.12255/128464.
14. "Tinnin to Write Feature Stories," *Floyd County Hesperian*, October 19, 1989, http://collections2.swco.ttu.edu/handle/20.500.12255/278785.
15. Shaun Kelley, "Midnight Raider Searches for New Trailer," *University Daily*, October 19, 1989, http://collections2.swco.ttu.edu/handle/20.500.12255/126824.
16. Ibid.
17. Ibid.
18. Ibid.
19. Leanna Efird, "Masked Rider Committee Seeks New Suit for Roof," *Daily Toreador*, October 3, 1989, http://collections2.swco.ttu.edu/handle/20.500.12255/128480.
20. "Bronze Masked Rider Statue Ready for Viewing by Public," *Lubbock Avalanche-Journal*, August 19, 1990.
21. Associated Press, "Tech Alum Says 'Neigh' to Masked Rider Statue," *Galveston Daily News*, May 6, 1990, https://www.newspapers.com/newspage/13893764/.
22. "Bronze Masked Rider Statue Ready for Viewing by Public."
23. "New Masked Rider Presented Reins," *University Daily*, March 2, 1990, http://collections2.swco.ttu.edu/handle/20.500.12255/126810.
24. Stacey Sandberg, "Masked Rider Duty Includes Hard Work, Honor," *University Daily*, September 28, 1990, http://collections2.swco.ttu.edu/handle/20.500.12255/128174.
25. Charrie South, "New Masked Rider Received Midnight Raider Reins," *University Daily*, March 1, 1991, http://collections2.swco.ttu.edu/handle/20.500.12255/126901.
26. Ibid.
27. "Former Student New Masked Rider," *Borden Star*, March 6, 1991, http://collections2.swco.ttu.edu/handle/20.500.12255/17055.
28. Leslie Cranford, "Masked Rider No. 30 Lit up the Night with the 'Light Show,'" *Texas Tech University,* September 23, 2011, https://today.ttu.edu/posts/2011/09/masked-rider-no-30-lit-up-the-night-with-the-light-show-ride.
29. Amy Collins, "Tech Establishes Fund for Future of Masked Rider," September 5, 1991, http://collections2.swco.ttu.edu/handle/20.500.12255/128269.
30. Quay Owen, "Selling the Best," *Agriculturist*, April 25, 2018, https://ttu-agriculturist.com/2018/04/25/selling-the-best/.

31. Edward T. Wright, Letter to the Editor, *University Daily*, September 23, 1992; Steven E. Mathews, Letter to the Editor, *University Daily*, September 23, 1992, http://collections2.swco.ttu.edu/handle/20.500.12255/192761.
32. Kristie Davis and Jake Rigdon, "Masked Rider Loses Job, Pending Appeal," *University Daily*, September 18, 1992, http://collections2.swco.ttu.edu/handle/20.500.12255/192758.
33. "Texas Tech Horse, Rider, Bowl Over Ref," Associated Press, September 16, 1992, https://www.newspapers.com/newspage/138484311/.
34. "Texas Tech Mascot Under Scrutiny," Associated Press, September 18, 1992, https://www.newspapers.com/newspage/14061538/.
35. Kristie Davis, "Spence Retakes Hold of Raider's Reins," *University Daily*, September 23, 1992, http://collections2.swco.ttu.edu/handle/20.500.12255/192761.
36. "The 1993 Bum Steer Awards," *Texas Monthly*, January 1993, https://www.texasmonthly.com/articles/the-1993-bum-steer-awards/.
37. Tom FitzGerald, "NFL Officials Take Hard Knocks," *San Francisco Chronicle*, December 20, 2008, https://www.sfgate.com/sports/article/NFL-officials-take-hard-knocks-3180009.php.
38. Letters to the Editor, *Daily Toreador*, October 23, 1992, http://collections2.swco.ttu.edu/handle/20.500.12255/192783.
39. "Tortilla Tossing Mystery: Do You Know How Tech's Tradition Started?" KAMC, September 9, 2013, https://www.everythinglubbock.com/news/kamc-news/tortilla-tossing-mystery-do-you-know-how-techs-tradition-started/.
40. Kristie Davis, "Masked Rider's Reins Change Hands," *University Daily*, April 5, 1993, http://collections2.swco.ttu.edu/handle/20.500.12255/192862.

## CHAPTER 7

1. Kristie Davis, "Future of Masked Rider Uncertain After Retirement of Midnight Raider," *University Daily*, May 3, 1993, http://collections2.swco.ttu.edu/handle/20.500.12255/192881.
2. Ibid.
3. Kristie Davis, "HSC, Surgery Department Donate New Masked Rider Horse," July 23, 1993, http://collections2.swco.ttu.edu/handle/20.500.12255/192899.
4. Ibid.
5. Jennifer Gooch, "Masked Rider Gets New Mount; Mount Gets New Name," *University Daily*, September 7, 1993, http://collections2.swco.ttu.edu/handle/20.500.12255/192912.
6. Davis, "HSC, Surgery Department."
7. Kristie Davis, "Committee Mulls Over Name for Masked Rider Horse," *University Daily*, July 27, 1993, http://collections2.swco.ttu.edu/handle/20.500.12255/192900.
8. Gooch, "Masked Rider Gets New Mount."
9. Leslie Cranford, "Masked Rider No. 30."
10. Jennifer Gooch, "Masked Rider Gets New Mount."
11. Jennifer Gooch, "Masked Rider Keeps Hold of Reins," *University Daily*, March 31, 1994, http://collections2.swco.ttu.edu/handle/20.500.12255/193021.
12. Ibid.
13. Jennifer Gooch, "Masked Rider Reins Change Hands Again," *University Daily*, April 25, 1994, http://collections2.swco.ttu.edu/handle/20.500.12255/193037.
14. Ibid.
15. Tara McQueen, "A Dream Come True: Masked Rider Prepares for Season," *University Daily*, August 29, 1994, http://collections2.swco.ttu.edu/handle/20.500.12255/193068.
16. Jennifer Gooch, "Masked Rider Reins Change Hands."
17. Ibid.
18. Tara McQueen, "Mascot Riding High for 40 Years," *University Daily*, August 29, 1994, http://collections2.swco.ttu.edu/handle/20.500.12255/193068.
19. Tara McQueen, "Masked Rider Receives Anniversary Saddle," *University Daily*, September 2, 1994, http://collections2.swco.ttu.edu/handle/20.500.12255/193072.
20. *Masked Rider Amy Smart with Her Saddle*, Southwest Collection/Special Collections Library, Texas Tech University, accessed February 21, 2021, https://swco-ir.tdl.org/handle/10605/84628.
21. McQueen, "Masked Rider Receives Anniversary Saddle."
22. Arni Sribhen and Bryan Adams, "Tech Mascot Dies," *University Daily*, September 6, 1994, http://collections2.swco.ttu.edu/handle/20.500.12255/193073.
23. Ibid.
24. Susan Shepard, "Double T's Last Ride," *SB Nation*, https://www.

sbnation.com/longform/2014/9/10/6126977/texas-tech-football-mascot-profile-lubbock-texas, last visited February 21, 2021.

25. Sribhen and Adams, "Tech Mascot Dies."
26. Cord Crenshaw, Letter to the Editor, "UNM Mascot Showed Poor Taste," *University Daily*, September 9, 1994, http://collections2.swco.ttu.edu/handle/20.500.12255/193075.
27. Brent Spraggins, "Search for New Horse Begins."
28. "Tech to Keep Mascot," *Manhattan Mercury*, September 7, 1994, https://www.newspapers.com/newspage/425184573/.
29. Spraggins, "Search for New Horse Begins," *University Daily*, September 8, 1994, http://collections2.swco.ttu.edu/handle/20.500.12255/193074.
30. Amy Osmulski, "Committee Scouts for Temporary Horse," *University Daily*, September 15, 1994, http://collections2.swco.ttu.edu/handle/20.500.12255/193079, http://collections2.swco.ttu.edu/bitstream/handle/20.500.12255/193079/UD_1994_09_15.pdf.
31. "Substitute Horse Chosen for Homecoming," *University Daily*, September 23, 1994, http://collections2.swco.ttu.edu/handle/20.500.12255/193085.
32. Amy Osmulski, "Tech Rides with Another Horse," *University Daily*, November 1, 1994, http://collections2.swco.ttu.edu/handle/20.500.12255/193112.
33. Brent Spraggins, "Officials to Study Safety Guidelines," *University Daily*, September 9, 1994.
34. Allison Reid, "Living the Fearless Life," *The Agriculturist*, Texas Tech University Department of Agricultural Education & Communications, July 26, 2019, https://ttuagriculturist.com/2019/07/26/living-the-fearless-life/.

## CHAPTER 8

1. Lisa Ray, "New Horse Makes First Appearance," *University Daily*, April 3, 1995, http://collections2.swco.ttu.edu/handle/20.500.12255/193183.
2. Dana Neal and Marsha Gustafson, "Masked Rider Tradition Makes a Return to the Past," *Texas Techsan*, Fall 1995, 36–37.
3. Lisa Ray, "New Horse Makes First Appearance."
4. Michael Sommermeyer, "LUBBOCK—JoLynn Self," *Texas Tech University News & Publications*, March 8, 1995, https://swco-ir.tdl.org/handle/10605/359876.
5. Jaime McDonald, "Masked Rider Saddles Up April 1," *University Daily*, March 23, 1995, http://collections2.swco.ttu.edu/handle/20.500.12255/193176.
6. Lisa Ray, "New Horse Makes First Appearance."
7. Jaime McDonald, "Masked Rider Saddles Up."
8. Kandis Wenk, "Masked Rider Program Celebrates 50 Years," *Daily Toreador*, October 11, 2004, http://www.dailytoreador.com/archives/masked-rider-program-celebrates-50-years/article_54ad4227-1a7a-55b1-a56e-43da8e995f1c.html.
9. Carrie Kilman, "Raider Alley, Tailgating Party Planned Before Game," *University Daily*, September 15, 1995, http://collections2.swco.ttu.edu/handle/20.500.12255/193238.
10. Neal and Gustafson, "Masked Rider Tradition Makes a Return to the Past."
11. Jared Parcell, "15-Yard Penalty Ousts Tortilla Tossing," *University Daily*, September 12, 1995, http://collections2.swco.ttu.edu/handle/20.500.12255/193235.
12. Ginger Pope, "Self to Take Over as Masked Rider," *University Daily*, November 8, 1996, http://collections2.swco.ttu.edu/handle/20.500.12255/193436.
13. Wenk, "Masked Rider Program Celebrates 50 Years."
14. Ibid.
15. April Castro, "Tech's Newest Masked Rider Takes Reins of Family Tradition," *University Daily*, March 15, 1996, http://collections2.swco.ttu.edu/handle/20.500.12255/193333.
16. Ibid.
17. Ibid.
18. Amy Head, "New Advisers Seek Goals for Tech's Student Activities," *University Daily*, August 26, 1996, http://collections2.swco.ttu.edu/handle/20.500.12255/193383.
19. Associated Press, "Texas Giants Merge with Big 8," *Nevada Daily Mail*, February 27, 1994, https://news.google.com/newspapers?id=1zkwAAAAIBAJ&sjid=_N8FAAAAIBAJ&pg=5906,3123357&dq.
20. Amy Head, "Masked Rider Tradition Continues," *University Daily*, August 26, 1996, http://collections2.swco.ttu.edu/handle/20.500.12255/193383.
21. Ginger Pope, "Masked Rider Committee Disbanded," *University Daily*, October 7, 1996, http://collections2.swco.ttu.edu/handle/20.500.12255/193412.
22. Ibid.

23. Ibid.
24. Ibid.
25. Ginger Pope, "Committee's Future Uncertain," *University Daily*, October 15, 1996, http://collections2.swco.ttu.edu/handle/20.500.12255/193418.
26. Pope, "Masked Rider Committee Disbanded."
27. Ibid.
28. Pope, "Committee's Future Uncertain."
29. Ginger Pope, "Mascot Committee's Duties Upheld," *University Daily*, October 16, 1996, http://collections2.swco.ttu.edu/handle/20.500.12255/193419.
30. John T. Montford and Joseph Daniel McCool, *Board Games: Straight Talk for New Directors and Good Governance* (Santa Barbara: Praeger, 2016).
31. Ginger Pope, "Mascot Safety Methods Proposed," *University Daily*, October 18, 1996, http://collections2.swco.ttu.edu/handle/20.500.12255/193421.
32. Ginger Pope, "Group Seeks Masked Rider Substitute," *University Daily*, November 1, 1996, http://collections2.swco.ttu.edu/handle/20.500.12255/193431.
33. Pope, "Self to Take Over as Masked Rider."
34. Michael Sommermeyer, "Texas Tech University Masked Rider Becky McDougal," *Texas Tech University News & Publications*, September 11, 1997, https://swco-ir.tdl.org/handle/10605/359980.
35. Ibid.
36. Ibid.
37. Ibid.
38. Ibid.
39. Ibid.
40. Ibid.
41. Michael Sommermeyer, "Masked Rider Transfer of Reins," *Texas Tech University News & Publications*, April 2, 1998, https://swco-ir.tdl.org/handle/10605/359982; Caren Carnefix, "Getting a New Brand," *University Daily*, April 6, 1998.
42. "'98–'99 Masked Rider Takes the Reins," *University Daily*, March 30, 1998.
43. Amy Wood, "Unmasked Spirit," *La Ventana* 74 (1999), Texas Tech University, 114, http://hdl.handle.net/2346/48677.
44. "Masked Rider Through the Years," *Lubbock Avalanche-Journal*, October 16, 2012, https://www.lubbockonline.com/picture-gallery/news/local/2012/10/16/masked-rider-through-the-years/969900007/.
45. "Spring Football Game on Tap," *Texas Tech Athletics*, Texas Tech University, March 26, 1999, https://texastech.com/news/1999/6/21/Spring_Football_Game_on_Tap.aspx.
46. Leslie Folmar, "Tech Searches for 40th Masked Rider," *University Daily*, January 15, 2001, http://www.dailytoreador.com/archives/tech-searches-for-40th-masked-rider/article_37863f16-238a-58b5-952c-22c92d6f59cf.html.
47. Will Frederick, "Wells Fargo Contributes to Program," *University Daily*, September 1, 2000, http://www.dailytoreador.com/archives/wells-fargo-contributes-to-program/article_7ea1b98d-bef4-5ff3-b614-837f8907a8c6.html.
48. Ibid.
49. Angel Wolfe, "Rider Stands Larger than Life," *Daily Toreador*, September 11, 2000, http://www.dailytoreador.com/archives/rider-stands-larger-than-life/article_d6f66869-abe8-5a0b-b3c4-3eff2f777e43.html.
50. "SGA Checks off School Year's Laundry List," *University Daily*, February 18, 2001, http://www.dailytoreador.com/archives/sga-checks-off-school-years-laundry-list/article_9670bb84-970f-5aa0-bfdd-a5170e27d755.html.
51. "New Masked Rider Event Advisory," Texas Tech University System News and Publications, April 18, 2001, https://swco-ir.tdl.org/handle/10605/358753.
52. Mara McCoy, "Tech Reps Follow Bush Transit to DC," *University Daily*, http://www.dailytoreador.com/archives/tech-reps-follow-bush-transit-to-d-c/article_2e613d0d-36ed-5b6f-a544-4628a41260d6.html.
53. Whitney Wyatt, "Carruth Grabs Reins as 2001–02 Masked Rider," *University Daily*, April 23, 2001, http://www.dailytoreador.com/archives/carruth-grabs-reins-as-2001-02-masked-rider/article_581c3665-05bf-51ff-8084-8c7c74fe297a.html.
54. Whitney Wyatt, "Ceremony to Ring in New Rider," *University Daily*, April 20, 2001, http://www.dailytoreador.com/archives/ceremony-to-ring-in-new-rider/article_726af5e9-dd3d-50f5-b211-77b0c1b1362f.html.
55. Wyatt, "Carruth Grabs Reins."
56. Wyatt, "Ceremony to Ring in New Rider."

## CHAPTER 9

1. Pam Smith, "Masked Rider, Horse Involved in Accident," *University Daily*, August 27, 2001, http://www.dailytoreador.com/archives/masked-rider-horse-involved-in-accident/article_931e2630-004a-5f1d-b84d-cba3c1fb7fcb.html.
2. Pam Smith, "Rider's Horse Put to Sleep Because of Injuries," *University Daily*, August 28, 2001, http://www.dailytoreador.com/archives/riders-horse-put-to-sleep-because-of-injuries/article_5786b356-5c9c-538a-804c-4d5555640d1c.html; John Davis, "Black Phantom Raider Put to Sleep after Collision," *Lubbock Avalanche-Journal*, August 28, 2001.
3. Davis, "Black Phantom Raider Put to Sleep."
4. Smith, "Rider's Horse Put to Sleep."
5. Smith, "Wells Fargo Commits to Finance New Mascot," *University Daily*, August 29, 2001, http://www.dailytoreador.com/archives/wells-fargo-commits-to-finance-new-mascot/article_6ed4540d-3be8-502c-8d19-dd40f3eccd59.html.
6. Smith, "Rider's Horse Put to Sleep."
7. Davis, "Black Phantom Raider Put to Sleep."
8. Ibid.
9. Ibid.
10. "A Big Loss for Tech," *Lubbock Avalanche-Journal*, September 4, 2001.
11. Smith, "Wells Fargo Commits."
12. Pam Smith, "RaiderGate's Debut Attracts Students, Fans, with Live Band and Barbecue," *University Daily*, September 10, 2001, http://www.dailytoreador.com/archives/raidergate-s-debut-attractsstudents-fans-with-live-band-and-barbecue/article_34bff75d-f4e2-59e2-816d-226ce9c94eed.html.
13. Pam Smith, "Midnight Looms as Masked Rider's Interim Horse," *University Daily*, September 10, 2001, http://www.dailytoreador.com/archives/midnight-looms-as-masked-riders-interim-horse/article_59e45314-b025-54f3-8bd8-168fc9783536.html.
14. Pam Smith, "Second Horse Earns Interim Mascot Status," *University Daily*, October 5, 2001, http://www.dailytoreador.com/archives/second-horse-earns-interim-mascot-status/article_9464c566-1339-5f73-8869-39809ae34e69.html.
15. Pam Smith, "Rider's Backup to be Ridden; Primary Horse Still Unclear," *University Daily*, October 11, 2001, http://www.dailytoreador.com/archives/rider-s-backup-to-be-ridden-primary-horse-still-unclear/article_e156357a-71a1-51f8-b34a-7cd7df26b52f.html.
16. April Tamplen, "Masked Reader," *University Daily*, March 7, 2002, www.dailytoreador.com/archives/masked-reader/article_266b1dd7-ebb6-5655-8b73-99e1934f5422.html.
17. Natalie Knox, "Former Tech Masked Rider Reflects on Past Year," *University Daily*, April 26, 2002, www.dailytoreador.com/archives/former-tech-masked-rider-reflects-on-past-year/article_2189382e-b570-5f9e-abaf-701d630daf07.html.
18. Ibid.
19. Tamplen, "Masked Reader."

## CHAPTER 10

1. Susan Shepard, "Double T's Last Ride," *SB Nation*, https://www.sbnation.com/longform/2014/9/10/6126977/texas-tech-football-mascot-profile-lubbock-texas, last visited February 21, 2021.
2. Natalie Knox, "Rider Revealed," *University Daily*, April 22, 2002, http://www.dailytoreador.com/archives/rider-revealed/article_90f5e001-69d3-5a11-a3a3-03c40f2e7af6.html.
3. Nikki Siegrist and Heidi Toth, "Masked Rider Begins as Mysterious 'Ghost Rider' in 1930s," *University Daily*, March 10, 2003.
4. Knox, "Rider Revealed."
5. Ibid.
6. Matthew Muench, "Masking the Mascot," *Daily Toreador*, April 22, 2003, http://www.dailytoreador.com/archives/masking-the-mascot/article_0cfe4e12-dc0b-523a-a0f7-a25ab839cf21.html.
7. Ibid.
8. Ibid.
9. Ibid.
10. Ibid.
11. Ibid.
12. Matthew Muench, "Next Masked Rider Revealed at Ceremony," *Daily Toreador*, April 17, 2003, http://www.dailytoreador.com/archives/next-masked-rider-revealed-at-ceremony/article_08ce676c-d8e5-5943-a530-bc91c819e58d.html.
13. Andrew Bell, "Red Raider Reigns," *University Daily*, April 26,

2004, http://www.dailytoreador.com/archives/red-raider-reigns/article_98368ca1-6872-522b-bdd9-8ec0e7b33a0a.html.

14. Mike Mandel, *The Masked Rider*, 2003, tile mosaic located at Jones AT&T Stadium west entrance, Texas Tech University System Public Art Collection, https://ttuspublicart.com/collection/the-masked-rider/.
15. Allison Reid, "Living the Fearless Life," *The Agriculturist*, July 26, 2019, https://ttuagriculturist.com/2019/07/26/living-the-fearless-life/.
16. Bell, "Red Raider Reigns."
17. Kandis Wenk, "Masked Rider Program Celebrates 50 Years," *University Daily*, October 11, 2004, http://www.dailytoreador.com/archives/masked-rider-program-celebrates-50-years/article_54ad4227-1a7a-55b1-a56e-43da8e995f1c.html.
18. Tom Otterness, *Tornado of Ideas*, bronze sculpture located on west side of the Student Union Building at Texas Tech University, Texas Tech University System Public Art Collection.
19. Scott Slemmons, "Horse and Rider Sculpture Replicas Available for Sale," Texas Tech Today, April 19, 2005, https://today.ttu.edu/posts/2005/04/horse-and-rider-sculpture-replicas-available-for-sale.
20. Kelly Gooch, "Traveling Ranch Horse Team Established at Tech," *University Daily*, February 24, 2005, http://www.dailytoreador.com/archives/traveling-ranch-horse-team-established-at-tech/article_ca5587bf-d86a-5955-863d-3c847aa6a779.html.
21. Kelly Gooch, "Burgin Named 2005–2006 Masked Rider," *University Daily*, April 25, 2005, http://www.dailytoreador.com/archives/burgin-named-2005-2005-masked-rider/article_aff790ce-06cd-5f52-a25a-0fee98d29995.html.
22. Cory Chandler, "Tradition Continues as Masked Rider Announced," Texas Tech University System Communications & Marketing, April 22, 2005, https://swco-ir.tdl.org/handle/10605/358804.
23. Ibid.
24. Illuminated Clothing by Janet Hansen, https://enlighted.com/p/texas-tech-masked-rider.
25. Illuminated Clothing by Janet Hansen, http://janethansen.com/portfolio/#wearables.
26. Illuminated Clothing by Janet Hansen, https://janethansen.com/i/bio.
27. Cory Chandler, "Amy Bell Named New Masked Rider," Texas Tech University System Communications & Marketing, April 21, 2006, https://swco-ir.tdl.org/handle/10605/358831.
28. Ibid.
29. Jeremy Reynolds, "Tradition 'Reins' as New Masked Rider Takes Over," *University Daily*, April 23, 2006, http://www.dailytoreador.com/archives/tradition-reins-as-new-masked-rider-takes-over/article_f9ff2fd9-10f6-5969-ba10-c7143b4e01c2.html.
30. Danielle Novy, "Masked Rider 'Unmasked,'" *University Daily*, September 18, 2006, http://www.dailytoreador.com/archives/masked-rider-unmasked/article_5e3de844-c125-5bbb-b09a-4b505109a40f.html.
31. Ibid.
32. Cory Chandler, "New Masked Rider Takes Reins during Transfer," Texas Tech University Office of Communications and Marketing, April 20, 2007, https://swco-ir.tdl.org/handle/10605/358844.
33. Ibid.
34. Ibid.
35. Ann Luu, "Spirit of the Masked Rider Continues with Hartzog," *University Daily*, April 20, 2008, http://www.dailytoreador.com/archives/spirit-of-the-masked-rider-continues-with-hartzog/article_a1be9297-1c86-5dd1-885f-2348ed195fe8.html.
36. Ibid.
37. Ibid.
38. Chandler, "New Masked Rider Takes Reins."
39. Ibid.

## CHAPTER 11

1. Joe Garza, "Daily Ticket: News to Know," *Fort Worth Star-Telegram*, November 6, 2008, https://www.newspapers.com/image/654626705/?terms=texas%20tech%20ratings&match=2.
2. Chris Cook, "Masked Rider Set to Make Historic Ride," *Texas Tech Today*, Texas Tech University, March 31, 2009, https://today.ttu.edu/posts/2009/03/masked-rider-set-to-make-historic-ride.
3. Katie McDowell, "Living the Dream," *Agriculturist*, Texas Tech University Department of Agricultural Education & Communications, Fall 2011.
4. Wikipedia, "AT&T Stadium," https://en.wikipedia.org/wiki/AT%26T_Stadium#Major_events; Wikipedia, "2009 Texas Tech Red Raiders Football Team," last modified June 28, 2022, https://en.wikipedia.org/

wiki/2009_Texas_Tech_Red_Raiders_football_team; Jason, "Cowboys Stadium / Texas Tech vs Baylor / Nov. 28th, 2009," November 29, 2009, YouTube video, 7:02, https://www.youtube.com/watch?v=Bka7S7TPFVg.

5. Madilyn Edwards, "Life After the Mask," *Agriculturist*, Texas Tech University Department of Agricultural Education & Communications, November 27, 2017, https://ttuagriculturist.com/2017/11/27/life-behind-the-mask/; Cory Chandler, "Tradition Continues: Raider Red Revealed and New Masked Rider Takes the Reins," *Texas Tech Today*, Texas Tech University, April 20, 2010, https://today.ttu.edu/posts/2010/04/tradition-continues-raider-red-revealed-and-new-masked-rider-takes-the-reins.
6. Lauren Ferguson, "Reins Passed on to 50th Masked Rider," *Daily Toreador*, April 17, 2011, https://www.dailytoreador.com/lavida/reins-passed-on-to-50th-masked-rider/article_e12b36b6-6942-11e0-b01e-001a4bcf6878.html.
7. McDowell, "Living the Dream."
8. Blayne Beal, "Masked Rider Named One of AP's Top College Mascots," *Texas Tech Today*, August 23, 2010, https://today.ttu.edu/posts/2010/08/masked-rider-named-one-of-aps-top-college-mascots.
9. "New Masked Rider Makes His First Ride," YouTube video, 3:13, posted by *Lubbock Avalanche-Journal*, July 11, 2011, https://www.youtube.com/watch?v=zOshZnTHzdc&ab_channel=LubbockAvalanche-Journal-A-JMedia.
10. Matthew McGowan, "Behind the Mask: Tech's New Masked Rider Takes the Reins," *Lubbock Avalanche-Journal*, May 3, 2011, https://www.lubbockonline.com/story/news/local/2011/05/04/behind-mask-techs-new-masked-rider-takes-reins/15235719007/.
11. Ibid.
12. Ibid.
13. "New Masked Rider Makes His First Ride," YouTube video.
14. Leslie Cranford, "Ashley Wenzel Chosen as New Masked Rider," *Texas Tech Today*, April 20, 2012, http://today.ttu.edu/posts/2012/04/ashley-wenzel-chosen-as-new-masked-rider.
15. Ibid.

## CHAPTER 13

1. Kelsi Hancock, "Changing Masks: Where Are Our Masked Riders Now?" *Agriculturist*, Texas Tech University Department of Agricultural Education & Communications, Fall 2013, https://www.depts.ttu.edu/aged/agriculturist/fall2013/pdfs/kelsi_feature.pdf.
2. Leslie Cranford, "Texas Tech Purchases New Horse for Masked Rider," *Texas Tech Today*, January 18, 2013, https://today.ttu.edu/posts/2013/01/texas-tech-purchases-new-horse-for-masked-rider-2.
3. Ibid.
4. Ibid.
5. Ibid.
6. Leslie Cranford, "New Masked Rider Takes Reins During Transfer," *Texas Tech Today*, April 19, 2013, https://today.ttu.edu/posts/2013/04/new-masked-rider-takes-reins-during-transfer-7.
7. Cranford, "Texas Tech Purchases New Horse"; Leslie Cranford, "Texas Tech Names New Masked Rider Horse," *Texas Tech Today*, April 19, 2013, https://today.ttu.edu/posts/2013/04/texas-tech-names-new-masked-rider-horse-2.
8. Ibid.
9. Cranford, "New Masked Rider Takes Reins."
10. Brittany Hoover, "Former Masked Rider Goes on 'Last Ride' Before Being Laid to Rest," *Lubbock Avalanche-Journal*, May 31, 2013, https://www.lubbockonline.com/local-news/2013-05-31/former-masked-rider-goes-last-ride-being-laid-rest?v=.
11. Eva Hopping, "Letter of the Day: Coke Hopping's Last Texas Tech Ride," *Lubbock Avalanche-Journal*, May 26, 2013, https://www.lubbockonline.com/story/opinion/editorials/2013/05/26/letter-day-coke-hoppings-last-texas-tech-ride/15090855007.
12. Sean O'Neal, "Dale Brisby's Netflix Show Teaches Viewers How to be Cowboys for the Instagram Age," *Texas Monthly*, September 24, 2021, https://www.texasmonthly.com/arts-entertainment/dale-brisby-netflix-how-to-be-a-cowboy/, accessed January 24, 2023.
13. Blake Ursch, "Friends Remember Tech's First Masked Rider," *Lubbock Avalanche-Journal*, August 2, 2013, https://www.lubbockonline.com/article/20130802/NEWS/308029792; American Quarter Horse Association, "Joe Kirk Fulton," Hall of Fame Human Inductees, https://www.aqha.com/hall-of-fame-human-inductees/-/asset_publisher/kz1Wsqd1xkSs/content/joe-kirk-fulton.
14. Callie Jones, "New Masked Rider Takes Reins at Transfer Ceremony,"

*Texas Tech Today*, April 18, 2014, https://today.ttu.edu/posts/2014/04/new-masked-rider-takes-reins-at-transfer-ceremony.

15. Ibid.
16. Ibid.
17. "55th Masked Rider Wraps Up 'Ride of His Life,'" April 21, 2017, 1:59, https://www.youtube.com/watch?v=upkP4V-CCQA&ab_channel=TexasTechUniversity.
18. Amanda Castro-Crist, "Texas Tech Names New Masked Rider for 2017–18 School Year," *Texas Tech Today*, April 21, 2017, https://today.ttu.edu/posts/2017/04/laurie-tolboom.
19. Chris Cook, "Communicators in a Cart: Laurie Tolboom," on *PBS Texas Tech Public Media*, 12:59, January 2, 2018, https://www.pbs.org/video/laurie-tolboom-4nr7ip/.
20. Amanda Castro-Crist, "2018–19 Texas Tech Masked Rider Unveiled at Transfer of Reins," *Texas Tech Today*, April 20, 2018. https://today.ttu.edu/posts/2018/04/masked-rider.

## CHAPTER 14

1. Castro-Crist, "2018–19 Texas Tech Masked Rider Unveiled."
2. Holly Clanahan, "The Masked Rider Rides Again," *America's Horse*, American Quarter Horse Association, November 2018, https://aqhadigital.panoramac.com/AMH/AMHDM/2018_11/html/Pair.php?p=9&vc=0.
3. Texas Tech Masked Rider, "Today I drive home with an empty horse trailer," Facebook, November 25, 2018, accessed August 10, 2022, https://www.facebook.com/TTUMaskedRider/posts/pfbid08oLuuVbH394XQJ7ep-SyVZzncbhX9rvtJ1tDGo2uireLBgyHDAKyfWE37XNwzbizDl.
4. Texas Tech University, "2019–20 Texas Tech Masked Rider Unveiled at Transfer of Reins," April 22, 2019, YouTube video, 2:00, https://www.youtube.com/watch?v=Rr4wqk2hEBw&ab_channel=TexasTechUniversity.
5. Texas Tech Department of Agricultural Education & Communications, "CASNR Experience: Emily Brodbeck is the 2019–2020 Masked Rider," August 21, 2019, YouTube video, 3:09, https://www.youtube.com/watch?v=AU-n6h2QkP4&ab_channel=TexasTechDepartmentofAgriculturalEducationandCommunications.
6. Amanda Castro-Crist, "Texas Tech Spirit Program: Cody the Quarter Horse Rides Again," *Texas Tech Today*, October 4, 2019, https://today.ttu.edu/posts/2019/10/Stories/spirit-cody-returns.
7. Amanda Castro-Crist, "Texas Tech Spirit Program Welcomes 59th Masked Rider," August 10, 2020, https://today.ttu.edu/posts/2020/08/Stories/2020-Transfer-of-Reins-Cameron-Hekkert-feature.
8. Ibid.
9. Ibid.
10. Ibid.
11. Texas Tech University College of Arts & Sciences, "Innovation Never Stops: The Series," September 30, 2020, YouTube video, 2:08, https://www.youtube.com/watch?v=2rg5yjsL_6Q; Texas Tech University College of Arts & Sciences, "Innovation Never Stops: Part 1: Chasing Dreams," October 5, 2020, YouTube video, 2:17, https://www.facebook.com/watch/?v=965307520618208.
12. "Outgoing Masked Rider Reflects After Taking on Role During Challenging Times," April 23, 2021, https://www.kcbd.com/2021/04/23/outgoing-masked-rider-reflects-after-taking-role-during-challenging-times/.
13. Amanda Bowman, "Ashley Adams Named 60th Masked Rider," *Texas Tech Today*, April 23, 2021, https://today.ttu.edu/posts/2021/04/Stories/ashley-adams-named-60th-masked-rider.
14. Hannah Egbert, "The Horse of a Lifetime," *Agriculturist*, Texas Tech University Department of Agricultural Education & Communications, May 5, 2022, https://ttuagriculturist.com/2022/05/05/the-horse-of-a-lifetime/.
15. Elyssa Sanders, "New Pastures," *Texas Tech Today*, April 29, 2022, https://today.ttu.edu/posts/2022/04/Stories/New-Pastures.
16. "Fearless Champion's Final Run; Texas Tech Mascot Ending Reign at Oklahoma State Game," *Lubbock Avalanche-Journal*, November 17, 2021, https://www.lubbockonline.com/story/news/2021/11/17/texas-tech-mascot-fearless-champion-ending-reign-oklahoma-state-game/8657911002/.
17. Paul Tubbs, "Transfer of Tradition Part 1," *Texas Tech Today*, May 26, 2023, https://today.ttu.edu/posts/2023/05/Stories/Transfer-of-Tradition-Part-1.

# INDEX

Publication of this book
was made possible by the
generous support of
the Helen Jones Foundation, Inc.